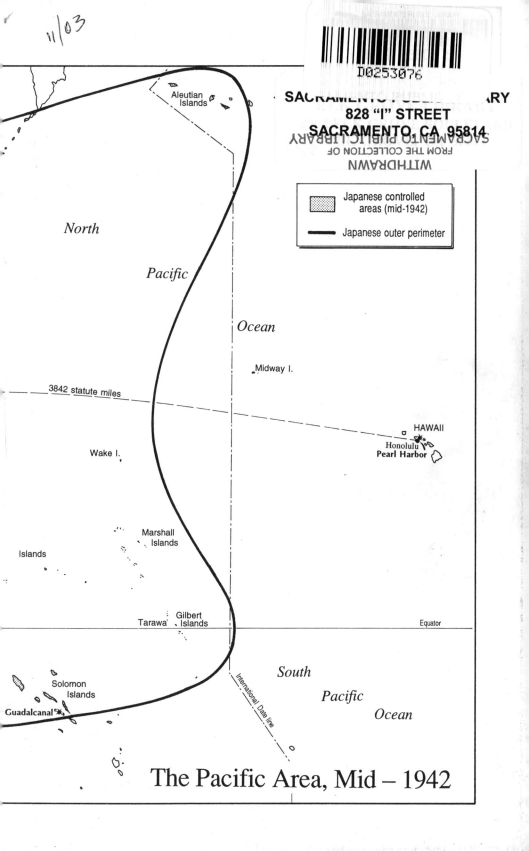

11/03

D0253076

SACRAMENTO PUBLIC LIBRARY
828 "I" STREET
SACRAMENTO, CA 95814

WITHDRAWN
FROM THE COLLECTION OF
SACRAMENTO PUBLIC LIBRARY

Japanese controlled
areas (mid-1942)

Japanese outer perimeter

North

Pacific

Ocean

Midway I.

3842 statute miles

HAWAII
Honolulu
Pearl Harbor

Wake I.

Marshall
Islands

Islands

Gilbert
Tarawa Islands

Equator

South

Solomon
Islands

Pacific

Guadalcanal

Ocean

International Date line

Aleutian
Islands

The Pacific Area, Mid – 1942

ELK GROVE LIBRARY
8962 ELK GROVE BLVD.
ELK GROVE, CA 95624

BattleFire!

ELK GROVE LIBRARY
8962 ELK GROVE BLVD.
ELK GROVE, CA 95624

BattleFire!

Combat Stories from World War II

Colonel Arthur L. Kelly

THE UNIVERSITY PRESS
OF KENTUCKY

Publication of this volume was made possible in part by a grant from the National Endowment for the Humanities.

Copyright © 1997 by The University Press of Kentucky

Scholarly publisher for the Commonwealth, serving Bellarmine College, Berea College, Centre College of Kentucky, Eastern Kentucky University, The Filson Club Historical Society, Georgetown College, Kentucky Historical Society, Kentucky State University, Morehead State University, Murray State University, Northern Kentucky University, Transylvania University, University of Kentucky, University of Louisville, and Western Kentucky University.

All rights reserved

Editorial and Sales Offices: The University Press of Kentucky
663 South Limestone Street, Lexington, Kentucky 40508-4008

01 00 99 98 97   5 4 3 2 1

Title page: USS Bunker Hill hit by a Japanese suicide attack. Courtesy of the National Archives.

Library of Congress Cataloging-in-Publication Data

Kelly, Arthur L., 1925–
    BattleFire! : combat stories from World War II / Arthur L. Kelly.
        p.   cm.
    Wartime experiences of twelve Kentuckians based on interviews the
author held with them.
    Includes bibliographical references (p.) and index.
    Contents: Pearl Harbor, Leyte Gulf, and Okinawa : signalman 1st class Lee Ebner, U.S. Navy —The Bataan Death March and Camp Cabanatuan : corporal Field Reed Jr., tanker, U.S. Army —Kamikaze attacks in the Pacific : lieutenant John Barrows, aircraft carrier pilot, U.S. Navy — Monte Pantano, Monte Cassino, and beyond : lieutenant colonel Benjamin Butler, infantryman, U.S. Army — The air war over Germany and Stalag 17 : sergeant Bernell Heaton, B–17 bomber gunner, U.S. Army Air Force — Normandy, Holland, Bastogne, and Stalag 4B : captain Willis McKee, airborne surgeon, U.S. Army — New Guinea and the Philippines : technician fourth class Thomas Murphy, combat medic, U.S. Army — Normandy and Lorraine : staff sergeant Paul Mudd, infantryman, U.S. Army — Depth-charge attacks in the Pacific : torpedoman first class Hanly Davis, submariner, U.S. Navy — Bastogne and Germany : technician third class Robert Haney, radio operator, U.S. Army — Iwo Jima : Paul and Joe Simms, U.S. Marines and hometown friends.
    ISBN 0–8131–2034–9 (alk. paper)
    1. World War, 1939–1945—Campaigns.   2. United States—Armed Forces— Biography.   3. World War, 1939–1945—Kentucky.   4. Kentucky—Biography. I. Title.
D743.K396   1997
940.54′2—dc21   97–16930

This book is printed on acid-free recycled paper meeting the requirements of the American National Standard for Permanence of Paper for Printed Library Materials.

∞ ❀

Manufactured in the United States of America

To the combatants, both the living and the dead

Contents

Illustrations

Acknowledgments

My heartfelt appreciation goes to all the interviewees who shared their combat experiences with me even when reviving painful memories brought tears or activated old nightmares. I'm thankful for their courage and cooperation in preserving their stories for posterity.

Midway through the process I asked Gurney Norman, author and English professor, for his opinion and advice about telling the combatants' stories in a book. His encouragement provided the spark I needed to get started, and I thank him for his help.

Author Joe Nickell's enthusiastic response to the five stories he read before leaving Kentucky kept my spirits up. I'm grateful to him for taking time from his busy schedule and for his encouraging words.

I owe a debt of gratitude to James Klotter, author, state historian of Kentucky, and director of the Kentucky Historical Society, for editorial help with the manuscript, and especially for professional advice on the process of writing and producing a book.

I particularly thank my young friend Russell Harris, award-winning writer and military historian, for his editing skills and his expert advice on military history, especially for details relating to the Bataan Death March. I look forward to reading the book he is writing on the subject.

Unfortunately, Bernell Heaton, a good witness whose friendship I had enjoyed, died before I finished writing his story. Fortunately, Paul Sears, a retired professor, former special assistant to the president of the University of Kentucky, and a former prisoner of war at Stalag 17 with Heaton, volunteered to check that chapter for accuracy. I am grateful to him for that and for his information about the air war over Europe and the long march out of Stalag 17.

For friendly and efficient assistance I am indebted to the staff of the U.S. military libraries at Fort Knox, Fort Benning, Carlisle Barracks, the Department of the Army's Military History Center, and the Military Records and Research Library in Frankfort, Kentucky. Maj. John J. Moore's monograph on the Pantano operation in Italy, provided by the Fort Benning Library, was especially helpful for important details about that battle. I also thank Tom Fugate, curator of the Kentucky Military History Museum, for research assistance, especially on military weapons and equipment.

Special thanks go to Terry Birdwhistell and Jeffrey Suchanek, oral historians in the Special Collections Department, Margaret I. King Library, University of Kentucky, for their continuous support over a long period. Working with them for the past ten years has been beneficial and a pleasant experience.

I owe a large measure of gratitude to my family and friends who helped me in a variety of ways: first and foremost my wife, Jane; my children, Sue Anne Ballard, Dan Kelly, Deborah Hissam, Steve Kelly, and Khrista Lee, and my stepchildren, Susan Dickinson and Sally Ray; my brother and sisters and their spouses, especially Jane and P.S. "Bubby" Barber and Tillie and John Kelly; my friends Don Armstrong, Ron D. Bryant, Robert Cocanougher, the late Roy Gibbs, Forest Grider, Enoch and Glenda Harned, Paul Honeycutt, Larry Hood, Nicky Hughes, Joe Leone, Mary Lou Madigan, Russell McClure, Harold Milburn, Charles P. Roland, Julia Simms, Al Smith, Jeanne Suchanek, Karen Warford, and all the others who helped me in many ways.

Introduction

A 20-millimeter round crashed through the fuselage and exploded beside Bernell Heaton's right leg. Blood ran down into his boot. Collecting himself from a stupor, the young Kentuckian squeezed through the narrow door of the B-17 bomber and jumped. But a strap on his parachute caught on the door handle, and wind from the propellers banged him against the fuselage in a rhythm like a beating heart. Above him a crew member worked desperately to free him.

Soon Heaton was falling feet first into the empty blue. Thousands of feet below him, a white cloud blanketed the earth. The lack of sensation surprised him: he felt nothing and heard nothing, could not even sense that he was falling. The contrast between the noises he had just left—voices cracking on his intercom, machine guns chattering, engines roaring, and ear-splitting explosions—baffled him. The sensation of being suspended in the blue sky in complete silence gave him an eerie feeling. He had to force himself to concentrate. He worried about when to pull the rip cord. If his parachute opened too soon, a German fighter might attack him. Without waiting, he pulled it. But the chute did not open.

World War II, one of the most tragic events in human history, plucked millions of ordinary American men like Heaton out of their communities, trained them for war, and hurled them into the strange reality of combat thousands of miles from home. This book records the experiences of a dozen Kentuckians among the millions of young American men who fought, suffered, and spilled their blood around the globe and who struggled daily just to stay alive in the midst of violence, chaos, and fear. These stories do not focus on world leaders, generals, tactics and strategies, or major battles. Rather they recount each individual's combat experiences from his first action to his last. All twelve lived to tell their own stories, stories of human kindness and courage, of people at their best in the worst of times.

These accounts are based on my interviews with World War II veterans from Kentucky. More than a hundred such interviews were recorded, and the audio tapes have been deposited in the Special Collections Department, Margaret I. King Library, University of Kentucky. Selecting among them was difficult, but I tried to choose the stories that best represent the breadth and depth of the combat experience. The next question was how to present those memories to the reader. Although powerful in the simple starkness of the words on tape, verbatim interviews sometimes left gaps or lessened the impact of what was occurring. I decided therefore to use the interviews as key sources for written narratives that could use secondary sources to verify details and supply the context needed for full understanding. Works such as the *United States Army in World War II* series and Thomas Parrish's *Simon and Schuster Encyclopedia of World War II* (see the list of sources for these and others) depicted the larger actions swirling around the combatant, often out of his sight or focus. The stories in and of themselves are so dramatic and powerful that no invention on my part was necessary; therefore, my own voice can be heard only in supplying information that the combatant could not have known at the time. My task was to capture the essence of what the combatants experienced.

I conducted follow-up interviews with the protagonists when it was possible. Six long sessions with Ben Butler—plus recourse to books, maps, and phone calls to other veterans who served with him in Italy—made a difference. For example, my mental image of Butler's rescue of Elbert Gourley altered after I interviewed Gourley himself and then discussed it again with Butler. Unfortunately, however, Field Reed found it too painful after the initial interview to rehash the Bataan Death March and his suffering in the prison camps. His personal validation of my version of his experience would have helped; lacking it, I removed from Reed's story a horrific episode that I wanted to include but could not verify.

Long-term or archival memory is crucial to this book. Despite popular skepticism about the validity of old memories, noted psychologists Alice and Howard Hoffman confirmed the value of long-term recollection in their 1990 work *Archives of Memory,* based on a study of Howard's own memory of his World War II experiences: "There is a subset of autobiographical long-term memory which is so permanent and largely immutable that it is best described as archival. From this perspective archival memory consists of recollections that are rehearsed, readily available for recall, and selected for preservation over a lifetime of the individual. They are memories selected much as one makes a scrapbook of photographs." Like Howard Hoffman, the men I interviewed often had trouble remembering exact places, dates, and names. Usually, I was able to fix dates by reference to independent sources. Many names, however, remain nearly impossible to recover; consequently, characters are often identified only by rank or last name.

The demographics of the Great Depression and World War II era dictated that many men, like several in this book, came from rural areas. Some had never crossed a big river, much less a mighty ocean. From newspapers, radio broadcasts, and newsreels, they learned of the dark war clouds gathering before the storm, and most sensed the infamy of forces at work in Germany and Japan. Yet not until they discovered the horror of Hitler's concentration camps, the brutal Death March, and the Japanese mistreatment of American POWs did they understand the scale of the evils that had been perpetrated on humankind.

World War II was the most destructive global episode in human history. More than fifty million people died of war-related deaths. It wounded hundreds of millions more, left major cities in Europe and parts of Asia in charred ruins, displaced millions to refugee camps, and—with the bombing of Hiroshima and Nagasaki—ushered in the nuclear age. Although the United States was spared the destruction of its cities and the killing of its women and children, the conflict still cost the nation some 400,000 young lives, and 600,000 more returned to America's shores wearing purple hearts awarded to them for spilling their blood in other parts of the world. Many were also affected—physically or mentally—for the rest of their lives. Nearly every American family grieved over the loss or debilitation of a son, brother, loved one, or friend. Of the 300,000 Kentuckians who put on their uniforms and went off to war, 7,900 died in the armed services, and 5,100 of those were killed in action.

Such statistics are overwhelming enough but help little in understanding the depth of suffering wrought by the war. Union Civil War veteran and United States Supreme Court Chief Justice Oliver Wendell Holmes once said in an address to fellow veterans: "We have shared the incommunicable experience of war. We have felt, we still feel the passion of life to its top. In our youth our hearts were touched with fire." Those who have not been in combat cannot fully understand the "incommunicable experience"; readers of this book can share it only within the limits of the power of words to recreate the actions, passions, and emotions of men in battle. Nevertheless, the powerful stories of these combatants may help all of us to better comprehend the ugly face of war and all that American combat veterans endured.

I chose to collect World War II stories and write this book out of appreciation for what these men did for our present and future generations. We as a nation owe our deepest gratitude to the generation that endured the Great Depression, won World War II, and created and sustained a postwar era of great economic growth. Their extraordinary war experiences ought to be shared and preserved for posterity. They have earned the nation's gratitude and a space in its public memory.

Pearl Harbor, Leyte Gulf, and Okinawa

Signalman First Class Lee Ebner
U.S. Navy

High on the signal bridge of the battleship USS *West Virginia*, twenty-one-year-old Lee Ebner, a native of Pineville, Kentucky, and three other signalmen looked out over Pearl Harbor packed with U.S. Navy ships. In five minutes his 4:00 to 8:00 A.M. watch would be completed, and he was looking forward to breakfast. After a hard week of serious training at sea and the tension of feeling that a war with Japan was coming, the fleet was enjoying a lazy Sunday morning while moored in the womb of the harbor. The band was setting up on the *USS Nevada* behind him. A few of Ebner's 1,541 fellow crew members were ashore attending church services, some were sleeping off a Saturday night hangover; those on duty were going about their business.

Suddenly, two planes zooming in from his left at a hundred feet above water grabbed his full attention. Surely the Army Air Force was not making mock attacks on the ships anchored in battleship row, he thought. Then, as the roaring planes bored in toward his ship, the rising sun emblem glared at him and he knew. He saw the pilots' faces and head-fitting leather caps when the planes crossed the *West Virginia*'s bow only fifty feet above him and less than a hundred yards to his front. But it didn't dawn on him that torpedoes were snaking their way through the water behind the planes.

The passing planes drew Ebner's eyes to his right front onto two dive-bombers diving for the navy airfield on Ford Island. He saw two bombs released, and followed them down. Just as the shock and sound waves arrived from their explosion, the "squawk box" barked, "General Quarters, General Quarters. This is no drill." Although things were breaking so fast that he could not take it all in, he knew this meant war. Someone said, "Get inside," and they darted into the silo-shaped superstructure that supported the signal bridge and the conning tower bridge and slammed the steel door shut.

Signalman First Class Lee Ebner was on the *West Virginia* when it was attacked at Pearl Harbor, but his worst experience of the war awaited him at Okinawa. Courtesy of Lee Ebner.

High above the main deck, his heart pounding, Ebner tried to figure out what was going on outside and wondered what he should do to stay alive. The signalmen didn't have a gun station to man during general quarters, so he stayed put. Then the torpedoes with half-ton warheads smashed into the port side of his ship. The first salvo buckled the 16-inch armor belt well below the waterline and knocked out the ship's power. Standing in the dark, Ebner could not separate the noise of torpedo explosions from the other battle sounds, nor could he feel the *West Virginia* rolling to the left (fortunately, the order to counterflood the starboard side brought the ship

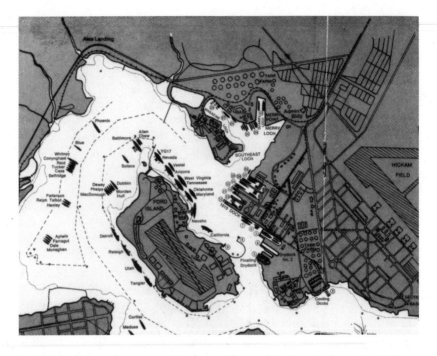

Pearl Harbor, December 7, 1941. Courtesy of the Pearl Harbor Survivors Association.

upright), but he did feel the vibrations ripple through the ship's 680-foot steel body. The next two torpedoes ripped a hole almost 200 feet long in the ship's side. Ebner felt the ship shudder for what seemed like five minutes.

Ebner's mind was racing: He wondered, "How are my friends making out?" "Were they really Japanese planes?" "How did they get here?" "What is coming next?" "Are there troop ships out there getting ready to invade Hawaii?" "What are my parents in Louisville going to think when they get the news?" and "What should I be doing?"

Suddenly, a lull settled over battleship row, and someone said, "Let's get out and see what we can do." What Ebner saw when he stepped out into the light on the signal bridge overwhelmed him. He could neither believe nor comprehend the degree of destruction and wreckage. Trying to focus on events all around him, he saw that his ship was sitting on the bottom of the harbor. He looked at the thick smoke billowing up from the burning oil slick on the water forward and aft, and from a raging fire on the front end of his ship. He noted the neat hole made in the signal bridge by an unexploded bomb. Another bomb had detonated and killed his captain, Mervin S. Bennion. To the rear on his ship he saw twisted metal and wreckage everywhere. A smokestack was missing; so was the ship's seaplane on the fantail, and the other one, on top of the No. 3 turret, was mangled. About 200 yards to his ship's right rear he could catch only glimpses of the *Arizona* through the thick smoke, but he knew she was in trouble and wondered how his friends on her were doing. He had no idea then that more than a thousand sailors were already entombed in her water-filled compartments with perhaps a few still alive in isolated air pockets. Immediately in front of the *West Virginia* he saw the *Oklahoma* do a slow roll to the left, rolling and rolling until she came to rest upside down. In the midst of this devastation, his best friend, Gene Merrill from Asheville, North Carolina, joined the men on the signal bridge, and the little group started moving toward the rescue boat. In this grim setting it was good to have his friend's company.

They moved down flights of stairs to the main deck and forward along the port side toward the rescue boat, part of which was above the level of the main deck. Somehow, someone discovered that there were men still alive in the top compartment near the rescue boat. Standing on the steps in water and oil up to his ankles and only his upper body above the main deck, Ebner formed a link in the rescue chain. He would bend down and hoist a limp form up to someone standing on the deck. When Ebner hauled them up into the light, he noted their faraway stares and how the whites of their eyes stood out against their blackened faces. After gently loading the six oil-soaked sailors on one boat, Ebner and seven other sailors from the *West Virginia* boarded another rescue boat and headed for the nearby submarine base, where they offloaded and moved under a shade tree, hoping to be out of sight of the Japanese planes of the second wave. Gloom and anxiety engulfed the little group. They didn't know the status of many friends; they had lost their home; of their personal things they only had what they wore on their backs. They didn't think they were a worthy target for the enemy planes, but they thought that an invasion might be coming any time. A thoughtful and brave lady came out of an officer's quarters and brought them a pan of sandwiches. The act of kindness in the midst of chaos was deeply appreciated.

At 10:00 A.M. the attack ended. Two waves totaling 363 planes from six Japanese aircraft carriers had done their damage. Except for the three American aircraft carriers and their escorts, which were at sea, many ships of the U.S. Pacific fleet either rested on the bottom of the harbor or were floating wrecks with raging fires burning out of control. As they walked to the assembly point for ship crews, Ebner saw smoke rising in patches throughout the harbor and on the airfields. He felt the enormity of the destruction and the sadness that hung over the island.

At the assembly point, they joined about forty others from the *West Virginia* and signed in. Here they tried to figure out what was coming next,

The USS *West Virginia* on fire and resting on the bottom at Pearl Harbor. The *Tennessee* is in the background. The smoke at right is coming from the *Arizona*, which went down with about 1,000 men aboard. Altogether 2,000 were lost in the attack. U.S. Navy photo.

where they were going to be assigned, and who had survived. It would be some time before Ebner would learn that more than 2,000 Americans had been killed in the attack, including 101 crew members and a few officers from his own ship. That afternoon when they asked for men to stand watch on the *Tennessee,* Ebner, thinking he might have a new home, readily volunteered.

The *West Virginia* had pinned the *Tennessee* against Ford Island and protected it from the destructive power of the torpedoes. Ebner's old ship, though, was still burning, and he helped fight the fire. On the waterline near the starboard side of the *Tennessee,* he saw a dead Japanese pilot lying face down with his parachute at his side. He didn't dwell on it. He figured he would see more of them. As darkness approached, soldiers and sailors alike became nervous and so trigger-happy that when American planes came in, antiaircraft guns opened up all around.

The next day Ebner and a friend were assigned to a destroyer, the USS *Mahan,* and they went to sea, leaving the catastrophic Pearl Harbor scene behind physically—but it would never leave his mind.

It was after participating in naval battles around Guadalcanal and other actions in the Pacific that Ebner's ship joined Gen. Douglas MacArthur's invasion force in the Philippines.

On a dark night in Leyte Gulf, on October 24, 1944, lightly armored amphibious ships and boats of every kind moved about cautiously, carrying ammunition, supplies, and troops ashore. Since the Japanese had assumed that General MacArthur would keep his word and return to the Philippine Islands, they had a plan to destroy the amphibious ships. Following the American landing on Leyte on October 20, all available fighting ships in the Japanese navy moved at full speed toward the Philippines in three powerful groups. To protect the landing craft and supply ships from the Japanese naval force approaching Surigao Strait, the southern gateway to the gulf, Adm. Jesse Oldendorf had drawn his task force of fighting ships into formation at the northern mouth of the strait. One of the twenty-eight destroyers poised for battle in the task force was the USS *Newcomb*. One of its sailors was Lee Ebner.

On the conning tower bridge of the *Newcomb*, Signalman Ebner listened nervously to the crackling radio and heard the torpedo boats at the southern end of Surigao Strait reporting contact with the southern Japanese naval force. He had known for hours that the dreaded ship-versus-ship battle was coming, and in the darkness of the night the clanging battle alarm had jarred the tense sailors, already at battle stations, to their feet. Now Ebner knew the fighting had started, but he had no idea that he was about to participate in the greatest naval battle in history.

Glued to the radio, his duty station, he followed the action as Admiral Nishimura's southern force of two battleships, one heavy cruiser, and four destroyers quickly pushed the American torpedo boats aside and pressed on up the narrow strait. Ebner's eyes probed the darkness to no avail. Not knowing what lay ahead was what bothered him most.

Poised in the middle zone of the northern mouth of Surigao Strait, the *Newcomb*, leading two other destroyers, glided back and forth, awaiting orders to begin its torpedo run down the strait into the angry fury of the Japanese big guns. Other American destroyers maneuvering on both sides of and deep into the strait were also waiting. Ebner had no illusions as to the danger of what they were about to do. Anxiety hounded him. The torpedo run was a first for him; he wanted to get it started and get it over with.

Suddenly, Ebner's full attention focused on the excited voices blaring over the radio. Orders and reports saturated the air waves as the destroyers down the strait started their torpedo runs in the darkness in groups of three and four; they delivered torpedoes, scored some hits, and hustled to clear the target area. Then, at 3:30 A.M., Ebner heard the order to the *Newcomb* to launch the attack. His heart pounded faster in his chest.

In response to the captain's orders, the engine room rang up high speed, and down the strait Ebner's ship raced, leading its three-destroyer pack. Fortunately, Ebner was not aware that in peacetime simulations of torpedo attacks the umpires would usually declare the lead destroyer sunk or out of action within minutes. He did know, however, that when the Japanese picked up the approaching U.S. destroyers on their radar, they would consider the ships life-threatening predators and aim their big guns at them. He knew the angel of death stalked them, and he felt the tension that shrouded the ship.

In what seemed like forever to him, they plowed straight down the middle channel, leaving a visible white foaming trail in their wake. The approaching danger focused Ebner's mind like coming upon a rattlesnake in the darkness; he listened closely and watched with all the attention he could muster as the distance between his ship and the enemy's big guns dwindled. Then, like a violent lightning storm, the big guns on six American battleships, which were "crossing the T" at the mouth of the strait to his rear, lit the sky in the distance with flashes, firing salvo after salvo down the strait. Ebner watched in awe as the big tracer shells, weighing over a ton, rose rapidly in bunches of twos and threes and streaked and roared overhead. The series of shells formed a glowing arch, matched by that of the Japanese counterbattery.

The *Newcomb* continued at full speed. The lightninglike flashes from the guns front and rear, the reflection of the tracers on the water, and the glow from a raging fire on a Japanese ship just over the horizon silhouetted the ship in ghostly light. The wait for the release point became more unbearable as the scope of the battle continued building and the gap continued shrinking. Ebner had to summon all his inner strength to beat off panic. Fortunately, he didn't see or hear the enemy shells hitting to the left and right of the *Newcomb*.

Turning right to run nearly parallel to the foe's new westward course, the *Newcomb* began firing its torpedoes—"number one," "number two"— while the ship's heavy-caliber guns pounded away at the target as well. According to the *Newcomb*'s fire controlman, both torpedoes and guns were aimed at the battleship *Yamashiro*; others said later that it was the Japanese destroyer *Asagumo*. Ebner knew only that flames were billowing up from the enemy ship hit by the *Newcomb*'s guns before she had finished firing her own spread of torpedoes. As enemy shells exploded near the *Newcomb*'s stern, it seemed to Ebner that the last torpedo would never splash down and snake its way toward the target.

Finally, the shout "Torpedoes away!" echoed throughout the ship and the *Newcomb* heeled over in response to the captain's order "Right full rudder." Ebner breathed a great sigh of relief; even though he knew he was still in mortal danger, the smoke screen made by *Newcomb* to cover her white wake as she zigzagged northward at full speed gave him some comfort. But the feeling didn't last long.

At 4:07 A.M., just as the USS *Bert W. Grant,* the last destroyer following the *Newcomb,* started wheeling northward, shells exploded all around and on top of her and inside her compartments. Seeing the violence of the exploding shells and the raging fire that billowed up from the ship as she went dead in the water demoralized Ebner. He would have felt even worse had he known at the time that the *Grant* had been hit not only by seven Japanese 4.7-inch projectiles but also by eleven American 6-inch armor-piercing shells.

It was about 6:30 A.M. when the *Newcomb,* with the badly damaged *Grant* in tow, steamed out of Surigao Strait. Despite his near total exhaustion, Ebner took a moment to observe with pride his old ship, the *West Virginia.* Having been raised from the bottom of Pearl Harbor, she was one of the six Pearl Harbor avengers in the battleship line that fought with the *Newcomb* against the Japanese southern force.

By this time, Ebner had experienced a wide range of dangerous naval combat actions. He had participated in the critical battle of Santa Cruz in the dangerous waters off Guadalcanal. In different ships he had helped fight off air attacks and engage surface ships and a submarine. At Iwo Jima his ship had to weave its way out from under incoming rounds from a shore battery. But the most violent and life-threatening action still awaited him—at Okinawa.

On the morning of April 1,1945, while American army and marine divisions waded ashore on the beaches of Okinawa, uptight crewmen of the USS *Newcomb* stood watch offshore, ready to respond to whatever the Japanese might try. Ebner knew the *Newcomb* was getting dangerously close to the main islands of Japan, but he was not aware of the new peril in store for the 1,300-ship armada swarming off the west coast of the island in support of the invasion.

The Americans wanted the island for air bases and as a springboard for invading Japan. The Japanese, determined that the Americans would not get it, developed a new sort of offense. On a limited scale they had used suicide planes before, but now they marshaled more than 1,500 pilots and planes for suicide attacks on American ships. The kamikaze ("divine wind") pilots were dedicated to flying planes loaded with high explosives directly into the ships of the invasion armada. There were also suicide boats and non-suicide planes allocated to the task. According to the plan, after the Allied ships were sunk or driven off, the Japanese army would leisurely destroy the ground forces on the island.

On April 6, 1945, the *Newcomb* plowed the waters some fifty miles north of the invasion area to help form a shield for the aircraft carriers and other heavy ships and to give early warning of danger. Like stirring up a hornet's nest, the early-warning ships drew the fury of the kamikazes.

At dusk, Ebner and the other crewmen manning the twin 40-mm anti-aircraft guns starboard and forward on the *Newcomb* saw specks in the sky coming their way. He watched intently as American fighter planes engaged the approaching specks in a dogfight. In the distance they looked like bumble-bees chasing bumblebees. He saw first one and then another burst into flame, then another and another, like someone flicking burning matches in the twilight. The burning specks blazed and left smoking trails streaking toward the sea. Knowing their lives were at stake, the nervous sailors intently watched the action and pulled for the American fighter planes. Although there must have been fifteen kamikazes knocked out of the sky, others came on, getting bigger as they approached. With pounding hearts, the gunners readied their weapons.

Ebner heard first the familiar boom, boom on the port side as the 5-inch guns opened up, then the shorter-range twin 40s began firing as the planes neared. Ebner thought, "This is it, they're going to get us." The flak gunners scored continuous hits, but still a plane continued its dive, louder and closer, until with only seconds to spare it burst into flames and, crossing over the back of the ship out of control, plunged into the water just twenty feet off the starboard side.

Within seconds another kamikaze lowered its nose and streaked for the ship, zooming through curtains of steel as the busy guns scored minor hits. At the last moment the ship executed a sharp turn, and the plane crashed and exploded in the *Newcomb*'s wake, sending up a huge geyser.

Skimming the waves while approaching from the port side, the next kamikaze aimed amidships. The port-side gunners lowered the sights of their 5-inch, 40-mm, and 20-mm guns and kicked up water all around the plane while it closed at full throttle. For a moment water and smoke obscured the target, and the gunners thought they had him—until he burst into view again. Still on course and narrowing the gap, the plane roared through exploding flak and spray, skipped off a gun mount, and slammed into the ship's afterstack. The *Newcomb*, in the midst of a dodging maneuver, rolled heavily to one side. The blast threw some sailors into the sea and others against objects as fire engulfed the area and escaping steam hissed. Ebner felt the heat, felt the ship vibrate and lose speed. He continued to think the end was at hand but could not dwell on it, because the fourth kamikaze peeled off and started for the *Newcomb*'s starboard side in his gun station's zone. One of the first salvos hit it, broke off a wing and sent it crashing into the sea several hundred yards out.

Two more kamikazes aimed for the *Newcomb* simultaneously. Ebner, busy passing ammunition, couldn't sort out all the fast-moving action and noise going on around him until one and then the other kamikaze hit his ship. The first one plowed into the midsection with a gigantic explosion. The concussion squeezed Ebner, and the shock wave tore open a giant cavity and shook the ship like a massive earthquake. The ship went dead in the water, its engine rooms a mass of rubble. Roaring flames soared upward out of the wrecked ammunition magazine compartments. Ebner knew he had lost some more friends. The second kamikaze, wounded and wobbling, crashed into the forward stack on the port side. Its explosion shot roaring flames around the superstructure, engulfing Ebner and his gun crew but disappearing as fast as it came, leaving his exposed hair singed and a strange odor in the air. He knew he was on death's doorstep, and he envisioned his mother grieving over him. Still he passed and loaded ammunition.

Destroyed guns to his left rear fell silent but not the 5-incher mounted over the bow. In front of the ship, at full throttle and nearly touching the water, yet another kamikaze aimed for the gun. As exploding shells kicked up water in front of the death carrier and the gap narrowed between foes, Ebner knew that the gun crew's lives and most likely his own depended on the outcome. Frozen, he watched the uptight crew, eyeball-to-eyeball with the Japanese pilot, gallantly stand their ground and work their gun. Finally, the left wing of the seventh kamikaze took a hit. It swerved, slid across the deck, and slammed into the destroyer *Leutze* that had just come alongside to aid the *Newcomb*.

Firefighters extinguished the flames, and in less than an hour another destroyer had the *Newcomb* in tow. Yet the presence of enemy planes in the brightly moonlit sky kept Ebner and his weary crew on their gun all night as they were towed out of the area. Fortunately, thanks to the need to focus on his job and to the numbness that had set in, Ebner was spared the shock of seeing the dead and hearing the moans of those suffering from severe burns and wounds. Early the next morning, while leaving the ship for reassignment, he found a close friend from Louisville lying on a stretcher among other wounded men waiting to be evacuated. He paused for a moment and told his friend, "Don't worry, I will write my mother and ask her to tell your mother that you are all right."

Looking over the severely damaged ship as he departed, he could not believe that she had managed to stay afloat. He worried about who would be listed among the dead, yet he felt relieved and glad to be alive. It would be some time before he would learn that seventeen of his shipmates had been killed, twenty were missing, and fifty-four had been wounded in that action. Nor did he know then that seventy men who had been either blown overboard or forced to jump by roaring flames had been rescued by other ships during that awful night. Later still, he heard from others that six of the sailors killed were close friends with whom he had shared both good times and the extreme hazards of battle.

Just over four months later, on his new ship at Subic Bay in the Philippines, Ebner heard men shouting, "The war is over." The word rippled through the harbor. Sailors on shore and ships shouted and jumped with joy. Ships' gunners started firing and filling the skies with flak and flares. Ebner just sat down and rested his chin in his hands and stared at the deck. He thought about his friends who weren't there to celebrate and about the suffering and destruction that he had seen since Pearl Harbor, and he just didn't feel like celebrating. Soon bottles and cans of beer were moving from hand to hand and celebrants were going wild with good cheer. Still the only one unable to join in, Ebner just watched. He wondered if something was wrong with him.

The Bataan Death March and Camp Cabanatuan

Corporal Field Reed Jr.
Tanker, U.S. Army

Wearing grim expressions, Pfc. Field "Jack" Reed and two friends sat down to eat at the post exchange. All morning, after hearing the shocking news about the Japanese sneak attack on Pearl Harbor, the perplexed National Guardsmen from Harrodsburg, Kentucky, and other tankers from the 192d Tank Battalion had cleaned weapons and hustled about preparing positions to defend Clark Field on Luzon in the Philippines. Outside, the airfield's B-17 bombers and P-40 fighters, after being airborne much of the morning, lined the runway while the pilots and crewmen gulped down a meal. About 12:20 P.M., only ten hours after the Japanese had struck Pearl Harbor, Reed heard the roar of sixty-eight planes getting closer and closer. Someone "reckoned" they were the new B-17 bombers expected from the States. Suddenly, ear-splitting explosions shook the ground with the violence of an earthquake. Reed and his friends sprang to their feet and streaked for the door.

Outside, with his jaws ajar and heart pounding, Reed looked down the runway and watched whistling bombs falling and exploding. Debris and smoke rolled down the runway through the parked aircraft toward him. Planes burst into balls of fire, sending up plumes of smoke. Airmen, tankers, and Filipino employees ran in every direction, some falling never to rise again. His mind could not digest the chaos and confusion or tell him what to do. Finally, some instinct sent him running to the company area a little farther down the runway.

At full speed he zigzagged, darting first behind a tree then behind a piece of equipment to get something between himself and the hostile planes that were attacking from all directions like angry wasps. Bombs and bullets peppered the area around him as he darted from one temporary cover to another. One bomb tore into the post exchange he had just left. Large and small steel fragments whistled or fluttered past him, bouncing off steel equipment and shearing off tree limbs; clumps of dirt thrown up by the explosions

Corporal Field "Jack" Reed survived the Bataan Death March. Courtesy of Field M. Reed.

rained down on him, and acrid smoke filled his nostrils. Shock waves from the closer explosions shook the ground under his feet when he ran and under his belly when he hit the ground. At times, concussion would steal his breath and make his ears ring. Still he continued the mad dash, determined to get to the company area—why, he didn't know.

As he reached it, a sergeant shouted, "Man your guns!" Reed and another soldier dived into a .50-caliber machine gun dugout. Trying hard, he managed to steady his hands enough to help break open the ammunition and load the weapon. Then Reed grabbed the gun and fired wildly, swinging from one plane to another. The firing helped to settle him down, and soon he was selecting and tracking the best target as he engaged it. It bothered him when he saw his tracers rip through one approaching plane without knocking it out of the sky.

In the midst of the battle noise and chaos, Reed saw American fighters running full throttle down the runway, trying to take to the air as Japanese fighters swarmed over them. Some American planes, hit before they could rise off the runway, burst into flames and careened out of control. Others barely off the ground took hits, exploded, and tumbled to the ground. Another left a smoke trail, glided down, and crashed hard into the ground. To stay in control, Reed had to fight off the host of emotions racing through his mind.

He saw enemy planes coming in from nearby Fort Stotsenburg to the west and zooming in from the east, the south, and the north, strafing and bombing from all directions, bringing noises, ungodly sights, odors, and chaos that he had never experienced in field training. War games in Louisiana a year before had not prepared him for the fear caused by the heat from the fireballs, the shock waves, the ground vibrating beneath him, and the bomb fragments whizzing by his head. His mind could not sort out the realities of death hovering over his dugout. Again and again he said, mostly to himself, "What in the hell is going on?" Still, he kept firing away, realizing now that he needed to husband his dwindling supply of ammunition.

Sgt. Zemon Barddowski's halftrack, at the edge of a banana grove just across the runway, caught Reed's attention when a Japanese plane spewing bullets flew straight at it. The bullets, kicking up dirt, made two tracks as they streaked toward Barddowski and his crew. It gave Reed encouragement and a sense of pride to see Barddowski stay at his machine gun in the face of death and pound away at the flying predator until finally he scored a killing hit. As the plane painted the sky with a descending smoke trail, someone shouted gleefully above the battle noise, "He got the son of a bitch, he got the son of a bitch!"

As suddenly as it began, the Japanese attack stopped. The hostile planes gathered in the sky and headed away to the north, leaving in their wake roaring fires, billowing smoke, and destruction. Distorted bodies lay scattered about; wounded civilians and soldiers were pleading, moaning, or dying quietly. As the violence and din disappeared with the hostile planes, it took Reed a moment to realize that the angel of death had gone too. Relief and a good feeling of being alive replaced the awesome burden of fear. Still, shock and disbelief gripped him as he surveyed the devastation and pandemonium. A state of numbness helped him to block out some of the horrible scenes, but he had to check on his friends from Harrodsburg to see for himself how they had fared.

Touring the battlefield in the Company D (Harrodsburg unit) area, Reed heard someone under a tank screaming, "I'm hit, I'm dying!" Reed and others gently pulled him out and huddled over Fred Leonard, another native of Harrodsburg. Leonard's eyes staring out from his bloodied head revealed his fear, but he didn't die. Not so fortunate was Robert S. Brooks, an inductee, a native of Scott County, Kentucky, and the only African American in Company D. Miraculously, however, Brooks and Leonard were the only casualties in the unit.

Farther out, Reed and some others stumbled upon the dead Japanese pilot that Barddowski had shot down. Reed stared down at a bloody body missing both arms and legs, but he didn't feel sorry for the dead man. He thought the pilot had gotten what he deserved. When a chaplain came and told the men standing around to bury the Japanese, none were in the mood to do it, and one soldier demonstrated his feelings by strolling over and pissing on the body. Then all the Americans turned and walked off, leaving the outraged chaplain shouting words that fell upon deaf ears.

That was just the beginning; more difficult and deadly ordeals awaited. The tankers endured four more air attacks on Clark Field before they moved north on December 22, 1941, and met the Japanese amphibious forces landing at Lingayen Gulf.

Making his first resupply run near the front lines, Reed knew that somewhere toward the beachhead Company A waited in hiding for the gasoline and ammunition carried by the two trucks from headquarters company. But he didn't like what he saw and heard as he drove the lead truck toward the enemy. After crossing the Agno River near Carmen, he saw one dead and mutilated horse after another, all freshly killed. Some, still wearing their bridles and saddles, had fallen on the sides of the road; others lay on the road in pools of blood. He didn't know what had happened to their riders from the U.S. Twenty-sixth Cavalry Regiment, but the Japanese airplanes making dive-bombing and strafing runs a few miles ahead told him what had happened to the horses. Reed strained to keep his eyes on the planes and the road at the same time.

Finally, he and "Mule" Henderson saw Company A's sign pointing off the road to a clump of trees on the right. The tankers, hidden from air observation but out of ammunition and running low on fuel, were glad to see them. No one, however, noted that it was Christmas Eve in their joyful greetings to the resuppliers. Reed surveyed the fast-moving situation with anxiety. He heard the high-pitched sound of enemy dive bombers and exploding bombs a short distance up the road. The rattle of automatic weapons told him that the front lines were getting too close to be ignored. Everyone hurried to unload the 55-gallon drums of gas and the boxes of 37-mm shells. The serious-minded men cracked no jokes now but exchanged what information they could without slowing down the resupply task. Reed labored hard to fit the pieces together, to grasp the immediate danger, and to comprehend what perils he might soon have to face.

After unloading his truck, he focused his attention on the wounded man stretched out on the back of a tank. Captain Walter H. Wright, a National Guardsman from Janesville, Wisconsin, wanted to talk. As Reed and others gathered around him, he said, "You fellows take care of yourselves. And watch these little bastards, because there are a lot of them." With those last words, he died. Before they left, others told Reed to stay on the roads, because the dry-appearing rice paddies would deceive a driver, and urged him to hurry along or the Japanese might cut him off.

Back at battalion headquarters just south of the Agno River, others coming and going exchanged grim information. Reed learned from Grover Brummett, a fellow Harrodsburg Guardsman, that in the first tank-versus-tank battle near the landing beach on December 22, 1941, a platoon from Company B lost all five of its tanks. Brummett didn't know the details, but both men knew that there were just 108 tanks in the only two tank battalions in the Philippines and that such an outcome was a serious matter.

The Japanese army pushed the defenders off one delaying line after another and drove everything before them toward the south. This fast-moving situation created chaos and a dangerous, confused world for Reed. Most of the time, only the tank units acting as a covering force were in contact with the enemy and they were scattered over a wide front. Moving north of Cabanatuan at a snail's pace on December 28, Reed labored to keep moving through the masses of Filipino troops and civilians making their way south. On their faces he saw traumatized expressions and their eyes revealed their fear. The heavy-laden civilians carried chickens and other treasured possessions on their backs and heads; some had overloaded carts drawn by carabaos. Untrained and frightened Filipino soldiers mingled with the crowd. These helpless men, usually without their weapons, were in disorder and out of control, though the two well-trained Philippine Scout regiments withdrew in good order and moved with unit integrity.

With horn blaring, Reed and Henderson sliced through the masses moving in the opposite direction. They stopped for a moment at a little village and worked their way through the melee into a liquor store whose

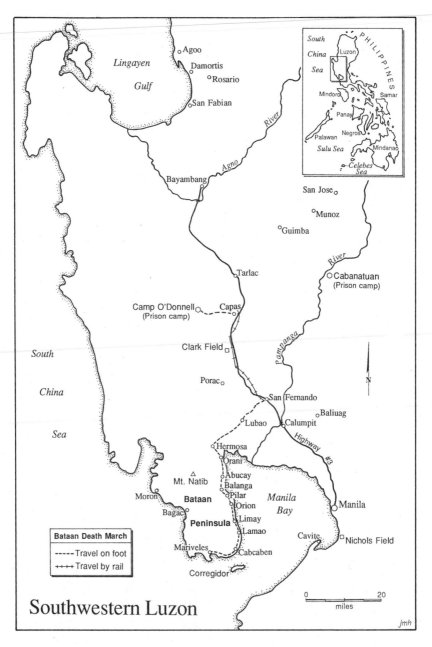

[Map of Southwestern Luzon]

owner had apparently given up on being paid for his wares. There they and some Filipinos helped themselves to all the bottles of rum they could carry. From then on Reed and Henderson took good care of their prize. Now and then they would take a little nip, though taking care to stay sober.

Continuing their one-truck resupply operation, Reed and Mule worked day and night driving over clogged roads, searching out the scattered tank units, delivering ammunition and fuel to the exhausted tankers. Sometimes they got in front of the tanks, and sometimes elements of the Japanese army infiltrated behind them and the tankers. On several occasions they had to run and gun their way out. Once, while Mule was driving, Reed noticed in the rearview mirror a Japanese soldier running alongside their truck. He grabbed his submachine gun, kicked open the door, and shot the enemy soldier before he could get his rifle unslung.

At the supply pickup points, trying to piece together the puzzle of what was happening, they would quickly swap stories with the other truck drivers. Then while the truck was being loaded, they would catch a nap on the ground, often without eating. But things moved so fast that no one seemed to know what was going on. Early in the ordeal Reed had heard that Company D had lost all seventeen of its tanks north of the Agno River. Many of these fellow National Guardsmen were, like him, from Harrodsburg, Kentucky, and he wondered and worried about them.

It was General MacArthur's plan to gather both his northern and southern forces and hold out on Bataan Peninsula until reinforcements came from the United States. Near the Calumpit Bridge, the main gateway into Bataan, Reed watched in awe as men and machines clogged the arteries that converged from north and south and streamed across the bridge over the Pampanga River. He knew the engineers were going to blow the big bridge as soon as the army had crossed it. The tankers crossed just as the New Year arrived.

About the time the American engineers blew the bridge, Reed received some good tidings at last. Lt. William Gentry, also from Harrodsburg, had led his own and another platoon from Company C in an attack at Baliuag, a little village about six miles north of the Calumpit bridge. Gentry and the tankers had knocked out six or seven Japanese tanks without losing any of their own.

One month after the start of hostilities and the successful completion of the long-existing withdrawal plan, General MacArthur's forces on Bataan. On January 9 the weary, hungry, and dirty tankers of both battalions, in desperate need of a respite, assembled in a bivouac area near the east coast about eight miles behind the main battle position, on the Abucay-Moron line. It was a welcome relief for Reed and the other tankers who had been fighting day and night, snatching only catnaps when they could. As men moved about replacing worn-out tracks, working on engines, and doing other much-needed maintenance, Reed and others took advantage of the change from near-constant driving to bathe in a creek, mend clothing, and eat food prepared by cooks for the first time since the bombing of Clark Field. But the half-ration being issued did not appease his appetite. They had been told there would be ample supplies in Bataan and fortified positions so that they could defend themselves until reinforcements arrived from the States. But rumors were flying wildly, and Reed began to have doubts.

Thirty-six of the two battalions' 108 tanks had been lost during the fight to get into Bataan. The 194th Tank Battalion, to which Harrodsburg's Company D of the 192d was attached, had lost twenty-six. While the remaining tanks were being redistributed so that each platoon had three (instead of the usual five), Reed moved about the bivouac area gathering bits of information. He learned that his Harrodsburg friends and others in Company D had swum and rafted the Agno River, because the bridge there had been blown before their tanks could cross, and that all of the Harrodsburg men had made it to friendly lines after walking several miles.

Later, after the tanks were back in action, Reed and Henderson made a resupply delivery to Company D and another company hidden from air observation in a grove in the foothills of the mountains near the Pilar-Orion area. While there, Reed and Henderson volunteered to take a jeep to an artesian well and get the men some drinking water. Cruising along, they came over a hill and looked right into the barrel of a big Japanese self-propelled gun. Reed did a screeching U-turn and raced back to tell the tankers that the only road out was blocked. For twenty-four hours the Japanese artillery pounded their position. While enemy shells exploded in their midst, the tankers pondered the option of going by foot over the rugged mountain. Reed, Henderson, and the men of Company D decided to fight their way out, but a few tankers chose to abandon their equipment and climb out, hoping to get to the west coast and into the hands of friendly forces. Finally, however, a Filipino force counterattacked and helped the tankers clear the area.

Each passing day made life more difficult. Not only did the defenders have to deal constantly with the hazards of combat, but they also contended with disease and near-starvation. Added to the problem of surviving were rumors and more rumors that taunted Reed and the others. The wishful thinking worsened after General MacArthur left for Australia in March. The most troubling stories held that reinforcements and supplies were not coming.

The Japanese, with bulldog tenacity, drove the Americans and Filipinos off the main defensive line to the rear defensive line farther down the peninsula. Low on ammunition, the tankers had to be selective about their targets. Also low on gas, they had to turn their radios off, often making it harder for Reed and Henderson to find them. Being twenty-one gave Reed some advantage over the eighteen-year-old boys, who needed more protein. His farming background and hunting skills also helped: in the jungle he hunted monkeys, birds, lizards—anything that moved or crawled. He and the other defenders had already eaten the meat taken from the few horses the Twenty-sixth Cavalry had left; later, the hungry troops ate the horses' oats. More and more of Reed's skinny friends came down with malaria.

Reed operated out of the battalion headquarters and bivouac area in the dense jungle about a mile above the southern coastline at Mariveles. Increasing exhaustion and hunger gnawed and tugged at him, body and soul. Although they made fewer supply runs over shorter distances, Reed and Henderson had to keep a constant lookout for the hostile airplanes that frequently circled overhead. Trying to supplement the daily 920-calorie diet, they also kept their eyes searching for wild chickens. When they spotted one, they shot it, dug a pit, dropped the chicken in, and waited. When an iguana fell for the bait, they quickly started a fire and soon feasted on the big lizard's roasted tail. They shot monkeys and took them to the company kitchen, where the cooks boiled them. But Reed didn't like the taste of the tough monkey meat, nor did he like the sight of a skinned monkey; it looked too much like a baby.

For several days a small group of Japanese soldiers who had landed behind the main battle lines in the vicinity of Reed's bivouac area concealed themselves during the day and learned the tankers' names. Then at night they lay outside the perimeter and called for Jack and others by name, asking for help. The tankers knew not to respond, but it kept them awake. So did the knowledge that there were hostile airplanes flying too high to be heard; only when the falling bombs exploded in the jungle treetops did Reed know Japanese flyers had paid them a call. It was nerve-racking not to know when or where the bombs would fall.

Before a tank and infantry team drove the Japanese operating behind the main line out on a point—where they jumped off a cliff onto the beach, choosing suicide over surrender—Reed saw how difficult it had been for the tanks to operate in the rugged jungle in the Anyasan Point and Silaiim Point areas. One tank had been knocked out of action by a magnetic mine slapped on it by a hidden enemy soldier. He saw a disabled tank that had been filled with dirt and watched other tankers dig around until they discovered that the dead crew had been buried in their own tank. They had waited quietly for darkness to unbutton their hatch, whereupon the Japanese dropped in a grenade, killing the crew, and then filled the tank with dirt.

On April 3, 1942, a reinforced Japanese army launched a major attack against the undernourished and weakened Bataan defenders. Desperate for food, Reed decided to check out the rumor that the U.S. Navy had food stored at nearby Cabcaben. He and Henderson commandeered a jeep that had enough gas in it to make the twenty-mile round trip from their bivouac area. Fortunately, at Cabcaben he met Sam Darling, a pharmacist's mate from Danville, Kentucky. Though reluctant to break navy regulations, Darling agreed to give them some food, provided they kept it quiet. They readily promised not to tell a soul. Darling took them into a large tunnel complex filled to the brim with canned goods and gave his excited and happy new friend from an adjoining Kentucky county a few cans of C rations, peaches, and tomatoes.

On their way back they discussed what they should do about their promise not to tell. It didn't seem right to Reed that all that food was there while the army was going hungry. For the time being, they decided to squirrel the food away and share it with just a couple of friends. At Cabcaben for a second time, Reed listened intently as Darling repeated the story told by the crew of a submarine that had surfaced the night before to take on food and supplies. Reed, hungry for any good news, smiled as Darling told how the American sub had sneaked into Tokyo Bay and waited for a new ship to come off the skids, and then had sunk it. But before the sub could escape, it had to take a lot of depth charges while it lay quietly on the bottom of the bay. Reed hoped it was a true story. Returning this time with several cases of food and two cartons of cigarettes, he and Henderson decided that they had a higher moral obligation than their pledge to remain silent. They told their supply officer about the food stored in the tunnels.

Having the cases of food—now being shared with a larger circle of friends—was like having boxes of gold, but it did not lift Reed's spirits much; it was too late. He could clearly see that the end was coming: the front lines were collapsing; there were no reinforcements; and he knew that they would be subject to brutal treatment if not death at the hands of the Japanese. The tankers had already exchanged stories of Japanese brutality in China and Burma. And earlier, when the defenders had overrun a Japanese hospital, Reed had seen for himself evidence that the enemy had shot their own wounded to keep them from falling into the hands of the Americans. Rumors that Gen. Jonathan Wainwright was about to surrender made the tankers angry. Reed and some friends talked about what they should do and decided they would fight to the last man—with rocks if necessary. Thinking that the Japanese were not going to take any prisoners and that he was not going to get out of Bataan alive, Reed mentally resigned himself to death.

Early in the morning of April 9, 1942, word came down to destroy all equipment, because General Wainwright had surrendered all his forces on Bataan. There was no place to go and nothing they could do, and Reed felt the despair that hung over the bivouac area. While they worked frantically to burn, bury, and blow up their equipment, the Japanese bombed and strafed them. In the confusion Reed barely noticed the earthquake that shook the ground beneath his feet.

In the column leaving the bivouac area, the somber men moved quietly with their emotions in turmoil. Reed struggled to get his feelings under control. A prayer would cross his lips now and then and disappear. He glanced back and forth, searching for the Japanese machine gunners he expected would open up any minute. He felt that President Franklin Roosevelt and the army had let them down. They had been told at the beginning that they were fighting a retrograde action, part of a strategic plan to gather them on Bataan where food, ammo, fuel, and other supplies would be sufficient to enable them to fight until reinforced. He knew that the tankers had done their part to buy time for the United States, and it had pleased him that General Wainwright had told the defenders to hold their heads high, for they had fought the good fight. But now their heads hung low. He had to beat down his anger to stay alert. Still, other converging emotions constantly distracted him. He felt thankful that the folks at home were safe from this mess, but he worried about how his wife, Joanna Coleman, would take the news of their surrender. Hungry and half sick, he thought, "If they kill me, so what?" Someone else said, "Hell, they ain't going to kill all of us." A little ray of hope shown through, and he thought maybe this danger would pass.

At the assembly point near Mariveles, Japanese soldiers met them. With disbelief and contempt Reed looked at the small, bedraggled soldiers and said to himself, "We are surrendering to those little bastards." Humiliation drove his spirits down even further. Angry guards shouted orders in Japanese and waved their hands, pointing first to the prisoners and then to the ground. Finally, some of the new POWs got the message and hurriedly started throwing the things they had carried out of the bivouac area into a pile; others, startled and confused, milled around trying to protect themselves from being hit with rifle butts. In the midst of the angry shouts and confusion, Reed saw a guard run his bayonet through a prisoner. The American's knees buckled and he slumped to the ground. After seeing another POW stabbed to death on the ground, Reed thought, "I have got to get out of here at the first opportunity."

Standing at attention in a formation of four ranks, Reed had to control his rage as a guard stuck his hands in Reed's pocket and took whatever he wanted. Reluctantly, Reed handed over his watch and wedding ring. Reed and Joanna had married while they were still in high school, and it hurt to part with his wedding ring. But he still had an important possession untouched by the Japanese—his canteen.

Moving out toward Cabcaben on what historians would later name the Bataan Death March, Reed pondered what lay ahead and what he had to do to stay alive. Still weighing about 200 pounds, he knew he was in better shape than many of his peers, but it was already obvious to him that he must concentrate on staying alive. The signs were everywhere. Just off the road he saw a hundred contorted and bloodied bodies scattered over the ground of the compound Americans had set up for Japanese POWs, and word came back that the Japanese had machine-gunned their own soldiers who had surrendered.

The long snakelike column of four men abreast in groups of about one hundred clogged the road to Cabcaben and beyond. Past Cabcaben the column moved northward on the road along the east coast of Bataan. Reed's group was near the rear of the long column of some 10,000 Americans and 65,000 Filipinos. Soon the thin, exhausted, hungry, thirsty, and in some cases sick men began falling to the ground. Now and then shots rang out. Word rippling up and down the column confirmed Reed's suspicion that those too weak to be helped up were being shot or bayoneted. Near Cabcaben the sudden, loud boom of Japanese artillery at the airfield grabbed Reed's attention. He knew the artillery shells roaring over his head were aimed at the Americans on Corregidor, five miles away. Just as he came within a few feet of the guns, he was horrified to see a huge shell, roaring like a freight train, rise out of Corregidor and head for the Japanese artillery. The American shell exploded in the middle of the Japanese battery and a hot, jagged fragment about the size of a nickel slashed through the flesh of Reed's leg and lodged against the bone. With his ears ringing, he took note of the blood running down his leg but didn't dwell on it. Although the prisoners were caught in a duel between Japanese and American artillery and Reed feared for his life, he was glad to see the American gunners pounding the Japanese.

Before the prisoners reached Orion, the guards had Reed's group sit. He pulled his pants leg up and looked at his now festering wound. The POW next to him said: "If nobody is watching, I've got a mess kit knife here in my pocket. Maybe you can get that metal out." Reed took the knife and, despite the pain, worked it under the shell fragment and pried it out. To stop the bleeding, he scooped up a handful of mud and plastered it over the wound.

Farther up the clogged road, Japanese troops were moving south in trucks. While both the convoy and Reed's group were halted, Reed's attention shifted to a Japanese officer who ranted and railed at the guards for shooting and wounding two POWs. Following the officer's orders, the guards hastily dug a shallow hole in the soft dirt, picked up the wounded prisoners, pitched them into the grave, and started to bury them alive. The horrified victims thrashed about, clawed their way to the edge, and grabbed the guards' legs. The guards beat the wounded men's heads and bodies with shovels. More guards with shovels pushed the bleeding and mangled POWs to the bottom of the grave while dirt was hastily thrown over them. The battered prisoners clawed their way out again. More beatings and more shoveling followed. Finally, the thrashing in the grave stopped, and the grunts and moans turned to silence. Only the noise of continued shoveling could be heard. The memory of the grunts and moans and the men's panicked expressions moved Reed and his group to tears before they moved on. It puzzled him that the officer would reprimand the guards for shooting the POWs and then idly stand by and watch their cruel murder and burial. But there was no time for reflection. He had to get his mind back on the business of surviving.

The hot sun that bore down constantly on the laboring, suffering column took its toll. Near Orion, about halfway up the peninsula, Reed's dehydrated body demanded water. He had drained the last drop from his canteen a day and a night before, and now his tongue had begun to swell. He knew that if he did not get water he would die of thirst. He also knew that if he made a break for one of the many artesian wells beside the road, the guards would try to kill him. But the sight of cool water streaming from a well and his overwhelming thirst drove him to break rank and make a dash for it. While he was filling his canteen a shot rang out. Reed dived to the ground as the bullet whizzed by. Fortunately for him, other prisoners too broke rank and distracted the guards, who clubbed the thirsty POWs with rifles to force them back into ranks. During the confusion Reed, unnoticed, crawled back as fast as he could. He had managed to save a little water. Approaching Pilar, three miles farther north, five POWs broke ranks and made a mad dash for another well. The guards shot and wounded all five and then bayoneted them to death. Reed licked his dry lips as he watched in disbelief, and his spirits sank even further.

Constant agony dogged Reed and the other prisoners every step of the way, and death stalked them around the clock. Near Hermosa, just out of Bataan, Reed and his group of weak, exhausted, and thirsty men snaked their way through a crowd of friendly Filipinos gathered on both sides of the road. Full of compassion, they shouted words of encouragement and sneaked the Americans small portions of food and water. The masses of sympathetic civilians in the rear squeezed their front ranks closer to the road. The infuriated guards shouted and gestured, motioning to the Filipinos to get back, and then started attacking the people with bayonets and rifles. In the midst of the general shouting and shoving, Reed watched out of the corner of his eye as one guard stuck his bayonet into a screaming baby. The force ripped the infant out its mother's arms. While the woman wailed in agony, the guard struggled to get the bayonet out of the child and then, shouting and screaming, hit the side of the mother's face with the bloody bayonet. Others were stabbed before the people in the rear caught on and started making room for the civilians nearest the road, now in total panic.

Walking on, Reed knew not to look directly at the terrible scene. He had seen others bashed just for looking at a Japanese act of brutality. Nor could he feel sorry for the mother or think about the awful act; he had to concentrate on what was happening around him in order to survive. If a prisoner became distracted for a moment, he could find himself in trouble—hit in the head with the butt of a rifle by Japanese soldiers in trucks going in the opposite direction, or attacked by the guards. Always there was some threat hanging over the POWs' heads. By this time not even thoughts of prayers entered Reed's mind, only the need to maintain constant vigilance throughout the day.

Nights were no better. Usually, Reed's group would be moved off the road and jammed together in a sitting position. All night he sat pressed together with the others, unable to stretch out his legs. When the guards passed around a bucket of water, a fast prisoner could manage to get a canteen cup full. For several days at a time Reed's group got no food, and when they did, it was only a handful of rice. Some prisoners with dysentery had saturated their pants, and a terrible odor hung over the cramped POWs. Later, after reaching Hermosa, they were herded into pens that had been occupied by other groups. Packed in like sardines, Reed and the others had to sit or stand all night in human feces. Although he didn't have dysentery himself, Reed's coveralls were coated with filth.

Reed and Lonnie C. Gray were the only two of the sixty-six National Guardsmen from Harrodsburg in Reed's marching group. The Guardsmen had been separated from the start: some, like Reed and Gentry, had transferred out of Company D before the march began; some had gone with Morgan French to Corregidor on a boat commandeered at Mariveles; and others were scattered about in different groups. But somewhere beyond Hermosa and before they reached San Fernando, Reed ran into Lt. William Gentry and Lyle C. Harlow. Seeing them alive lifted Reed's spirits, though other than Gray, Harlow, and Gentry he didn't know who had survived the last battles before surrender or who had survived the march to this point. It would be some time before he learned that none of the Harrodsburg guardsmen had died on the march. The weary Kentuckians exchanged lessons learned on how to stay alive, talked about the odds of surviving this ordeal, and pondered whether escape into the jungles or the mountains was possible or desirable. Soon they were on the road again—in their own separate worlds.

Not far from San Fernando two or three POWs stumbled and nearly broke rank before others could help them along. Unfortunately, in the confusion Reed relaxed his guard for a moment, and a shouting and enraged Japanese soldier wheeled and jabbed the Kentuckian with his bayonet. For a moment the blow stopped Reed in his tracks. Fortunately, the jab wasn't meant to kill, and the guard jerked the bayonet out and left Reed bleeding, adding another difficulty to the task of staying alive.

By now some of the men with malaria were delirious and had to be carried along by others. Occasionally a weak man would fall and could not summon the strength to stand. If his fellow POWs couldn't get him up before a guard got there, he was doomed to death by a bullet or bayonet. No one knows the exact number who perished on the death march. Some estimate as many as 10,000 Filipinos and 700 Americans; Reed himself saw about twenty Americans killed between Mariveles and San Fernando.

When they reached San Fernando, the POWs were jammed into suffocatingly hot railroad cars for a nightmarish journey to Capas, about ten miles from their final destination at Camp O'Donnell. On the railroad cars the living did not know who among them had died on their feet until the survivors got off the train, making room for the dead to fall. Fortunately, Reed had decided to take the advice of a friendly Filipino who told him and others that those who volunteered for a detail would be working for Japanese engineers, and he thought they would get better treatment there. The detail loaded on a truck and in a few hours arrived back at Mariveles—where Reed had started on the agonizing march several days earlier.

For a couple of months Reed's detail filled in shell holes in the roads and rebuilt bridges. As long as they worked hard, they were treated reasonably well. One Japanese engineer who spoke English would sometimes sit and converse with the POWs. For Reed, any semblance of decent treatment ended with this detail; from there he was sent to the infamous Camp Cabanatuan.

In 1943, Reed and about 800 other POWs were assigned to work at Nichols Airfield, a few miles southeast of Manila. There they labored for months, usually moving earth and construction materials in the blazing sun or sometimes toiling in mud above their knees. Every day some of the abused, neglected, diseased, and underfed POWs died.

Captured American servicemen are guarded by Japanese troops just before the brutal Bataan Death March. Courtesy of the Kentucky Historical Society.

One day, Reed could not keep up with the crowd running across the airfield, everyone trying to avoid being the last to meet the chow truck. Having finished last, Reed knew what awaited him. While most of the guards ate in a Nipa hut, three of them tied Reed to a nearby post. One guard hit him across the back with a pick handle, another whacked him with a belt, and a third rammed his fist into Reed's stomach. For thirty minutes, while the other guards and POWs ate, Reed's tormenters circled him and jeered, alternately beating him on the body and over the head. One blow to an eye sent blood dripping down his cheek; a hit to the side of the head made his eardrum bleed. Finally, unconsciousness delivered him from the agony. It was not the only beating he had received for being the last POW to get to the chow line, nor was he the only one beaten, but it was the worst during his six-month stay at Nichols. His eardrum was permanently damaged.

Another time, after a hard day's work, a Japanese called "the white angel" by the Nichols Airfield detail (because he wore a Japanese commander's white uniform) rode in a limousine behind the column of weary POWs, pushing them toward the camp at the usual fast pace. On the road Reed's closest friend, suffering from dysentery and too weak to go on, fell to the ground. An excited guard ran over and plunged his bayonet through the helpless prisoner and continued stabbing him until the man was dead. Outraged by this brutal act against his friend, Reed threw caution to the wind and with all his might struck the guard under the chin. The blow broke the Japanese soldier's jaw. Other guards quickly unleashed their fury against Reed, and back at camp they put him in the sweatbox under the blazing hot sun. For fourteen days Reed stayed coiled up in a box about two by three by four feet. Three times a day he got a ball of rice. An old bucket served as a toilet. Heat and painful cramps consumed most of his attention. Still, he grieved over his friend, and when he thought about the murder it further embittered him toward his captors. Though it had been obvious that his friend had been too weak to get up, the Japanese tried to justify the killing on the grounds that the POW had tried to escape. This gross injustice and evasion of responsibility added to Reed's bitterness and frustrations.

When at last they released him, Reed could not stand up, and for a few days he had to crawl to his food, to the latrine, or wherever he had to go. When the Japanese realized Reed could no longer work at the airfield, they shipped him to Bilibid prison in Manila. By then the emaciated prisoner's weight had dropped from 200 pounds at the time of his capture to about 100 pounds.

One morning after Christmas of 1944, back at Cabanatuan, Reed sat up on the bamboo floor, looked at another Harrodsburg tanker who slept next to him, and realized that Ben Devine was too weak and too sick to get up. Every day after work on the camp farm, Reed nursed, fed, and cared for his friend, who was suffering from malaria, dysentery, and the effects of malnutrition. But after about a week he saw the faraway stare on Devine's face that indicated his sick friend was giving up. Reed knew Devine's life would soon slip away if he didn't do something. But what? He reminded Devine that Ruth, the pretty wife he had married just before going overseas, was waiting for him and that his family wanted to see him again. Devine said, "There isn't any need to go on. There isn't any need for any more suffering. There is nothing in the future, just more of the same."

By now Devine's lips were scabbed over and sticking together. After work Reed gently washed the scabs off, pried Devine's mouth open, and forced water down his throat, but Ben would not eat. Reed knew that sometimes a person with the "thousand-mile stare" would snap out of his despondency if you could make him mad, but nothing worked on Devine. There was no response. One evening Reed came in from work and saw maggots working between his friend's lips. Mercifully, the angel of death came that night and took Ben while Reed slept.

By the end of 1944, the 500 POWs still living at Cabanatuan were all in bad shape. Many not much better off had been sent to labor camps in Japan on the "Hell Ships." Of the Harrodsburg Guardsmen only Reed, Bill Gentry, Charles Quinn, and Garret Royalty remained at Cabanatuan. To stay alive the POWs would risk their lives and steal food while working in the vegetable crops. Compassionate Filipinos from a little village down the road periodically appeared beyond the camp fence and threw sugar cakes to the Americans. They also sang popular American songs in English, slipping bits of news about the progress of the war into the lyrics to lift the prisoners' spirits. And there had been signs that their ordeal might soon be over. The friendly Filipinos had told them that American and Allied forces were closing in on the Philippines. In September, Reed's spirits had shot upward when he saw the first American air attack against Japanese targets on Luzon. The large formation of airplanes from aircraft carriers told the prisoners that powerful forces were within striking distance. Still, it was an ever present challenge to stay alive, and they had to use their collective wits and skills in every way possible. To supplement their rations, Reed and others, at the risk of their lives, found a way to sneak out of camp at night to steal food. Using their discarded plaster cast for the ingredients, the prisoners manufactured pills that looked exactly like sulfa pills and traded them for food to guards seeking treatment for gonorrhea. To prepare the food without getting caught, they established ingenious networks to warn of approaching guards.

After hearing that the Americans had landed at Lingayen Gulf on January 9, 1945, Reed and others organized a pool, gambling on the exact day, hour, and minute the Cabanatuan prisoners would be liberated. But he and others talked and worried about being lined up and massacred before that could happen. Had he known that on December 14, 1944, Willard R. Yeast and Joseph B. Million, fellow Guardsmen from Harrodsburg, had been herded into trenches with 150 others at Palawan Island, doused with gasoline, and set on fire, he might have panicked.

One day, guard activity picked up in and around the camp, and prisoners were put to work building a platform. One guard who was a Christian and shared information with the prisoners whenever he could told Reed that Tomoyuki Yamashita, the commanding general of the Japanese forces in the Philippines, was going to speak to them. All the POWs who had the strength to walk were gathered in front of the platform and forced to sit down on their knees. Reed remembers that the Japanese officer he assumed was Yamashita spoke through an interpreter, saying essentially: "We hate you damn people. If I had my way, I would line a machine gun up here and kill every damn one of you. But Tokyo won't let me do it. We are not going to win this war. We know that. But as far as we are concerned we have won this war because of the economic distress we've caused in your country, the turmoil we've caused. We've won our war, because we are going to get our fish and rice regardless of who feeds it to us. You sons of bitches, we hate you. Some day, some way, we'll whip you. Some day, some way, we'll conquer you."

It took a moment to soak in, but one day Reed and his friends realized that the guards had disappeared. The prisoners who were still mobile began scouting around, and soon they had a plan. Some headed for the farm cattle and started a roundup; some gathered firewood; others rigged up grills and assembled butchering equipment. Like a beehive, the camp hummed with excitement and movement. At the slaughtering site, weak and emaciated men wrestled with the cattle, joking and laughing about their plight as they tried a range of ideas to get the job done.

When the aroma of steaks on the grills spread throughout the camp, the festive mood moved up another notch. The POWs were about to have their first decent meal since the bombing of Clark Field. Before long, hungry men were gorging, and it wasn't long until Reed, like most of his friends, had severe stomach cramps. Some of the celebrants lost everything they had eaten.

In a few days seventy-three new guards appeared and took control of the camp. Traffic was building up on the road just north of the camp as convoys of Japanese combat troops being redeployed by General Yamashita rushed by. The prisoners, watching, sensed that their fate would soon change. They did not know that General MacArthur, leading the approaching American army, had had reports that caused him to fear the Japanese might massacre the POWs rather than let them fall into the hands of the Americans.

On the evening of January 30, 1945, Reed and his friends sat chatting along the outside wall of their bamboo barracks. A guard at the front gate clanged the gong, as he did routinely on the half-hour. Reed figured it must be about 7:30 P.M. In minutes, a shot rang out. All conversations ended, and Reed hastily looked around to see if a prisoner was trying to escape. Almost immediately there was a second shot. Reed thought, "if they missed him the first time, maybe they will miss again." Then all hell broke loose. Rifle and automatic weapons fire filled the air in and around the camp. Reed hit the dirt, face down, and wrapped his arms around his head. What in the hell were the Japanese up to now?

He had no way of knowing that Lt. Col. James Mucci and part of his Sixth Ranger Battalion were systematically wiping out the guards in the towers, bursting through the main gate, annihilating the off-duty guards in their barracks and the 150 Japanese soldiers temporarily bedded down in the camp, and knocking out the tanks in the tank shed. Only when he heard the Rangers shouting, "Head for the main gate!" did Reed realize that they were being rescued. He and others ran toward a gate they had been using, but giving some POWs a firm shove, the Rangers quickly rerouted them to a gate they hadn't used before.

Half running and half walking, skinny POWs converged on the gate. Behind them, Rangers carried on their backs and in their arms about 170 who were nonambulatory. In just twelve minutes the firing was down to a few scattered shots in the camp. Reed saw the Rangers' wounded and dying surgeon, Capt. James Fisher, being attended to on the ground. Nearby, a Ranger stepped behind eight Japanese guards with their hands up and one at a time slit their throats. Reed watched it but never gave it a thought as he hurried along. Within thirty minutes of the first shot, a red flare shot into the air, the signal that all POWs had cleared the camp. Reed heard a big explosion and machine guns firing, 300 or 400 yards to his right. He didn't know the Philippine Scouts and guerrillas were inflicting heavy casualties on a Japanese combat unit that happened to be bivouacking in the vicinity and had launched an attack trying to get to the POW camp.

In the moonlit night 511 weak POWs, in a long column stretching out about a mile, moved happily toward friendly lines some twenty miles away. Water buffaloes pulled carts loaded with the men too weak to walk; those who could walk followed the carts. When a water buffalo gave out along the way, friendly Filipinos quickly replaced it and added more carts during the night for the men who collapsed.

About ten miles north of Cabanatuan the column had to enter a mile-long section of a main highway the Japanese had been using to move forces at night. Although Colonel Mucci had blocking forces deployed, he worried that they might not be able to hold out long enough to allow the column to clear the dangerous stretch of the road. Reed wasn't aware of these problems. He was in a state of ecstasy, thinking about his wife, his two children, and the rest of his family, rejoicing that the end of his purgatory was in sight. Despite his physical condition, he thought he could walk any distance necessary to get out of there. Tired, weak, and weighing only about a hundred pounds, he nevertheless moved with a spring in his walk. The open wound that had plagued him ever since he had operated on himself during the Death March continued to drain. The arm the Japanese had broken with a pick handle hung in a sling. Two teeth knocked out left a gaping hole in his smile. The dry beriberi caused by malnutrition ached like a bad tooth, as it would for the rest of his life. He was deaf in his right ear from the beating at the airfield. But none of this reduced the warm glow that embraced him.

By 8:00 A.M. the column had covered about fifteen miles and arrived at Sibul, a tiny village where friendly Filipinos waved American flags, fed the former prisoners, and provided an additional twenty carabao carts. Here

Former American POWs march to an evacuation hospital on Luzon after rescue by the Sixth Ranger Battalion's raid on the Japanese prison camp at Cabanatuan. Courtesy of the Kentucky Historical Society.

for the first time Mucci made radio contact with Sixth Army headquarters at Guimba. The good news about the raid rippled through army headquarters.

At 11:00 A.M. the lead Ranger ran into a friendly patrol who advised him that trucks and ambulances awaited the men a short distance down the road. Reed welcomed the friendly airplanes that circled overhead. In an hour the convoy arrived at Guimba, where American soldiers cheered, waved, shouted words of encouragement, and gave the V for victory sign. As those who could walk hastily unloaded, the crowd gathered in closer, shook the hands of the long-lost Philippine defenders, patted them on the back, and told them what a great job they had done and that America was proud of them. In the midst of the good cheer and jubilance, tears rolled down Reed's cheeks. Wide smiles and wet cheeks surrounded him. It was the best day of his life. He was a free man again.

Kamikaze Attacks in the Pacific

Lieutenant John Barrows
Aircraft Carrier Pilot, U.S. Navy

On his first combat mission, in the summer of 1942, Lt. (jg.) John Barrows proudly flew his Dauntless dive bomber on the wing of the group leader. He looked forward to the anticipated action. Flying ahead of three squadrons at 18,000 feet and above solid cloud cover, he felt exhilarated. His eyes constantly swept the cloud formation, looking for an opening to the Pacific below. Then the clouds parted and all eyes in the group focused on three Japanese destroyers and one cruiser in the vicinity of the island of Bougainville. Tense with excitement, Barrows dropped his right wing and peeled off the formation into a descending forty-five-degree turn. At the right moment he pitched the nose down into a seventy-degree power dive.

Diving at 250 knots and a hundred yards behind the skipper, Barrows was sure he could sink the enemy cruiser. Over a hundred times he had practiced hitting targets, and he had beaten the other pilots in bombing competition in the States, thus earning his position of wingman to the skipper. His confidence soared as he concentrated on the moving target. The twenty-five-year-old pilot dived through the puffs of smoke from antiaircraft shells with some anxiety but not much fear; he was still too young and too ignorant to understand the danger. At 2,500 feet he released a 1,000-pound bomb and started pulling up. At 1,000 feet he was out of the dive and climbing for the assembly point.

Back safely on the aircraft carrier *Sangamon,* the pilots could now joke and laugh about little things that had happened on the mission. Openly, Barrows bragged about sinking the cruiser while visions of the Distinguished Flying Cross danced in his head. But then his friend Ben Harrison, who had followed him in the dive, announced, "Barrows—you missed." His high spirits evaporated. The others, however, continued to celebrate, for the group had sunk two destroyers and one cruiser.

Lieutenant John "Jug" Barrows, a U.S. Navy pilot on the aircraft carrier USS *Bunker Hill*. Courtesy of John Barrows.

The U.S. Navy was then operating in a high-risk area inside the Japanese outer perimeter in the Pacific. Barrows did not know until the last moment about the Guadalcanal invasion plans that would crack that perimeter, but on August 8, 1942, the day after the U.S. Marines landed, he fought in the Battle of Savo Island in the waters off Guadalcanal. It was the beginning of a desperate fight to control the shipping lanes in the area. So many American and Japanese ships were sunk in the waters of Guadalcanal that the place was named Iron Bottom Sound.

Even though Barrows knew that the outcome of the Guadalcanal invasion was still in doubt, he felt good about going ashore on August 20, 1942, when his Twenty-eighth Dive Bomber Squadron and others touched down on Henderson Field. Barrows reasoned that the enemy couldn't sink the island, but they might sink his aircraft carrier, the *Sangamon*, which he had just left.

Since Pearl Harbor, the Japanese had extended their outer perimeter several thousand miles into the Pacific by capturing island after island. The invasion of Guadalcanal was America's first offensive of the war. Had Barrows known that Tokyo had given Lt. Gen. Harukichi Hyakutake 50,000 men, based on the nearby island of Rabual, to drive the Americans off Guadalcanal, he might not have felt so secure.

The day after Barrows landed, his dive-bombing skills were put to the test. To help defeat the Japanese foot soldiers sent in to attack the eastern side of the four-by-seven-mile U.S. Marine perimeter around the airfield, Barrows bombed and strafed the enemy in close support of the marines on the ground. The proximity of the marines to the target made the task difficult, for he worried about killing an American by mistake.

The contrast between life on the ship and existence in the jungle didn't go unnoticed. On the ship he ate steak and eggs; on the ground he ate field rations, and every day they tasted worse. On the ship he slept between sheets; here he slept on a canvas cot in a hot and humid four-man tent. During his first night on shore Barrows's ears pricked up when a marine shouted in a loud and angry voice, "Turn those God damn lights out or I will shoot them out!" From then on they lived under blackout conditions.

About 2:00 A.M. someone shouted, "Air attack!" Barrows hastily slipped on his shoes and made a mad dash for a foxhole. He jumped in the first one he came to, right on top of a marine sergeant. Close on his heels, his friend Ben Harrison tumbled in on top of them. The old sergeant was not too happy with his uninvited guests, but the whistle of a falling bomb, getting louder as it neared the ground, distracted him. With his head down as low as he could get it, Barrow thought the bomb had his name on it. It crashed down within 150 yards, and the loud exploding-cracking noise and flying debris made his pounding heart beat faster. To cut the tension, the old sergeant tried to entertain the young pilots. He said, "Guadalcanal is the only place in the world where you can stand in your foxhole in mud up to your ass and have the wind blow dust in your face." He was right about this island just below the equator and about a hundred miles north of Australia.

During his first two-week stay on the island, one or two enemy planes came over every night at about the same time. But from then on Barrows and Harrison had their own foxholes. Harrison enjoyed a reputation of being a tiger in the air, but the bombing attacks petrified him. Barrows spread the word that Harrison was the only man in the squadron who could turn a corner with both feet in the air during a bombing attack.

One night while Barrows was in the control tower, a Japanese pilot called the tower in English and told Barrows in a friendly and nonthreatening voice that he had gone to college at the University of Oregon. While they carried on a conversation, the Japanese pilot continued his approach to the airfield, dropped his bomb, and departed.

Barrows was worked hard; as one of the more skilled bomber pilots, he was designated to support the marines when the enemy was close to the "friendlies." Some days he would fly three missions. Such a schedule, plus the mud and dust, made staying clean a challenge. The numerous crocodiles in the nice, fresh river that ran near the airfield made a leisure bath there impossible, so to beat the reptile threat Barrows and friends rigged a shower.

One day Barrows's friend made a dash to the river, scooped up a bucket of water before the crocodiles could react, and poured it through their makeshift shower head while the exhausted Barrows hurriedly soaped his grimy and dark-tanned body. In the midst of the joy of the shower, a white-skinned man with a towel wrapped around a pudgy midsection appeared and announced, "I'm a lieutenant commander and I'm ordering you out of that shower." Barrows thought about it and, although he realized the risk of disobeying an order, informed the intruder in no uncertain terms that he was not going to leave. The expected summons to headquarters was not long in coming. A navy captain asked Barrows to explain his conduct. Just as he finished telling his story, a short, gray-haired man stepped out from behind a curtainlike partition and said, "Son, any time a son of a bitch orders you out of your shower, you tell him to kiss your ass." It would be a little while before Barrows realized that his protector was Adm. William F. "Bull" Halsey.

One night an alarm came from the watchers behind enemy lines who warned of approaching Japanese airplanes or ships. Enemy ships were coming down the "slot," a large channel between the Solomon Islands leading down to Guadalcanal. In the wee hours of the morning men all around the airfield scrambled to get about 125 planes in the air to meet the challenge. Rudely awakened from his slumber, Barrows hurriedly dressed and joined other sleepy-eyed pilots converging on the briefing tent. With his head crammed full of information about the mission and how it would be conducted, Barrows concentrated on the things he had to do and rushed for his plane.

There he joined his gunner. Up and down the lanes around the airstrip, starting engines coughed and roared in the parking areas. Soon, planes with only dim flashing lights—a red light on the right wing, blue light on the left wing, and white light on the tail—were jockeying for position, the pilots trying to get to the takeoff spot at the end of the unlighted runway in proper order. Barely able to see and keep up with all the movement around him, Barrows strained to focus on the dim lights. He feared that he might get confused and plow into a moving plane on the ground or crash on takeoff.

Parked on the end of the runway a few feet to the right of Capt. Spencer Butts's plane, Barrows quickly ran his throttle forward and back to check the magnetos, at the same time watching the flashing lights of Butts's plane out of the corner of his eye. The moment Butts started moving down the metal-planked runway, Barrows started counting off the seconds to get the proper short distance behind his group leader. At the right moment he ran his throttle full forward and rolled down the runway. Two climbing left turns and he began flying parallel to the runway, opposite to the direction of take-off. He saw flashing lights on the trailing planes making their inside turns, but he couldn't see the lights of the planes still lifting off from the runway. At the assembly point in the sky the converging planes started a big circling maneuver so that the pilots could tidy up their formation.

Rolling out on the heading for the target and on the wing of what he thought was Captain Butts's plane, Barrows relaxed a little. Soon the rising sun began lighting the sky. A casual glance to his right caused him to jerk his head around and take a hard look. The young lieutenant couldn't believe that his group leader was not in the plane next to him. They had orders to maintain radio silence, but he was overwhelmed by the notion that the responsibility of leading this large formation of armed planes against a dangerous target—one that might threaten the whole Guadalcanal operation—rested on his shoulders. Finally, by the use of hand signals, word was passed through the flight formation, and the second in command came forward and took the lead. As it turned out, they didn't locate the enemy ships. Back at Henderson Field, Barrows learned that Butts's plane had lost power on takeoff and crashed into a coconut tree. Fortunately, he was not injured, and Barrows would again get to fly in the coveted position of the leader's wingman.

Barrows knew little about the general situation, but he sensed that the outcome hung in the balance. He knew that the two navies were locked in a mortal struggle to control the shipping lanes to Guadalcanal. Both sides needed to resupply and to reinforce their troops. When the American aviation fuel tanks ran dangerously low, Barrows lived in a chronic state of anxiety until they were topped off again.

While supporting the ground troops, he also participated in the navy battle for the shipping lanes. One day, while flying at 16,000 feet up the slot, Barrows looked over and saw Captain Butts pointing down at two grounded destroyers off Tulagi Island. Barrows realized that Butts wanted him to go down and identify the nationality of the ships. He dreaded the thought of leaving the relative safety of the formation, and knowing they were under radio silence, Barrows decided to pretend that he didn't see any hand signals. Soon his leader moved in closer and signaled in no uncertain terms that he wanted Barrows to leave the formation and do his duty. Finally, when Barrows began fearing his leader's wrath more than he feared being jumped by Japanese fighters, he dropped a wing and pointed the nose into a seventy-degree dive. But he wasn't happy.

After identifying the Japanese ships he flew in a circle at 3,500 feet and watched the dive bombers peel off and start their dive toward the grounded destroyers. Suddenly, out of the blue, two Japanese Zeke fighter planes jumped him. A dive bomber with a gunner in the second seat is no match for even one fighter and Barrows knew it. His pulse raced. Fortunately, in his maneuvers he discovered a cloud and quickly ducked into it. Coming out the other side, he nearly collided with a PBY, a big, slow American seaplane. The notion that both he and the PBY pilot were using the same cloud sanctuary at the same time amused him.

Back on the ground, Butts said to Barrows, "I had a hard time getting you to move up there," and that was all that was said.

After several more combat missions from his old aircraft carrier and from Henderson Field, and a bout with malaria, Barrows returned to the States. But, after about five months the pleasant stateside tour ended, and on January 24, 1945, he sailed under the Golden Gate Bridge. The first time he had left the United States to go to war, he had previously made only six landings on an aircraft carrier. This time he was an experienced pilot and one of the few combat veterans in the Eighty-fourth Dive Bombing Squadron of the Eighty-fourth Air Group on the USS *Bunker Hill.* This time he thought he knew what to expect.

The *Bunker Hill* approached Japan in the middle of February 1945 to participate in the navy's first dive-bombing mission in the Tokyo area. Barrows paid close attention to the intelligence officer's instructions about what the pilots ought to do if they were shot down. He didn't like the notion of giving up the pistol he carried in a pocket on his pants leg. Early in the war, he had resigned himself to the possibility of death; he was more concerned with how he would die. He knew about the Bataan Death March of 1942 and how the Japanese had brutalized prisoners of war. He dreaded the thought of protracted suffering before death. Knowing there would be more antiaircraft fire over Japan, he had thought about the consequences of being captured; he had already resolved that he was not going to be taken prisoner. Now he was being told not to resist, and that bothered him.

At 8:30 A.M. on February 25, 1945, twelve "Helldiver" bombers roared down the flight deck one after the other and climbed in a column formation behind their leader, Lieutenant "Jug" Barrows, to the assembly point in the sky. There they joined the air group's torpedo squadron and two of its fighter squadrons, and together they headed toward Tokyo.

As they reached the coast of Japan and continued on, Barrows took in the beautiful crazy quilt patterns made by the light blanket of snow covering the rice paddies. Forced down to 13,000 feet by clouds, Barrows became anxious as they approached the large Koizumi aircraft assembly plant, an untouched and easy target. He became more concerned and irritated when the group leader led the formation into a glide to 10,000 feet, a dangerously low nose-over point where they would start the dive for the target. Suddenly, his friend Hook Brothers, a pilot in the group's torpedo squadron, broke radio silence and shouted, "I'm hit. My engine is out. I'm going down!" Barrows listened intently to Lieutenant Commander Swanson, skipper of the torpedo squadron, telling Hook to bail out. "When you hit the ground," he said, "just stand there—don't resist. Our prayers go with you." In a little while Hook reported over the radio that he had landed safely on the ground.

Barrows glanced at the burning factory and the black smoke plumes rising high into the sky as his squadron left the area. He tried hard to concentrate on flying to keep from thinking about his friend. But after he and the others had landed on the ship, regardless of the unwritten rule that you don't dwell on or talk about the hazards of flying, they all discussed Hook's plight. They worried about his wife and family. Barrows had to struggle to get it all out of his mind.

On March 4, 1945, after twenty-two grueling days of flying combat missions over Japan, Iwo Jima, and Okinawa and about a 7,000-mile cruise, the USS *Bunker Hill* dropped anchor off Mog Mog, a little island southwest of Guam, where the pilots and sailors could let off steam and get away from the pressures of combat. Barrows hurried off the little boat that took them ashore, dumped his gear on his cot, and headed for the officers' club. The grass-covered shack wasn't much to look at, but it had what the pilots were looking for—more beer and whiskey than they could drink. Empty beer cans were everywhere.

Barrows and his friends drank and told war stories, drank and played softball, drank and played cards, drank and swam in the ocean. For ten days they hardly drew a sober breath. Still under the influence of alcohol on the tenth day, the squadron waited at the dock for the boat to take them back to the *Bunker Hill.* In spite of all the hard drinking, not all the pressure had been released. Suddenly, their skipper in a slurred voice shouted insults at the pilots from the aircraft carrier USS *Essex,* who were also waiting at the dock. When he insisted that it wasn't just the weather that caused them to fail to show up over Tokyo on a scheduled bombing raid, a fistfight started, and a free-for-all broke out between the two crews. Before it had run its course there were bruises, bloody noses, and one broken arm. Later, Barrows's friend Herb Wiley, a guitarist and composer, wrote a song titled "The Battle of Mog Mog." The ditty became their squadron's fighting song, and to this day they sing it at their reunions.

At dawn on March 19, 1945, the squadron took off to attack the great naval base of Kure on Honshu Island, Japan. Barrows was not with them; it was his morning to sack in. Two days earlier he had led a flight through intense heavy and medium antiaircraft fire over Japan, so he was pleased not to be scheduled for this mission. He woke up relieved and looking forward to a relaxed day—and he was having it until well into the morning when the general quarters bell rang out. Barrows rushed to the ready room and joined the other pilots not in the air.

When he stepped out on the deck after the all clear, the tall column of billowing black smoke from the USS *Franklin,* not more than 1,500 yards away, told him what had happened. First, the bombed aircraft carrier just sent up volumes of black smoke. Then Barrows saw aviation fuel–fed flames appear, grow, and spread. He hardly noticed the other pilots, quiet and solemn, standing beside him. He knew that a lot of sailors had been killed or wounded on the burning ship and that more would be killed as the bombs and ammunition stored aboard began to explode. The *Franklin* pilots had been over the same target areas where he had flown, and they flew the same kinds of airplanes as the *Bunker Hill* pilots. It was like watching kinfolks being wiped out. But self-preservation as well as empathy played on his mind. Watching the explosions, flames, and smoke made him feel vulnerable, jolted his confidence, and gave him a sense of urgency to get this war over with. The anti-Japanese feeling began to churn in his head. Eyes glued to the terrible scene, he lost track of time as he watched destroyers pull alongside the wounded ship, now filled with suffering and death. He admired the brave sailors on the destroyers who risked being blown out of the water while they helped fight the raging fires.

Returning from the Kure strike, the *Bunker Hill's* planes approached their carrier, but Barrows was so distracted that it took him a moment to realize his squadron was about to land. He hurried to the tower and took his place on "vulture row" with other pilots to watch the landings. The exuberant expressions on the faces of the returning pilots heading for the ready room and a debriefing told him that something big and exciting had occurred. Lt. C.J. Davis, the squadron's full-blood Indian from Oklahoma, even did an Indian victory dance with yells. Barrows soon learned that they had both reasons to celebrate and reasons to be sad.

They had arrived first over the Kure target area, ahead of three formations from other carriers. As the American planes passed to the northeast of Kure at 13,500 feet and approached their targets—the docks and the naval arsenal—the heavy antiaircraft fire increased in intensity, and to their great surprise the pilots saw a harbor packed with anchored Japanese combat ships. Immediately, they changed plans and started attacking the ships. They had bombed a battleship, a destroyer, and others. Lts. (jg.) H.R. Gordinier,

F.A. Swearingen, L.T. Hicks, and H.O. Timm had pounded a large aircraft carrier with four 1,000-pound bombs and eight 250-pound bombs. The gunners had seen bombs burst inside the carrier and smoke rising out of its hull.

Listening to the stories, Barrows felt left out. He regretted not having been a player in the great event. It would be a while before he would know that Lt. Charles Carper's gunner, M. Wilcox, had drowned when Carper ditched his severely damaged airplane in the ocean. Wilcox was the first person in the squadron to be killed in action. But what grieved Barrows most was the news about his friend Lt. (jg.) J.D. Welch. Some of Barrow's friends had heard Welch say over the radio, "I'm hit and heading east." They never heard from him again. Of the eleven planes one failed to return, one ditched, and four were hit by antiaircraft fire. Even so, Barrows wished he had been with his squadron in their moments of glory and loss.

That evening, saddened by the day's events, Barrows went to the galley to have a cup of coffee and be with friends. Someone brought two grim-looking pilots to his table and introduced them to Barrows. They told him that they were from the aircraft carrier USS *Hancock,* that they had made an emergency landing on the *Bunker Hill,* and that they had been on the Kure strike with Barrows's younger brother Dale A. Barrows, who also flew the navy's Helldiver bomber. First, they apologized for having to bring bad news, but they thought he would want to know. Then they said, "Your brother was shot down," but they hastened to add that someone had seen movement around an inflated life raft.

Barrows was stunned. He wondered how his widowed father would take this news. He knew that besides the heavy burden of fear for his missing son, his father would be filled with increased anxiety about his two remaining sons, both vulnerable to being hurt or killed in combat. He thought the strength of his sister, Viola Larson, would comfort their father; she had shown great steadfastness while dealing with the loss of her mother, a son, and her husband. Then he worried that his brother might be taken prisoner—but he didn't want him dead either. He hoped that if Dale was dead he hadn't suffered, or that if he was a prisoner he would not have to endure much suffering. He knew that he had to write a letter to the folks at home, and he dreaded it. The day had sapped his energies and drained his emotions. He would have to write it another day.

Early in the morning of March 23, 1945, Barrows sat in his cockpit on the flight deck with the propellers turning and roaring. At the go signal he released his brakes and shot down the flight deck. At liftoff, the worst possible moment, he lost power. His plane dribbled off the bow and fell like a rock into the ocean in front of the *Bunker Hill.* The bow wave sucked the plane under the ship before he could get out. The current and the forward movement of the ship twirled his water-filled plane, bumping and buffeting it against the hull. Gulping water, Barrows worked desperately to get out as the plane moved toward the four rapidly spinning propeller screws. He worked so hard trying to get out that he never gave the screws a thought, but his poor swimming ability crossed his mind. Suddenly, a powerful current sucked his plane into the large propellers—which instantly ripped the plane apart and popped him out into the ship's wake without a scratch.

Bobbing on the water in his yellow life jacket, he watched in disbelief as the carrier and her destroyer escorts continued on. It made him mad as hell, and although he was coughing and struggling to get air into his partially filled lungs, he managed to shake his fist at the ships as they disappeared over the horizon.

Then a lone destroyer came alongside the bobbing yellow life jacket and rescued the semiconscious pilot. Quickly, they drained the water out of Barrows and resuscitated him. He awoke to find his gunner, Airman 1st Class Sell, greeting him with a smile. The captain promised Barrows they would get them back to the *Bunker Hill* as soon as possible. The destroyer wired the carrier: "We've got one of your pilots." Barrows had to laugh when he found out how much he was worth: the destroyer told the *Bunker Hill* they would return him for fifteen gallons of ice cream. Later, alongside the *Bunker Hill,* the crews of both ships made ready to make the transfer at sea with a breeches buoy. In a state of good cheer, the destroyer crew shouted, "Send over the ice cream first." Sailors laughed and joked as Barrows was hoisted over to the carrier.

After bombing a target on Okinawa and while en route to the *Bunker Hill,* Barrows looked down at the mighty armada of over a thousand ships gathered in the waters off the island for the invasion scheduled for April 1, 1945. He saw the battleships in line plowing the waters parallel to the western shore of the island. He saw cruisers, destroyers, landing ships, and others. Farther out were several aircraft carriers, far more than he had ever seen before, each with its escort ships. He saw planes coming and going, landing and taking off. The carriers hummed with activity. Taking it all in made his confidence soar and gave him pride, even though he knew that the war had moved to Japan's back door and a ferocious battle awaited them. What he didn't know was that the Japanese were assembling over a thousand suicide planes to sink fighting ships and drive off the American fleets.

High over the *Bunker Hill* he flew in a circle, waiting his turn to get in the landing pattern. Just above the flight deck he entered the flight pattern on the downwind leg. Near the touchdown point—right hand on the stick, left hand on the throttle, and approaching stall speed—he kept his eyes on the signal officer's paddle for the signal either to touch down or to go around.

At the signal Barrows had to cut the engine or go to full power instantly. If he delayed in going to full power on a wave-off, he would be likely to stall and crash; if he touched down against a wave-off order, he faced certain court-martial. He was fully focused. On touchdown the hook caught the steel cable and jerked him to a sudden stop; he then quickly throttled up and taxied out of the way of the next plane in line to land, just seconds away from touchdown.

Later, on another mission of the preinvasion effort, he dropped the nose of his dive bomber seventy degrees and dived for the target. To keep the plane from exceeding its speed limit, he lowered the dive brakes. While he kept the nose pointed at the target, the altimeter whirled toward zero. He knew that hitting the target meant saving lives, so he was determined to take out the enemy gun emplacement. But at some point in the dive his mood changed from that of warrior to that of sportsman, and he became oblivious to anything being shot at him, so intent was he on scoring. He released the bomb; it hit the target; and a quick glance at the secondary explosion made him feel great.

Unfortunately, his total concentration had caused him to dive past the safe pullout altitude, and he was suddenly aware that he faced a violent crash. He snapped the stick forward and jerked it back, knowing that it was a dangerous maneuver. The plane shook and shuddered and stalled at high speed; engine torque flipped it over on its back. Quickly he pushed the stick forward again to catch it, to reduce the wing load, and to get it out of the stall before it fell out of control like a tumbling rock. To get the plane off its back he did a half roll. Meanwhile, the ground rose rapidly, and he did not yet have the plane under control so that he could level off or gain altitude. He was scared, busy, and running out of time. Another snap-jerk maneuver would stall it again and slam him into the ground, yet he needed to set the wing at the maximum angle to change from a dive to a climb. Too much wing attack angle would cause a stall, and the plane would fall to the ground; too little, and he would fly into the ground. He nursed it, keeping his eye on the ground and splitting the difference. Finally, at about treetop level, the crisis ended: he started gaining altitude. Joining his wingman, who had been circling nearby, he headed for home.

On the flight deck, he cut the engine, breathed a sigh of relief, and sat motionless for a moment. During the crisis, he had been too consumed with gaining control of the airplane to pray for help, and he didn't utter a prayer of thanksgiving now, but as he sat in the severely damaged airplane it dawned on him that an invisible helping hand had saved him. Suddenly he felt a communion with God that he had never experienced before; a warm, pleasant feeling surged through his veins and his soul. He knew now that he had a source to provide protection for whatever awaited him, and it gave him strength.

Feeling good about being alive, Barrows stood on the deck and watched the maintenance crew examine his plane. The stress placed on the wings while pulling out of the dive had damaged them beyond repair. The maintenance crew pushed his pride and joy over to the edge of the aircraft carrier and dropped it into the ocean.

On the morning of April 1, 1945, elements of Thirty-fourth Army Corps and Third Marine Amphibious Corps of the Tenth Army started wading ashore. Circling high above in his replacement plane, Barrows waited for a call for close air support by the air controller on the ground with the marines. He watched in awe as the landings progressed. Some of the landing craft loaded with troops circled the mother troopship, while others headed for the shore in waves. From his altitude they looked like little bugs in the water.

He had plenty of time to think. He hoped the island's constant pounding by the navy's big guns and airplanes had made it safer and easier for the soldiers and marines in the little boats. He had great respect for the troops going ashore to face violent explosions and weapons fire. His heart went out to them. The danger facing them, and their having to live in foxholes exposed to the weather, made him appreciate his decision to join the navy. He took stock of the awesome amount of military power in comparison with what he had seen at Guadalcanal some two and a half years earlier. Then, the Americans barely managed to hold that first island taken in the Pacific. Now, he sensed that it was just a matter of time until this terrible war would be over. He wanted to help hurry its ending. During the hard fighting for the island, Barrows flew daily bombing missions, often three hours or longer, in close support of ground troops.

On the morning of May 11, 1945, Barrows sat erect in the cockpit, both eyes on the signal officer on the flight deck. With his foot pressing hard on the brake pedal, he began easing the throttle forward. Fully focused, awaiting the signal to taxi out of the way of an approaching friendly plane, he barely sensed the flash a few feet over his head on the superstructure. The kamikaze's explosion hurled Barrows's plane over on its side, its wings still folded and propeller still spinning. Before it hit the deck, he knew what had happened, because Japanese suicide planes had been striking other American ships around Okinawa. He knew that he had to bolt out of his plane, now a death trap. He ripped open his buckles, dropped to the deck, and, in the chaos that surrounded him, darted between burning planes on the flight deck.

His mind raced, trying to take it all in so that he could decide what to do. He and every man aboard knew that tons of bombs and high-octane aviation fuel stored on the aircraft carrier meant disaster if a fire on board got out of control. His instinct, as he dashed for the edge of the ship, urged him to jump overboard as some were doing. But he was a poor swimmer, and although he had on his life preserver, he ruled that option out for the time being. Instead, he bolted down the catwalk on the side of the ship and raced with others for the fantail at the rear. Only a few passed him in the 400-foot dash. Running at full speed he heard another kamikaze crash through the flight deck toward the bow of the ship and explode. He felt the heat from the roaring fire. To bridge the gap between the catwalk and the fantail, Barrows and others grabbed a plank that had been blown off the deck, made a precarious bridge, and quickly crossed over.

On the fantail he joined a couple of hundred frightened sailors. The flight deck extended out over the fantail, whose open sides made it like a kind of porch on the rear of the ship. Thick, black smoke billowed high above. As the ship sailed on, air currents caught some of the smoke from the burning oil and pulled it into and around the fantail. Breathing became difficult. Men coughed and covered their noses with handkerchiefs. To cool his feet Barrows lifted first one and then the other off the hot deck. Now and then he would stand in a pool of water that dripped down from the hosing operations above on the flight deck. He watched an old chief approach a young sailor who kept making motions to jump overboard. The old salt in a calm voice said, "Son, you're not on fire, just stay where you are." He watched his friend Fred Swearingen take a rope about two inches in diameter, tie it to the rail, slide down it, and sit in the water free of the smoke-filled fantail. Only later did Barrows learn from Swearingen that it had worked fine until others slid down the rope and stripped him off.

Since Barrows had no special emergency duties, most of his thoughts were about staying alive. Still, he noted and admired the great seamanship of Commander Dyson. Dyson would roll the ship to its limits to slush and direct the large pools of water. His cool voice over the public address system, directing the emergency crews, calmed Barrows. When a cruiser came alongside to fight the fires and assist with other tasks, Barrows thought he was in good hands. His thoughts shifted to his friends in the squadron. He felt sure that the first kamikaze had penetrated the ready room, and he knew that all but he and the three pilots who had lined up behind him on the flight deck before the first hit had been in the ready room being briefed.

By midafternoon things began to calm down, and the grim task of locating and ministering to the wounded received more attention. Barrows joined a group to help remove some sailors who had been asphyxiated in the engine room. He tried to get to the ready room to check on his friends in his squadron, but for the moment there was no way for anyone to get there.

The carrier USS *Bunker Hill* is hit by a Japanese suicide attack off Okinawa, killing 372. The blast from the first kamikaze plane flipped over John Barrows's airplane (behind the running men). Courtesy of the National Archives.

As evening approached he joined others gathering on the flight deck for the first burial ceremony. Sailors were working diligently to finish enshrouding the bodies laid out in neat rows. Five-inch shells were placed between the legs of the dead, if they had legs, and the shroud tied securely around the body to hold the shell, whose weight would take the body to the bottom. A long line of silent and motionless men wrapped in their final garb lay stretched out over the deck before him.

He had been staring into the face of war for a long time, but that eerie scene amid the black and mangled wreckage was the worst. Fortunately, by then nature had anesthetized him, and like all combatants, knowing the atmosphere in which war moved, he had been inoculated with a measure of fatalism about violence and death. Still, now and then powerful emotions broke through and terrorized his spirits, especially when he thought about his many friends who lay among the dead. One of those friends was W.T. Jacks from Arkansas. To Barrows, Jacks had looked, talked, and acted like the great comedian Bob Burns. He had enjoyed Jacks's rare sense of humor and admired his coolness in combat. Now, all that was gone forever. When taps sounded and bodies started sliding down the ramp and splashing into the ocean, a cloud of gloom and agony engulfed Barrows and the ranks of the sailors on deck.

Later, under her own power, the *Bunker Hill* and her armed escort ships turned east and headed for the United States. Like his ship, Barrows did an about-face and turned his thoughts toward America. Once again, his destroyed dive bomber had been swept off the deck and thrown overboard. No more combat missions. No more circling over Okinawa waiting to be called down on a target in the face of antiaircraft fire. A great sense of relief came over him, and his spirits began to rise. The war was entering its final phase; he might not have to fight again. To while away the time on the long journey, he played poker and red dog with his surviving friends. More and more, as the days dragged on at sea, he anticipated the joy of family reunion, savoring his freedom from the responsibilities and dangers of combat and the drain it had put on body and soul.

As the mangled *Bunker Hill* approached the dock at Pearl Harbor, Barrows looked down and saw, to his elated surprise, two of the ship's pilots on the dock waving happily up at him and the other crew members gathering on deck. Awe and joy swept over the sailors who knew them as the story rippled throughout the crowd. Both Roland Ownby and H.R. Gordinier, members of Barrows's squadron, had been presumed dead; their roommates had already packed their personal effects for shipment home. But Gordinier and Ownby had been plucked out of the ocean and brought to Hawaii on another ship. For Barrows, it was as if his dear friends had risen from the dead.

Rarely did the subject of the two kamikazes come up on the final leg between Hawaii and the United States. But in the midst of the charred, gaping holes of the ship, their ghosts were there for those who dwelt on the reality of their surroundings. Some crew members had seen part of a kamikaze pilot's head on the deck near the impact area, and word of that sighting had spread after the chaos ended. Not until some forty-seven years after the event did Barrows learn more. In October 1992 he received a letter at his home in Versailles, Kentucky, from Herb Wiley, a *Bunker Hill* shipmate. The letter included a translation of a letter from a kamikaze pilot, purported to be one of those who had slammed into the *Bunker Hill*. Twenty-three-year-old Flying Petty Officer 1st Class Isao Matsuo of the 701st Air Group wrote to his parents on the morning of the *Bunker Hill* attack:

Dear Parents: May 11, 1945

Please congratulate me. I have been given a splendid opportunity to die. This is my last day. The destiny of our homeland hinges on the decisive battle in the sea to the south where I shall fall like a blossom from a radiant cherry tree. How I appreciate this chance to die like a man. Think well of me and know that Isao died for our country. May my death be as sudden and clean as the shattering of crystal.
    Written at Miyazaki on the day of my sortie.
    Isao

    The letter created much excitement among the survivors of Barrows's squadron, and it added yet another interesting topic for their conversations at their reunions.

FOUR

Monte Pantano, Monte Cassino, and Beyond

Lieutenant Colonel Benjamin Butler
Infantryman, U.S. Army

Helmet under his arm, Capt. Benjamin Butler stood over the graves of his friends near Oran, Africa. He could hardly comprehend that both his college classmates had been killed in the North African campaign and were buried side by side in the American cemetery. Both George Lawrence from Cadiz, Kentucky, and Virgil Beasley from Lexington had taken military science classes with Butler at the University of Kentucky. All had participated in the challenges and rigors of leadership laboratory, summer camp, and other activities offered in the university's ROTC program. They had shared the joys and hardships of campus life. Butler and Lawrence had roomed together for three years and had double-dated sisters.

For a brief moment Butler's reflections turned to Lawrence's widowed mother, and the thought of how grief-stricken she must be at the loss of her only child cast a deeper shadow of gloom over him. What did it all mean? Butler wondered, looking down at the graves. The silence and distance from home made him feel lonely and empty. He knew this war was necessary and that he would fight the Nazis to the end, but his silent friends reminded him of his own mortality. His thoughts turned to two other classmates from Kentucky—John Sherman Cole from Nicholasville, and Fred Hill from Somerset—who had also been killed in the North African campaign. Saddened, the combat veteran left the cemetery to continue his training and preparation for the invasion of Italy.

In September 1943 Captain Butler took his Company A, First Battalion, 168th Regiment, aboard the *Rajula,* an old Indian ship. Because it had been port-loaded rather then combat-loaded, he knew they were not going to make an amphibious assault landing. At Salerno, Italy, the Allied forces that had landed on September 9 were in danger of being driven off the beach by a major German counterattack. Butler's ship had to circle and wait. Finally, days later, his unit went ashore.

While Butler's men walked northward toward Avellino, threatening clouds moved over the area, and soon rain poured out of the blackened sky. The long column of soaking wet soldiers leaned into ever increasing winds as they struggled to keep moving. Butler held on to his helmet and turned his head away from the howling wind to get his breath. Debris flew and tumbled around the long column. The storm drenched and battered the exposed troops the rest of the day and most of their first night in Italy.

By October 6 the U.S. Fifth Army forces had fought across the narrow Naples plains, through mountain passes, and over rugged mountains on their way to positions generally along the south bank of the Volturno River. Butler's division, the Thiry-fourth, having seen only sporadic action in Italy, moved into an assembly area preparatory to crossing the river.

Patrols from the Fifth Army probed for crossing sites, and since Butler's was to be the First Battalion's lead company for the river crossing, he wanted to see the chosen site for himself. So on the chilly, rainy night of October 11, Butler and nine men waded in ankle-deep mud to the edge of the Volturno. Each of three groups, spread a few yards apart, lashed themselves together and slipped cautiously and quietly into the swift, swollen river. In chest-deep water they pushed against the current, holding their weapons over their heads. The moment they crawled out of the river, the enemy opened fire. Tracers from automatic weapons whizzed by, and mortars exploded in their midst. They pressed hard to sink their bodies deeper into the mud. They were in the German final protective fire zone, and Butler knew the German defense at this designated crossing site would wipe out his company. He ordered the patrol to pull back, slid over the bank into the river, and made for the other side.

At the designated assembly point Butler and the two men with him waited and waited for the other seven. They never returned. As daylight approached, Butler took the survivors to the rear. The moment they arrived at a point where the enemy couldn't see them, the exhausted men lay down on the ground and dropped off to sleep.

The next night Butler and the battalion commander accompanied another patrol farther down the river, near Limatola. The new patrol waded into the river, probing the depth with long poles. They soon learned that the river was over their heads and that there were no German defenses in the immediate area of the other side. They had found their crossing site.

After dark on October 12 the First Battalion moved quietly into its assembly area on the south side of the river near Limatola. Butler waited anxiously for the friendly artillery to start firing. At 1:45 A.M., ninety-six American guns thundered. Artillery shells roared overhead and splashed down over the river, across the division's eight-mile front. For fifteen minutes he

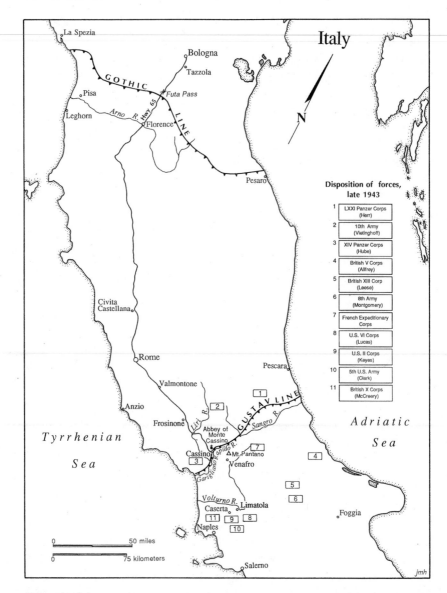

Italy

N

La Spezia

Bologna

Tazzola

GOTHIC LINE

Pisa

Futa Pass

Arno R. Hwy 65

Leghorn

Florence

Pesaro

Disposition of forces, late 1943

1	LXXI Panzer Corps (Herr)
2	10th Army (Vietinghoff)
3	XIV Panzer Corps (Hube)
4	British V Corps (Allfrey)
5	British XIII Corp (Leese)
6	8th Army (Montgomery)
7	French Expeditionary Corps
8	U.S. VI Corps (Lucas)
9	U.S. II Corps (Keyes)
10	5th U.S. Army (Clark)
11	British X Corps (McCreery)

Civita Castellana

Rome

Pescara

Valmontone

Anzio

Tyrrhenian Sea

Adriatic Sea

Frosinone

Liri R.

1

2

GUSTAV LINE

Sangro R.

Abbey of Monte Cassino

Cassino

Rapido R.

3

Mt. Pantano

7

Venafro

4

Garigliano R.

5

6

Volturno R.

Limatola

Caserta

11

9

8

Naples

10

Foggia

0   50 miles

0   75 kilometers

Salerno

jmh

[Map of Italy]

heard the guns thundering, the shells roaring overhead, and saw the exploding shells flashing in the night. When supporting infantry lifted their fire, which had pounded the crossing site, Butler led his company carrying their boats, to the bank of the Volturno, where they quietly slid their metal assault boats into the swift current.

On the river, an ear-splitting artillery round exploded in their midst. Private "Snuffy" Smith panicked, stood up, fell over the side, and disappeared into the darkness. The others rowed harder and faster. Soon about 200 heavily armed men slipped and slid over the north bank into enemy territory. While he was taking an azimuth to get oriented, an enemy mortar round exploded near Butler and knocked his compass out of his hand, leaving him shaken but unhurt.

In the moonlit night Butler quickly spread the men out in a line and led them in a running charge for the hills about half a mile from the river. Mortars rained down behind them and machine gun tracers zipped over their heads. Fortunately, the Germans had made the immediate north river bank area their final defensive line, and their machine guns were set high.

Yards away from the German bunkers on the hillside, Butler fired a green flare, signaling his breathless men to open fire. The sounds of cracking rifles and chattering machine guns quickly filled the air. Seconds after the sudden, intense fire ripped into the enemy's fortifications, the Germans quickly withdrew. Butler sent up a red flare, and the friendly artillery lifted its fire. In minutes, he had his assigned objective on top of the hill.

By November the Americans were ready to assault Marshall Albert Kesselring's massive defensive system, constructed across the Italian peninsula several miles south of Rome. The Allies called it "the Winter Line." Consisting of a heavy outpost and two strongly fortified main lines of defense, it was a formidable barrier.

On November 28, 1943, after a hot noon meal, the First Battalion of the 168th Infantry moved over rugged mountain country toward Filignano, the designated assembly area. At 4:00 P.M., to avoid enemy observation, Captain Butler halted the lead company short of the assembly point and awaited darkness. In a steady howling wind he and his men bedded down on the cold, muddy ground to get their last sleep before their next ordeal. They all knew they were going to attack the Germans in the morning.

About 1:00 A.M. Butler roused the men of Company A from their fitful sleep and resumed the march in the unrelenting wind. In two and a half hours the companies of the battalion were coiled up in their assembly area. Here they drew their basic load of ammunition, drank hot coffee, ate sandwiches, and made their final checks. Tension grew in the ranks as the silent men slogged northward on the narrow road in the little valley. American artillery fire exploded on the nearby mountain peaks to their left, as it had done for several days and nights.

On the line of departure along the road at the foot of Monte Pantano, Butler organized his platoons for the attack. At 6:00 A.M., carrying about sixty pounds on their backs and behind a rolling artillery barrage, Company A started the torturous climb to attack one of the many strong points on the Winter Line, in concert with other Fifth Army units. At first, the going was not so bad. But Butler knew what waited for him on top of the mountain, more than 1,500 feet above them, because one of his patrols had made it to the top and had seen the fortified position. The battalion's plan put him at the point of a wedge formation. He hoped that the artillery and mortar fire hitting the top of the mountain would keep the Germans pinned down, so that when he assaulted their position on Knob 1, they would be surprised.

Taking long strides, the slim, six-foot-tall captain led his company dangerously close to the exploding friendly artillery before he fired a green flare to signal the artillery observer to roll the artillery barrage another increment up the slope. In a couple of hours the units on the sides of the wedge formation—Company B on the left and Company C on the right—were out of sight in the brush and out of contact with Butler. His radio operator told him the battalion commander had sent a message for him to slow down. The message distressed Butler, who knew the Germans were pinned down. He paused, took a deep breath, and then instructed his radio operator to ask battalion to repeat the message and then turn the radio off before they could answer.

In a little while the battalion S-3 (operations officer), Capt. John Moore from New York, caught up with Butler and told him the battalion commander was deeply concerned about having his companies separated before the final assault; he wanted Butler to wait until the others caught up. But Butler thought surprise would be worth more than numbers, and he wanted to hit the Germans while they were down in their holes. He pleaded with the S-3 to permit him to charge on. Moore agreed and hurried back to inform the battalion commander.

The eastern slope of Pantano became drastically steeper as they approached the summit, and there were no trails to help them find their footing. Still, Butler hurried the exhausted men along. Near the summit and as close to the friendly exploding artillery rounds as he could get, he waited to the last seconds before lifting the artillery fire. The moment the friendly artillery stopped, Company A poured over the summit and charged through the German platoon's position. Three hours after Butler and his company had crossed the line of departure, fifteen Germans lay dead in their holes on the objective and five others had been captured by Company A before the enemy had time to recover from the American artillery fire. Knowing the Germans would counterattack and fearing they would do it before the rest of the battalion arrived, Butler promptly organized to defend Knob 1.

Monte Pantano had four knobs, their peaks about 400 yards apart. Butler now held one; the Germans still had the others and from their peaks could make things difficult for Company A. They could conceal troops and mortars, observe Knob 1, launch an attack, and provide automatic weapons support to an attacking force.

Butler coiled his platoons just below the crown of Knob 1 in an area about the size of a football field, with his automatic weapons generally oriented toward Knob 2, to the northwest. Soon mortar shells raining down and exploding in their midst told him the counterattack was coming. He knew the Germans would try desperately to cut him off and destroy his company before the rest of the battalion closed on his position, but he didn't know where they would strike. Then, suddenly, the attackers hit Company A on both flanks. Fire from enemy machine pistols (automatic handguns) splattered the rocky knob and ripped into the bodies of some defenders.

Standing below on a steep slope and behind Pfc. Bailey, a Browning automatic rifleman, Butler anxiously watched the cool movements of the little soldier. Wearing thick glasses, Bailey raised his head slowly out of his hole, glanced down the draw toward Knob 4, and then jerked his head down. Butler knew something was going on when he saw Bailey's head move up slowly and bolt back down again. Then Bailey rose up quickly in his hole and fired. His automatic rifle chattered and spewed out its clip of twenty bullets as he swung it back and forth. When it fell silent, Bailey looked back into the eyes of Butler and grinned. Both knew that he had done well, but at the moment only Bailey knew that he had cut down eight Germans. Similarly tenacious actions of others stopped the attackers on the left flank.

Meanwhile, the right platoon, fighting hard to hold its ground, began to give way under a savage attack. Butler gathered two squads from the left and had them fix their bayonets. They maneuvered to the right, plugged the hole, and drove the Germans off. Wounded and dead men, both Americans and Germans, lay scattered about—including three of Butler's seven lieutenants. But he still held his part of the bloodstained knob.

By noon, B and C Companies and the battalion forward command group had arrived. Lt. Col. Wendell Langdon, the battalion commander, gathered his company commanders where they could observe Knob 2 to finalize his plan of attack. At 1:30 P.M. B Company moved between A and C Companies and started their attack against Knob 2. Just as the lead platoon ran into a minefield at the bottom of the ravine, German mortar shells peppered all the companies in the battalion and kept it up for thirty minutes.

In his foxhole Butler heard the mortars thumping the ground all around him. A sound like a sudden soft wind meant the falling shells were dangerously close. Soon the chattering of automatic weapons added to the din as the Germans hit Company A's right flank. Someone yelled for the captain. Butler knew the risk of standing up while machine gun fire zinged by, but he leaped out of his hole—and just as he did, he heard the soft rush of wind before the mortar exploded in the empty foxhole. Butler glanced into the shattered hole and vowed to himself that he was not going to get back in a foxhole on Knob 1.

While Company B retreated back to Knob 1, Butler got Langdon to attach one of its platoons to him. By 3:00 P.M., the German attack had been beaten off, but many casualties lay scattered over the battlefield in the cold drizzling rain. Although he did not know all the details, Butler knew he was in a precarious situation. Ammunition was running dangerously low. Two-thirds of the way up, the mountain became too steep for a mule; men would have the nearly impossible task of dragging ammunition and supplies the rest of the way. Butler ordered the living to strip ammunition off the dead. Meanwhile, repeated requests went back to hurry with the ammo and hand grenades.

Before the fifteen new stretcher cases were ready for evacuation at the battalion aid station, word filtered up about the difficulty of getting casualties off the mountain: during the six hours it took battalion litter-bearers to get casualties down, the Germans often shelled them with heavy mortars. Both the wounded on stretchers and the litter-bearers were hit, some tumbling, sliding, or rolling to their deaths. Infantrymen on Knob 1 could not look forward to a non-life-threatening wound to take them safely out of danger. The bad news caused their morale to drop another notch.

Clouds drifted down and covered the mountaintop while the men of Company A, chilled to the bone in their lightweight field jackets, policed the battlefield and prepared for the next counterattack. Soon the clouds swept upward, clearing the fog, and when Butler glanced into the valley to the northeast he saw a German tank pointing its gun barrel toward his position. Almost immediately the barrel belched fire; in an instant he heard the booming noise, and the shell slammed into the mountainside below him. As the tank continued to fire, his eyes flipped back and forth from the gun to the impact points, like watching a tennis match, as the blossoming explosions crept up the mountainside in small steps. Suddenly his mind cleared, and he knew the tankers meant to clip the top of Knob 1. He shouted, "Hit the ground!" and dived behind a stack of six cases of C rations. The last tank shell crashed into the top case and exploded above Butler. Hot shock waves battered him against the ground and hurled ruptured cans and particles of food across the company's area. With his ears still ringing, Butler checked to see if he was hurt. He did not find a scratch, but the musette bag on his back was riddled.

The long hard day—which had started in the wee hours of the morning with the march to the line of departure, had continued with the exhausting climb up Monte Pantano, and had worn on with the fending off of two bloody counterattacks—finally came to an end. But there was no rest for Butler and his weary, wet, shivering men, or what was left of them. At dark, enemy artillery roared over the Americans' heads, apparently aimed at the battalion's supply line and its supporting mortars in the valley below. Soon, German mortar shells mixed with the freezing drizzle to rain down on Company A and the rest of the battalion. The pounding went on and on.

Butler, true to his vow, never thought of getting into his foxhole. He had noted that the mortar shells were clipping off the scrub bushes and little trees just inches above the ground. He thought his chances were as good or better if he stayed on his feet. He moved up and down the thin line, offering words of encouragement and telling his men to hold at all cost. Eventually, the noise and destruction from the exploding mortar shells ended, and German small arms opened up from Knobs 2 and 3. Then, twenty yards in front of Company A, the Americans heard the familiar crackling of machine pistols, and soon the charging enemy breached the line and occupied foxholes in a twenty- or thirty-yard slice out of Company A's position.

Butler did not want to let the Germans get more troops into the penetrated area; if they were allowed to reinforce their success, the whole battalion might be driven off the mountain. He stumbled down the mountain about a hundred yards to his seventeen-man reserve. He ordered them to fix bayonets and quickly briefed the attentive men. He told them that when he gave the word he wanted them to shout at the top of their voices so that they would sound like a hundred men. Then he said, "Follow me."

Observing the dark skyline and sensing the folds in the ground that he had been over again and again, Butler moved hurriedly toward the breach. At the nose of the penetration he gave the word. Shouts and screams rang out above the battle noises as the Americans charged the Germans, trying in the melee to avoid killing their own men. The crackle of a German machine pistol drew well-aimed American fire; a guttural voice drew a bullet, a bayonet, or the butt of a rifle. In a little while the Germans sprinted out of Company A's position. In his rush to get away one of them dropped the American machine gun that he was trying to carry back to his own lines. Soon Company A's line was restored. Butler had not lost anyone during the counterattack, but five dead Germans lay silent on the ground. Still, the dwindling ammunition supply left Butler and the battalion in a vulnerable situation. He knew they could not beat off another counterattack.

The Germans retreated just over a twenty-yard-wide ridge and hurled their wooden-handled grenades over the hogback into the Americans' position. Some of the Americans, fresh out of grenades, hurled rocks back.

Finally, at 10:00 p.m. the regiment's antitank company arrived on foot, loaded down with ammunition (mostly hand grenades) and some medical supplies. On their way back the ammo bearers picked up the twenty litter cases and carefully carried them down the steep mountain. In the darkness the infantrymen hurriedly distributed the ammunition. On the signal at 11:00 p.m., those in the forward foxholes rushed up onto the hogback no-man's-land and quickly hurled three hand grenades each down the steep slope into the Germans. Screams from men in excruciating pain told the Americans that their grenade barrage was on target. Later they heard the Germans digging in farther down the slope. Then, except for sporadic mortar attacks, the bloody battlefield grew quiet. Butler's men began rigging their shelter halves to catch drinking water from the drizzling rain and fine sleet.

Morning dawned with a blanket of misty, cold fog covering Monte Pantano. Around noon Colonel Langdon met Butler and the commanders of Companies B, C, and D at the artillery observation post to plan another attack on Knob 2. Visibility was near zero. But as Langdon, Butler, and Capt. Bruce Hair, commander of Company C, moved forward on the hogback into no-man's-land in front of Company A's forward line, the fog lifted and in seconds German mortar rounds slammed into the ground and exploded in their midst. Langdon and Hair crumpled to the ground.

Butler, watching Langdon's face turn ashen white, knew that the colonel's stomach and liver wounds were critical. Rather than wait for a litter-bearer, he grabbed Langdon's web suspenders and dragged him back over the ridge. The rough movement caused Langdon's head to double down toward his feet. Butler was unaware at the time that the manner in which Langdon was bent over restricted the bleeding and was a factor in saving his life. Hair, knowing he was under enemy observation, shouted, "Don't leave me, don't leave me!" At the aid station Butler sent litter-bearers to get Hair. Before the battalion commander was evacuated, he called off the plans to attack Knob 2 and ordered Butler and the others to hold what they had at all cost.

Soon the fourth German counterattack began, and for three hours the men of Butler's reinforced company and the rest of the battalion, fended it off. Americans spotted a number of enemy mortars on Knobs 2 and 3, engaged them with their own mortars, and scored several hits. For the first time since they had arrived on Pantano, the sky had cleared enough for the friendly artillery to register on enemy positions, assembly areas, and routes of approach.

Later that afternoon, as clouds drifted down, Butler said to Bronston, his machine gun corporal, "Let's watch and when the clouds cover no-man's-land we will sneak out and recover our machine gun," the one the Germans had dropped on their way out the night before. At the right moment they made a mad dash onto the ridge, but just as Butler reached out to smack down the gun's erect sight, the fog lifted. A bullet zipped close by his head and slammed into Bronston's neck, cutting the jugular vein. Butler let go of the machine gun, grabbed his bleeding, blood-soaked corporal, and frantically dragged him down the steep slope into the company's position. It was too late. Bronston was dead.

By the end of the second day, Butler and his thinning ranks had withstood four German counterattacks, periods of intense mortar attacks, and sporadic mortar and artillery attacks. All fear had been drained from his emotions; he was totally focused on staying alive and doing his job. He moved around the position, restationing infantrymen here and there, selecting positions for the newly attached platoon, and offering words of encouragement to the weary, cold, wet, numb men. When he wasn't under enemy observation or small arms fire, he walked about; under automatic weapon or rifle fire, he crawled.

Shortly after darkness had settled in on the second night, Butler heard the hobnailed cleats of German boots hitting the rocky, steep slope on the other side of the ridge and realized that the enemy was going to attack his position without the usual mortar preparation. Word was passed down the line: "Hold your fire." Tension rose as the men heard the Germans approach the crown of the hogback—and was released with the sudden firing of all the weapons of Companies A and B into the Germans as they appeared on the skyline. Dragging their dead and wounded, the Germans scurried off no-man's-land and down the other side of the ridge. Later they hit the flank of Company B, but the Americans fired their artillery defensive concentrations and broke up the attack. However, bringing artillery in close to friendly lines on a mountaintop is difficult and dangerous, and three volleys of an American artillery battery exploded in the midst of the battalion's own command group, near the aid station. Among the dead were three of the litter cases.

It was midnight when the German attack ended. Except for sporadic mortar and artillery fire, the battlefield quieted down. Butler continued to move about, reorganizing the lines and arranging for evacuation of the wounded. Now and then he found men suffering with trench foot; they too were sent down the mountain. As the night wore on, the temperature dropped and wet clothes began to freeze. By morning it was snowing.

Later on the third day Butler crawled up beside Pfc. John Hafer, who had a good view of Knob 2 from his position on the company's right. He told Butler, "I think I see movement down there in the minefield." Butler looked down the draw at the minefield between Knobs 1 and 2, about 200 yards away. On the left the Germans had built a rock roomlike structure without a roof against a stone fence that ran behind the minefield. Staring at the strange fortification Butler saw the top of a helmet moving. He said, "That's a Yank." In spite of the difficult task of keeping up with the status and whereabouts of his own men in combat, Butler always made the extra effort to know where they were, and he knew this man was not one of his. At a gathering at the aid station with the other company commanders, a heated debate opened about who, if anyone, should try to rescue the American soldier. Butler lost his patience: "I don't care who he belongs to, I'm going to get him. He has been out there two days and that's long enough." He instructed Sgt. Roger Caya to bring him three more medics with their red cross armbands. Butler himself laid down his weapon and picked up a red cross flag. Sergeant Caya said, "You don't have to go, sir." Butler knew that he shouldn't go, but he was so exhausted, numb, and emotionally drained that he didn't give a damn. And being a little put out with the other company commanders, he wanted also to show a little contempt for them.

On the ridge he waved his red cross flag and started down the steep slope. Butler knew that both the Americans and Germans had respected the red cross and allowed medics to rescue their wounded; nevertheless he nervously scanned the German-held knobs. In his mind's eye he could see German eyes following the little rescue party, and his heart pounded in his chest. He carefully picked his way through the minefield by watching for trip wires and disturbed dirt. When Butler appeared at the entrance of the stone structure, Pfc. Elbert Gourley looked up from his bloody, mangled foot and said, "Thank God. You've come." Carefully, they laid him on the stretcher. The German Schu mine that Gourley had stepped on had been designed to maim, not to kill.

Struggling to get the wounded man up the steep slope, the stumbling medics at the rear had to hold their end of the stretcher above their heads. When they reached the aid station at last, Butler tried to help Gourley get his mind off his wound by asking the wounded private where he was from. Gorley said, "Madison, Indiana." Butler said, "You won't believe this, but I grew up on a farm right across the Ohio River from you." Gourley's face lit up with a smile. Butler didn't know it at the time, but he would have a lifelong admirer in Gourley.

Later that afternoon Butler crawled up beside Hafer again. The private stared at one of the few large trees in the area. He said, "I think I see movement in that big tree on the right side of Knob 2." Butler knew there was a sniper over there somewhere; from the moment the company overran the Germans on Knob 1, the sniper had patiently waited to get Americans into his sights. Just after the initial assault he had left Lt. Irwin Horowitz mortally wounded. On the second day the same sniper had killed Bronston, the machine gunner. And on the third day he had killed Pfc. Armanda Damiani, who had been hoping to meet his uncles and aunts in Frosinone, near Rome.

Staring at the tree, Butler said, "Hand me your rifle, John." He cocked the rifle, took aim, and waited. The sniper's head moved slowly into view. Butler squeezed the trigger. A German body dropped from its perch in the tree and dangled on a rope fastened around its chest. Butler said, "That son of a bitch won't kill any more of our people."

Butler had often counseled his men about the danger of developing a deep-seated hatred for the enemy, but infantrymen both feared and hated snipers, feeling there was something unfair about their sneaky methods. Consequently, word of the sniper's death brought some good cheer in the ranks.

On the third day, after the regiment committed its reserve and captured Knob 2, Butler decided he should visit each of the sixty or so survivors in their fighting positions to tell them the good news that they would be relieved after darkness. He knew that each had lost some buddies and wanted to cheer them up as much as he could. But just as compelling as the need he had to lift their spirits, he felt was the need to express his respect and admiration for each of them. The manner in which they had conducted themselves in the face of death and the way they had accepted their suffering had made a lasting impression on him. At each position, when he heard the good news, a haggard-looking infantryman barely forced a weak smile before returning to an empty stare. Although Butler often spoke to his men about the need to control their emotions in combat situations, the depth of their suffering grieved him. His compassion for them grew deeper and deeper until, near the end of his visits, he had to struggle to hide his grief.

Shortly before darkness, as an unsettling quiet fell over the battlefield, Butler decided to take a last tour of the area. Normally, he liked to keep his battle positions tidied up, but as the ranks had thinned out and weariness set in, no effort was made to police the area after an attack other than getting the wounded to the aid station and removing the dead. He had been in a lot of fights, but nothing equaled the devastation of this drawn-out battle. The area was peppered with shallow craters, a few still smoldering. Rock splinters and broken stones dotted the landscape. The scrub bushes and small trees had been clipped off and shredded as if someone had mowed the area, leaving only splinters, mulch, and short stumps. Damaged equipment, broken rifle stocks, torn shelter halves, and helmets—both American and German—lay strewn over the battlefield. Most unsettling were the blood-stained bandages scattered over the wet ground.

At the place where the Germans had penetrated the position, he reached down and took a bayonet off a German Mauser rifle. He wanted it for a souvenir. Then he moved down to the place where about twenty men from Company A lay side by side. Butler looked down on the bodies, individually covered with blankets or shelter halves, and said a short prayer of thanksgiving for not being among them. This group wasn't all of the company's dead; a few had already been taken off the mountain. Butler knew them all, though he didn't know where each individual lay. The silent battlefield and the stillness of the dead gave him an eerie sensation. His thoughts turned to Pfc. Armando Damiani. Everyone in the company had been excited about Damiani's plans to look up the uncles, aunts, and cousins he had never seen when the unit reached Frosinone; Butler knew that Damiani's parents in the States were excited about the expected visit, too. But now Damiani's corpse, with a hole in the head from the sniper's bullet, lay silently among the dead.

He thought about others—Bronston, the machine gunner, also killed by the sniper; Abernathy, who was standing beside Butler when he got hit. Each lay there somewhere among the bloody corpses, motionless under a dirty shroud. Butler hoped they would rest in peace. He had noted that all the dead Americans he had seen had a smile on their faces, as if they had died at peace with themselves and the world, whereas he had observed that the dead Germans all had a look of anguish. He pondered the meaning of those different expressions but found no answer. He counted the dead and departed the sad scene, but the mental picture stayed with him.

At 9:00 P.M. the relief in place started, and by 3:00 A.M. it was complete. Of the 160 men in Company A who had come up the mountain, only about 60 walked off, and about half of those were either walking wounded or hobbling on frostbitten feet. Limping down the mountain after the others had departed, Butler sat down after he had descended the steepest part. It was early morning. He had much to think about, but with his weariness and numbness he could hardly collect his thoughts. His head was spinning slowly as he took off his shoe to examine the slight wound on the bottom of his foot. He was hardly aware of the small shell fragment in his hip or the one in his shin. He knew he and his men had fought well and felt good about that, but knowing that it was the last battle for many pained him. How many of the wounded would get back to the unit he didn't know.

As he unwrapped the bandage on his foot, the presence of Col. Frederic Butler (no kin) looking down on him with tears in his eyes went unnoticed. Only slowly did Captain Butler sense someone standing over him. He looked up and saw his regimental commander. Butler sprang to his feet and saluted. Colonel Butler touched him on the shoulder and said in a gentle voice, "Sit down, Butler. I ought to be saluting you." It startled and surprised the captain to see tears flowing down the colonel's cheeks. He had known Colonel

Butler as a tough, demanding, and hard disciplinarian. This compassionate side of his commanding officer moved Butler. For a brief moment their sad eyes met in silence. Both knew that for four days and three nights the unit had fought hard, suffered extreme hardships in miserable weather, and taken heavy casualties. At that moment Captain Butler didn't know that for his actions, he would receive the Distinguished Service Cross, the nation's second highest award for valor.

Though his unit was relieved of combat duties to replenish their ranks and do some more training, Butler knew they were getting ready to face the Germans' heavily fortified Gustav Line about ninety-five miles south of Rome, the strongest and last defensive segment in the Winter Line complex.

By early January 1944, Lt. Gen. Mark W. Clark's Fifth Army was in direct contact with the Gustav Line. South of Monte Cassino, a key terrain feature on the Gustav Line, Butler and his men waited in the assembly area. To get there, they had not only survived the bloody battle of Monte Pantano but had fought through nameless rain-swept valleys and sleet-lashed mountains. In the valleys, mud was axle deep. As one soldier said, "We walked in it, ate in it, and slept in it."

Monte Cassino overlooked the junction of the Rapido and Liri Rivers. At the foot of the mountain lay the little town of Cassino, and above the town, on the site chosen by Saint Benedict in 529 A.D., stood the famous Benedictine abbey. Clark had to have Monte Cassino to enter the Liri Valley, which contained one of the few approaches to Rome. He intended to take the entrance into the Liri Valley for a seventy-five-mile advance to Anzio, where the Fifth Army would land an amphibious force behind the Gustav Line on January 22, 1944. There the two forces were to link up and advance north to Rome. But the Germans meant to hold Monte Cassino at all costs.

In the afternoon on January 27, 1944, Butler and Company A waded into the cold, muddy Rapido. Since the Germans had diverted some of the water into the marshlike bottom to create a muddy obstacle for American tanks, the river itself was only knee deep where they were crossing about a mile and a half north of Cassino town. One of the four tanks that had tried to cross ahead of them had sunk out of sight in the quagmire. The other three, seeing the plight of the lead tank, made no further attempt to cross at this time.

On the far bank in mud up to their ankles, frightened men shouted, "Mines! mines! mines!" Short lengths of what looked like piano wire bristled to the front, left, and right as far as Butler could see. All the devices were armed and waiting to catch unwary feet. Up and down the line men pointed out trip wires. He ordered the men to dig in and phoned Lt. Col. Simon

Yanks slog through the mud en route to the Fifth Army front in Italy. Weather conditions in the winter of 1943–44 were appalling. Courtesy of the Kentucky Historical Society.

Castille, Langdon's replacement, to ask for engineers to clear paths through the minefield. Castille told him to wait.

Shivering in their muddy foxholes under observation by the German infantry in fortified positions, the Americans dared not move. Now and then an artillery round splashed down in the vicinity, the noise of the explosion muffled by the mud. Butler worried about the men getting trench foot or frostbite. Finally, after a long wait, Castille called to tell Butler the engineers couldn't help them until dark—about two hours away. Sighing deeply, Butler made a painful decision: he led his men down the steep six-foot bank across the dry portion of the river bed and back across the knee-deep water channel. Here they were out of sight of the enemy infantry and still on the sandy riverbed. Now they could move a little on drier ground and consequently reduce their chances of trench foot. He called the battalion commander and reported his move. Getting back to where they had been would take about five minutes, and no fighting would be necessary.

In minutes, Castille called to report that the regimental commander, against his wishes, had relieved Butler of his command. The shock jolted Butler; he shook his head in disbelief, and then he got mad. A bond of mutual trust and deep respect had been forged between him and the old-timers with whom he had suffered through the Pantano battle and others. When word filtered through the ranks, the men too became enraged. As he moved down the line to say goodbye—his devastation and bewilderment showing—they wanted to know who would relieve him, and why, and where he would go. Some cursed Col. Mark Weber,* their new regimental commander. As darkness fell, the old-timers, in a defiant mood, disappeared.

Reporting to battalion headquarters before dark, Butler explained to Castille that his withdrawal had not changed the tactical situation. Castille seemed puzzled about Colonel Weber's action. Later in the night, Lt. William Galt, from Company A, came to Butler with a worried expression and told him about the disappearance of the company's old-timers. Butler told Castille that they might have a mutiny on their hands. Castille asked Butler to do what he could to round them up. Meanwhile, Butler was taken off the unassigned list and reinstated in the First Battalion. Castille gave him the coveted position of battalion S-3. By morning the old-timers had come out of the wine cellars in a nearby village, dry and ready to get back to the nasty business of war.

On January 29, 1944, the 168th Regiment and a company of tanks got across the Rapido River and through the minefield north of Cassino. After tanks knocked out the German machine guns in their fortified positions, it looked as if the Gustav Line might be permanently breached. German headquarters controlling the action in the immediate area was overrun, and the enemy's coordination of tactical operations broke down. Without much effort, the First Battalion bagged and sent to the rear German soldiers trying to plug the breach. Butler enjoyed helping to round them up.

Later that night, though, he had to go to the hospital with an abscessed tooth. When he returned on February 1, 1944, the battalion was not in a combat formation but was being served a hot breakfast at the base of Monte Cassino, about a mile and a half north of the towering abbey, where the Gustav Line runs south to north before it bends back to the east. Butler thought the battle for the Gustav Line was over. He had no way of knowing what suffering and pain still lay ahead for the Thirty-fourth Division.

---

* Because I do not know the regimental commander's side of the story, I have used a fictitious name for him.

Butler's regiment continued the attack to the west with light opposition. Then, in concert with other Fifth Army units, it swung left and attacked southward, aiming for Monte Cassino at a point behind the abbey. According to plan, the 168th Regiment was to attack up, over, and down the mountain a few hundred yards west of the abbey and cut Highway 6 in the Liri Valley. By late afternoon around February 2, the battalion was ordered to stop for the night at Point 450, one peak in a forest of rocky peaks on the mountaintop, all mostly laced with deep ravines or gullies in an area northwest of the abbey.

The order frustrated Butler. A German prisoner captured a few minutes earlier had confirmed information from other sources that the German division defending the area had lost its combat effectiveness. Butler wanted badly to go on across the top, down the mountain, and across Highway 6. He vigorously pleaded his case with his battalion commander and persuaded him to seek permission from Colonel Weber to continue the attack throughout the night.

Weber responded by asking, "Does Butler think he is a field marshal?" Butler chose not to cross swords with his regimental commander and stopped arguing his case, but his intuition told him it was a serious mistake not to seize an opportunity to open the Liri Valley. The decision to wait and launch a coordinated attack on a larger scale would give the Germans time to reinforce the sagging Gustav Line.

The relative positions of the Germans and Americans was of critical importance. A few feet below and a few hundred yards north and west of the abbey the terrain on top of the Monte Cassino massif formed an oblong, bowllike shape. The long axis ran east and west. Points 450 and 445 were perched on the northern rim, and Point 444 rose on the southern rim. The 168th Regiment facing south controlled most of the northern rim. The Germans controlled the rim of the bowl from the west, south, and east. Anytime the Americans moved on the northern rocky ridge, the Germans could see them. To get to Highway 6 to the south, Butler's battalion would have to go down the southern slope of the northern rim, across the 200-yard-wide basin, up and over the southern rim, and then down the steep southern side of Monte Cassino.

On the morning of the coordinated attack the men of the First Battalion formed into two companies abreast, rose up onto the northern rim like troops coming out of their trenches in World War I, and moved down into the basin with American artillery fire whistling overhead. Morale was high, and Butler sensed a great victory. Soon, however, German machine guns from the west, south, and east blasted streams of bullets into the Americans, and enemy mortar fire pounded the men of the First Battalion. They had run into a hornet's nest, as had the rest of the units in the division. Butler, observing the action from Point 450, knew they were in trouble. With the help of friendly artillery, however, the battalion extricated itself and withdrew back over the northern ridge.

Three German prisoners of the First Parachute Division, captured during the attack, told Butler through an interpreter that they had been brought to the front on trucks during the night and had just arrived on top of the mountain. The information confirmed Butler's belief that his commanders had missed an opportunity to open the road to Rome. He was upset with them for not having pressed ahead when they had the opportunity, when by his reasoning the Germans had been too weak to stop them. Had Butler been able to predict the future, he would have been more than just upset.

Following that failed attempt to open the Liri Valley, miserable weather set in to plague the troops. The cold, damp, and windy weather coupled with the rocky terrain and the enemy's ability to observe their movements during the day created a harsh situation that challenged the Americans' mental toughness and physical stamina to the limit of their endurance.

After sleet glazed the rocks and night seeped in, Butler stepped out of the First Battalion's cavelike command post on the back side of the ridge and began the long trek down the mountain to pick up attack plans from regimental headquarters. A few steps down, his feet slipped out from under him, and like a sled he shot down the slope on his back. With his arms stretched out, he kept grabbing for something—anything—to no avail. A vision of broken bones flashed by in his mind. Suddenly, some sixty feet down, his feet hit something that bounced him upright into a sitting position and jarred him to a halt. Badly bruised and with a bleeding hand he continued more carefully on his way. As soon as he could, he got back on the winding mule trail and forgot about the shortcuts.

For the troops, chilled to the bone, a night and a day seemed an eternity. At most of the First Battalion's positions, any daylight movement reaped a sniper's deadly bullet or a swift mortar attack. Consequently, during the day the troops could only hunker down on the rock floor of their refrigerated rock shelters. On his nightly visits, Butler encouraged the men to improve their two-man, coffin-shaped shelters. He pooled the best ideas and shared them with all, but there was little they could do to relieve the suffering. Hoping to keep out the wind and snow, they would thicken their stone walls and place their shelter halves over the top and sides, anchoring the edges with rocks. But as snow flurries first dusted the mountaintop and then melted in spots in continuing cycles, with no fires to warm bodies or canned rations and little available water, morale was low and continued to slide.

Around February 6 the Germans added rockets to their arsenal to supplement the constant artillery fire. After one big shell, timed to explode after it had bored into the rock surface, had hurled rock splinters of varying sizes into the air, Butler watched in disbelief while the medics brought into the dugout command post seventeen soldiers who had been wounded as a result. Some had only bruises; others had broken bones, and a few had bleeding wounds. That one shell's addition to the long casualty list caused a higher degree of anxiety to sweep through the ranks.

But what really battered the morale of the American troops and added to their discomforts and woes were the rockets called "screaming meemies," that roared in around 2:00 A.M. The echoing mountains magnified the terrorizing noise long before the rockets splashed down in ripples of a dozen or so ear-splitting explosions. For about six hours the rocket attacks rattled and shook the ridge beneath the exhausted soldiers of the First Battalion. Anticipation of the attack, plus the noise and vibrations, made sleep even more difficult. Every night, living nightmares persecuted the Americans. The explosions—a constant reminder that they might be killed at any moment— plus the miserable living conditions hammered away at both their spirits and their bodies.

Soldiers operated in triple pairs: a pair on guard, a pair rubbing each other's feet to avoid frostbite (feet had to be rubbed every two hours), and a pair sleeping—if they could. Dressed in their poor-quality winter clothing, usually in two-man tomblike shelters, American soldiers stretched out their two blankets on their rock mattresses. Huddled together, back-to-back, they wrapped themselves in the blankets. A folded raincoat was the best they could do for a pillow. Besides the battle noises, life-threatening rockets, and hard beds, the constant cold wind howling down from the towering, snow-covered Mount Cairo whipped against their shelters and swept in through cracks and crevices. If their feet turned numb from the cold, they were in trouble and they knew it. Already some of their peers were losing toes in the hospital to the rear because of frostbitten feet.

When Butler wasn't making the all-night trip to and from regimental headquarters, he toured the battlefield. He wanted to gauge the troops' condition and morale and give them words of encouragement. About the fifth night after the foul weather had set in, Butler and his runner, Pfc. Baker, started making their rounds. Butler soon realized that the troops were approaching the limit of their endurance. He found men coughing and hacking. Some had stomachaches from eating cold, greasy cans of C rations (they tried to get the congealed grease off the top with their dirty fingers but could not remove all of it). Some had vomited, many were skipping meals, and a few had simply stopped eating. Because it was impossible to dig latrines in the rock, human waste added to the unsanitary conditions of the unbathed and unshaven men. For the first time, Butler had trouble getting them to talk.

Facing one young soldier in the dark with the cold wind gusting around them, Butler had to listen hard to understand what he was saying. In a quivering voice the soldier asked, "How much longer are we going to have to sit here and take this punishment?" When Butler gently laid his hand on the young man's shoulder, he could tell that the boy's teeth were chattering. Then the boy began to sob, and feeling his body shaking shredded Butler's emotions, but he knew that he must appear to be strong. Swallowing hard and squeezing the boy's shoulder, Butler said, "We will do everything possible to get you out of here as soon as we can. Keep on toughing it out."

Butler moved on to the mule train terminal on the reverse slope of Point 450, where he watched the Italian mule skinners and American supply personnel load the mules with empty water cans and broken equipment for the return trip to the supply base. When they led three mules toward a spot where three bloodstained American corpses lay on the ground, the mood of the loading party turned somber. Normal chatter ceased; only the Italian sergeant spoke, and in a hushed tone. The mules, scenting blood, snorted, reared, and pulled against the bit, trying to avoid what they knew was coming. In the snow-enhanced half-light of the night Butler watched the frightened mules thrashing and snorting near the three quiet and motionless corpses. Four mule skinners firmly held the first mule in place while four Americans quickly placed a corpse, face down, over the pack saddle. As the loaders pulled the stiff arms and legs down to strap them to the saddle, the trapped air in the corpse's lungs hissed and gurgled until the lungs were empty. An eerie sensation rippled through Butler's soul as he listened.

His eyes and thoughts turned to the still form of Sergeant Eldridge, waiting to be loaded. Together, they had crossed the Volturno River, climbed Monte Pantano, and forged a close bond while suffering and fighting the Germans. It pained Butler to watch his friend being loaded in the cold, dimly lit night, in such an undignified manner. No oratory, no bugle playing taps, no firing squads, no family—just a few strangers struggling to strap the sergeant's body onto a mule.

In less then a minute after the loading of the dead had started, the long train of about sixty mules started moving down the treacherous trail, and soon, the body of Butler's friend was out of sight. But in his mind's eye Butler still saw his friend's body swaying to the rhythm of the mule's hoofs. He listened to the mules' iron shoes striking the rock trail and thought about his friend's family and their isolation from their loved one on this, his last day on earth. The burp of a German machine pistol jolted him back to reality.

A pack mule train halts for rest somewhere in Italy. These animals transported supplies up to the fighting men on the rugged mountaintops and carried their dead back down. Courtesy of the Kentucky Historical Society.

Wiping cold tears off his cheeks with a grimy sleeve, he turned and left the scene, determined to do something to change his men's condition.

The next night, three hours after Butler started down the mountain, he arrived at the regimental command post, where the operations officer briefed him on the regiment's plan of attack. Butler shook his head in disbelief. He waited for a moment to get control of his temper, then described how the ranks had been depleted by casualties, frostbitten feet, respiratory problems, and stomach ailments. Colonel Weber looked down his nose at Butler and said, "You don't look so bad." The urge to tell his regimental commander off surged through Butler's mind, but the thought of being court-martialed for insubordination restrained him. He saluted and left.

Climbing the mountain with the aid of a seven-foot staff, Butler leaned into the cold, howling wind, sometimes leaning forward so far that his nose nearly touched the steep, rocky slope. The more he thought about what had just happened at the command post, the madder he got. Clearly, the colonel did not believe him or just didn't understand; perhaps he would have understood had he made the effort to visit the troops. The thought of Weber lounging around in his warm command post and eating hot rations while the troops suffered up on the mountain made Butler grit his teeth, and his contempt for the regimental commander reached new heights. He just thought it was morally wrong to ask more of the troops in their condition. Frustration nagged him every step of the four-hour climb back to the battalion command post, where he briefed the battalion commander. The next morning, the battalion launched a feeble attack that ended in minutes—in failure. The Americans were too weak to fight another battle.

At last, on the morning of February 12, 1944, word came that the Thirty-fourth Division would be relieved by the British army's Fourth Indian Division. That afternoon Captain Popple, a British officer commanding the Indian company slated to relieve the First Battalion, walked the American line with Butler. About 800 men of the First Battalion had started the fight to help open the Liri Valley; fewer than 200 men remained on the mountain. The others were dead or wounded or in the hospital for other reasons. And clearly, those remaining had reached their limit. Ashen-faced, unshaven men stared off into the distance. They were cold, stiff, and weak; their dirty clothes stank.

While Butler and Popple were in view of Point 593, a German sniper's shot rang out. Reminded that it was extremely dangerous to move around during the day, they hurriedly completed the tour. Returning, Popple said, "My God, Butler, this is pathetic. Half of those soldiers won't be alive tomorrow." Back at the command post, Popple called his battalion commander, explained the situation, and suggested that his company relieve the American battalion a day earlier than planned.

The relief in place started that night. Accompanying the Indians during the process, Butler saw some weak men get up with a little help and stagger to the rear. Others would stand up and then fall and have to be helped up again. A few, having lain on the cold, hard rock too long without hot food, were too stiff and weak to move. The Indians gently placed them on stretchers and carried them off Monte Cassino. The disturbing scene severely depressed Butler, but he had to admire the soldiers' mental toughness in those unbearable and life-threatening conditions. Mercifully, their ordeal was over.

Butler's tour on Monte Cassino, however, was not. In their haste to relieve the Americans, the Indians could not get some of their crew-served weapons up on the mountain, so he had to stay and teach them how to use the American weapons.

On February 14, Butler watched propaganda leaflets whirl in the wind over the abbey and surrounding terrain. He grabbed the first one that blew his way and read the Fifth Army's urgent warning to the Italian occupants to abandon the monastery at once. The British officers had told him of the Allied plan to bomb the abbey, and the thought of destroying one of the most venerable monasteries in Christendom saddened him. He had some knowledge of its historical value to Western culture, and he knew it contained great treasures of art, literature, and historical documents.

He had observed the enormous structure in awe while his American unit was approaching the Cassino town area from the east. Here, the towering monastery looming above Butler only about 700 yards from his position on Point 450 made him keenly aware of its presence. He felt as if he could reach out and touch it. Having observed it often for about a week and having seen no Germans in the building through its many windows, Butler wondered why the Allies wanted to bomb it. His American unit had had orders not to hit it, even with mortars. He clung to the notion that maybe the decision-makers would change their minds before February 16, the appointed day for the bombing.

He was not aware of the headlines sweeping the world about the issue; neither was he aware that the major newspapers in England and America had come down on the side of military necessity to bomb the monastery. He was vaguely aware of the tension between his American chain of command and the British chain of command (which included General Clark's British boss, General Sir Harold Alexander). A staff officer from the American Second Corps, commanded by Gen. Geoffrey Keyes, had recently called Butler to inquire about what he had seen, and Butler had reported that he did not believe any Germans were in the building. Generals Keyes and Clark did not want to bomb the abbey.

On February 15, at about 9:20 A.M., Butler heard airplanes droning from the south and looked up into the first clear sky for some time to see about thirty-eight American B-17 bombers approaching. He thought, "Somebody is going to catch hell today"—and then he saw dark specks falling and followed them down in disbelief. He and the Indian unit he was with had not yet moved to a safer distance. The bombs falling a day early puzzled him, so that it didn't occur to him to hit the ground. Instead, he just stood there with his mouth open. He saw the fins blow off of a couple of bombs and watched them tumble in the sky. The rest whistled down in clusters that exploded on, in, and around the abbey. Thundering shock waves shook the mountain and vibrated the rocky peak under Butler's feet. With horror he watched pillars of smoke, dust, and debris shoot into the sky, though he did not know at that moment that people were being slaughtered before his

The Benedictine monastery atop Monte Cassino commanded a view of the Rapido Valley, the entrance to the Liri Valley and the road to Rome. Courtesy of the National Archives.

eyes. When the smoke and dust cleared, the battered thick walls still stood, but their cream color showed scorched marks, the broken window spaces were larger, and the roof was severely damaged.

He did not know that Fifth Army soldiers who were not on Monte Cassino were cheering the event. Some had even come from the rear echelons to watch the bombers bomb the abbey. Apparently the Indian units were the only soldiers in the Fifth Army who did not know that the abbey was going to be bombed that morning. Important sectors of American and British media, on the basis of military reports and rumors, had whipped up a widespread belief that if the abbey did not contain German machine gunners, it certainly must contain German observers capable of directing barrages of killing artillery. Although the Germans had announced that they had declared the abbey off limits, many still thought the building housed the cause of the misery and failure suffered by the Americans. But those were not Butler's feelings, and he was not cheering. He felt only remorse.

Soon a second wave of heavy bombers pounded the abbey. When the smoke and dust blew off to the west, Butler saw ugly fissures in the 150-foot-high walls. He did not see the stunned and dazed civilian refugees who fled the abbey, or hear the hysterical and mournful screams of those trapped under fallen debris. But during perhaps the third of eight attacks, a bomb exploded in the midst of the Indian unit he was with, and splinters of rock and metal bomb fragments shot past Butler. He was not hit, but Captain Popple, the British officer who had commanded his company of Punjabis for years, wasn't so lucky.

Butler heard an uproar sweep through Popple's company, men wailing at the top of their voices like little children, and soon he saw distraught soldiers with tears streaming down their cheeks carrying their captain face down on a litter toward the aid station. The long, bleeding gash running up Popple's back convinced his charges that they were going to lose him.

At the time Popple was wounded, Butler had gone to the cave shelter behind Point 450 for a brief moment, but curiosity drove him back to watch the successive attacks take their toll on the abbey. Finally, at about 1:50 P.M., the last of some 250 bombers dropped its load and departed. Exhausted and depressed, Butler looked at the dust-covered ruins. He saw large sections of the long, thick walls beaten nearly down to the ground and other segments still standing, as if a giant beast had taken bites out of them. Here and there big jagged splinters protruded through the rubble. Butler's judgment had been correct: not a single German soldier had been in the building. But at least 142 Italian refugees lay dead or dying under the rubble. The abbott and the few monks who had chosen to stay remained safe in Saint Benedict's cell deep in the bowels of the abbey. Most of the great pieces of art and treasures had been removed by the Germans before the bombing, but Butler was not aware of this.

Several of the Indian soldiers too were wounded during the bombing attacks. After the last bomber left, the British battalion commander sent for Butler and told him, in a voice showing displeasure with events, that he could return to his unit. Butler gathered his personal belongings and headed down the long mule-train trail with a sense of sheer relief to be getting out of that hellhole. The Americans had lost the first battle for Cassino, but Butler felt lucky to be alive. As he made his way down, the second battle for Monte Cassino was about to begin. It too would end in failure after more suffering and death.

When Captain Butler rejoined his division nearly a hundred miles to the rear, near Naples, the First Battalion commander had transferred to another regiment, so he was given command of the battalion. They received replacements, replaced missing and worn-out equipment, and trained hard in preparation for the Anzio breakout. Shortly thereafter the division moved by ship to Anzio, where Butler stepped ashore on a secure beachhead about twenty miles wide and ten miles deep. It had not always been secure. When Hitler demanded that Kesselring remove the "abscess," the German Fourteenth Army had launched a series of attacks against the Anzio beachhead. The Allies had stabilized the lines after a German penetration. Now the action was mostly an exchange of artillery fire and air attacks.

Butler's battalion was positioned in the northeast corner of the beach-head, its right flank on the Mussolini Canal and its front on a branch that drained into the main canal from the west. Colonel Weber paid Butler a visit and ordered him to put an outpost about 500 yards out beyond the Mussolini Canal in an area that was in good tank-maneuvering terrain. Butler was convinced, given the situation and the terrain, that he could not come to the outpost's aid in time if it were attacked at night by German tanks. Having little faith in Weber's tactical judgment, Butler felt compelled to object. He summoned up his courage and said, "Sir, this is a mistake—we'll lose them if we put them out there." With furrowed brow and in a harsh voice, Weber said, "Put them out," and left. Butler gritted his teeth and complied.

About three nights later, Butler heard a trembling voice on his radio urgently asking that artillery fire be brought down on top of the caller's position at the outpost—"now!" Butler took a deep breath and authorized it. Soon, converging artillery rounds whistled overhead, speeding toward the outpost, and a chain of loud explosions rattled Butler's command post, a dugout in the bank of the canal. The radio fell silent. The battalion never saw or heard from the five men manning the outpost again. The loss of these young lives increased Butler's contempt for his regimental commander.

In March 1944 Butler stood at attention in a formation on the beach-head, looking up into the face of Gen. Mark Clark and listening to the cita-tion being read in a loud voice by the adjutant. He had had no forewarning that he would be awarded the Distinguished Service Cross for heroic action on Monte Pantano. After "That the President of the United States of Ameri-ca . . .," most of the words being read about his valor escaped Butler. The thought that his wife, Ruth, and his parents would hear about the news sent a surge of pride through his mind; countering that feeling, a sense of humil-ity engulfed the farm boy from Milton, Kentucky, as he thought of the men who had been killed or seriously wounded in the battle. He wished that somehow they could share in the honor of the medal that General Clark pinned on his field jacket. The feeling of euphoria stayed with him long after the ceremony ended—and before Clark left, he ordered Weber to pro-mote Butler.

Days dragged on as the Allied buildup for the breakout from the Anzio beachhead continued. Except for the exchange of artillery fire, patrolling, and air action, enemy action had virtually come to a halt. From his new

Then Captain Benjamin Butler receives the Distinguished Service Cross from General Mark Clark. Courtesy of Benjamin Butler.

position on the beachhead perimeter, Butler noticed that green vegetables had begun to grow in no-man's-land in the gardens of an abandoned farmhouse. At first he and his former Company runner, Pfc. Baker, sneaked out at night and quickly gathered green onions and artichokes. As the nights passed they got bolder. One night the "vegetable patrol," as they came to be known, went far out in front, to a point near a farm building. Suddenly Germans who were dug in under the building opened fire. Butler jerked a German machine pistol off his shoulder and fired back, but Baker, in fluent German, starting yelling at them to cease fire. He whispered to Butler, "Keep picking vegetables." Baker kept up a running conversation with the Germans, then paused and said in a low voice to Butler, "Slip on down the hill," and Butler hurried down. Baker soon caught up with him. "What did you say to them?" asked Butler. Baker said, "I cursed them out and they apologized."

As they hustled along, with their sandbags filled with vegetables, Baker hooked his toe into something and yanked it out of the ground. Butler heard him say, "Oh my goodness," and asked, "What's the matter?" Baker said, "I pulled up a big mine back here." Butler went back and felt around and discovered that it was an antitank mine, fortunately not booby-trapped. Butler reported the location of the minefield to the First Armored Division, which was slated to pass over that area during the breakout, now only two nights away. The night before the attack the division's engineers removed truck-loads of mines.

About four months after the first of three failed attempts at breaking the Gustav Line, the Polish Corps, now assigned to the Fifth Army, captured the abbey on Monte Cassino on May 18, thereby opening the Liri Valley. On May 22, 1944, the attack to break out of the Anzio beachhead started. That morning, a couple of days before the First Battalion was scheduled to be committed, Butler received orders to turn command of the battalion over to Maj. Kermit Hanson, who had been the S-2 (intelligence officer) at regimental headquarters. Butler reasoned that cronyism motivated the change. It seemed unfair, and he felt betrayed; nevertheless, with his anger under control, he reported to regimental headquarters, where he was made the assistant S-3.

About three nights later, at the regimental command post, Butler listened on the phone to a perplexed Captain Galt, the S-3 of the First Battalion, who informed Butler that he could not find the new battalion commander and that the battalion was not moving in the night attack as ordered. In the midst of the conversation, newly promoted Brig. Gen. Fred Butler walked into the command post. Butler stood up and greeted his old regimental commander. General Butler stared down at Weber and his staff asleep on their folding cots, then turned to Captain Butler and in a gruff voice asked, "Is the First Battalion moving?" Butler told the general that it was not and that Galt could not find Hanson. Put out, the general said, "I'll be back; see if you can get the battalion moving."

Butler woke his boss, the regimental S-3, and told him that the First Battalion was not moving, that the battalion commander could not be found, and that General Butler had seemed upset about events when he left the command post. The sleepy S-3 told Butler in a mind-your-own-business tone not to worry: "Hanson can handle it." He instructed Butler not to wake Colonel Weber. Butler thought it was a hell of a way to run a war but said nothing. Then General Butler, blocked by the clogged traffic arteries of the attacking beachhead forces, reappeared. Butler offered him his own bedroll, the only one not being used.

All night Butler prodded Galt to find Hanson and to get the battalion moving. Before waking General Butler as instructed, Butler woke Weber and explained the tactical situation and General Butler's concern. A confident Weber told Butler that he could handle "Freddie," his old West Point class-mate. With that he turned over and went back to sleep. About 5:00 A.M.

Butler woke the general, who sat up, glared at the sleepers, and asked if the battalion was moving. Butler reported that it was not. The general got up and stormed out of the command post. About 6:00 A.M. Galt told Butler that he had found Hanson asleep in a haystack.

Standing in the breakfast chow line, Butler saw a jeep come to a screeching halt at the command post. Maj. Gen. Charles Ryder, the Thirty-fourth Division commander, bounced out of the jeep and walked straight to Butler. Returning Butler's salute, he said, "Come with me." Walking downstream with his arm on Butler's shoulder, Ryder said, "Tell me exactly what happened last night." Butler told him. Ryder said, "Thank you," and hurried off.

Exhausted from forty-eight hours without sleep, Butler took his bedroll out into the spring sunshine. A commotion awakened him suddenly out of deep sleep. Barely awake, he managed to understand that Maj. Fred Clark, commander of the Second Battalion, had been wounded in action; the battalion had two companies cut off and surrounded and another company pinned down at Genarro Ridge in the foothills of the Alban Hills. Butler heard Weber tell his executive officer (XO) that he had to take command of the battalion. The XO walked toward his jeep, stepped in a hole, wrenched his knee, and left for the aid station on a stretcher. Weber then told his S-2 he would have to take command. The S-2, intentionally causing his hands to tremble, said, "I'm too nervous." Weber looked at his S-3 who, with his head down, wrung his hands and said, "I'm too valuable a man for you at a time like this." Grunting, Weber said, "I guess you are."

Butler, pretending to be asleep, was galled by what he had heard. Suddenly, Weber gave Butler a swift kick on the bottom of the foot and told him he was just the man needed to take command of the Second Battalion. Butler said, "Sir, I heard the others turn you down. I'm not going to turn you down. But by God, the next promotion that comes to this outfit should be mine." For a moment, Butler couldn't believe he had said it. He quickly gathered his gear, slung his carbine over his shoulder, and departed.

Near the front lines, Butler halted his jeep and started walking toward Genarro Ridge. The nose of the ridge pointed toward the beach; two streams had cut a gorge on each side about sixty feet deep. Approaching the nose, Butler could see where the German forces had hidden at the base of the bluffs before cutting off the two American companies. But he did not know the nature of the situation confronting the Second Battalion, his new command. Running into a platoon out of the Third Battalion and learning that it was lost, he commandeered the platoon in spite of the displeasure shown by the platoon leader.

Near the nose of the ridge where the two streams came together he ran into Company E, cowering in gullies, depressions, or wherever they could find cover from sporadic German bullets. A few had been wounded. Butler did not like what he saw. Long ago he had concluded that in most cases units pinned down could work their way out of trouble with fire and maneuver. Standing over the company commander stretched out on the ground, Butler asked, "What's the matter?" The commander said, "We're pinned down." Butler queried, "How come you are and I'm not?"

Soon, Butler had organized the available force and issued orders. Three platoons attacked abreast. The flanking platoons had part of their men sweeping the ravines. Butler moved with the commandeered platoon behind the center platoon. Later, he notified regimental headquarters that the battalion was out of the trap, digging in, and awaiting orders. He was told to hold his position. Butler put his command post in a wine cellar and went to sleep.

About midnight someone woke him up and told him a colonel wanted to see him. Col. Henry Hine, without returning Butler's salute, stuck his right hand out and said, "I'm glad to see you. I'm your new regimental commander. I know what has been going on around here, and I want you to know that I have full confidence in you." Assuming that Hine knew about the circumstances that had caused Weber to be relieved of his command and perhaps about the bad blood between him and Weber, Butler chose not to elaborate; instead, he thanked his new boss and told him that he would do the best he could for him.

No more than three or four days passed before a truckload of officer replacements arrived in the regiment, and Lt. Col. Joe Bourne appeared at Butler's command post with his personal gear. In an apologetic tone he said that he knew what Butler had been through, but that he had orders to assume command of the battalion. Butler understood how seniority worked in the army, but that did not ease his deep disappointment. Bourne made Butler his XO.

Meanwhile, the German forces began to crumble under the weight of the Allied forces at the Gustav Line and on the Anzio beachhead as the two came together while gaining control of the Alban Hills, the key terrain feature south of Rome. General Clark had two options: he could mass his forces for an attack to the east and capture Valmontone, as ordered, and hopefully trap and destroy the retreating German Gustav Line forces, or he could drive into Rome. Enticed by the prize of entering Rome, Clark directed his main effort toward the city and sent a smaller force eastward toward Valmontone. Fighting desperately and skillfully, the German Tenth Army managed to evade entrapment. The Allies entered Rome on June 5, 1944, to the cheers and hugs of the masses.

In a motorized task force screening the Fifth Army's left flank as it poured through the city at night, Butler passed Saint Paul's church, crossed the Tiber

River, and marveled at the sight of Saint Peter's dome silhouetted in the distance. He did not think about all the suffering and young lives lost while trying to get there; he was concentrating on not getting lost. Headlines swept the globe: "Rome Captured." But the well-earned fame and glory proved brief. The next day world headlines passed to the Normandy invasion, the greatest ever attempted.

Later, while observing the Second Battalion attacking on a ridge toward Civita Castellana, a resort town thirty miles north of Rome, Butler heard agonized screams from a wounded German soldier slumped over a barbed wire barrier at the edge of the town. With compassion for a suffering fellow human being, the medics asked Butler to let them go to his rescue. As four medics—their red cross flag whipping in the wind and red cross armbands revealing who they were—moved hastily with their stretcher to the wounded man, German SS soldiers darted out and captured the good Samaritans. The duped Americans watching the action could not believe their eyes. That the Nazi soldiers could not only let their own wounded soldier suffer but use him as bait to capture American medics boggled their minds. These men had not, to their knowledge, been in contact with the SS before and were unaware of the radical nature of many of its soldiers.

During the next day's advance, men of the Second Battalion came upon the four medics lying face down on the ground, each in a pool of his own blood, each shot in the back of the head. Word about the brutal killing quickly spread through the ranks. The Americans knew the repulsive face of war; they had lived in the midst of killing and being killed, but this hideous act exceeded the bounds of war as they knew it, and they were outraged. Frustrated men cursed the Nazis. Their mood swung to a revenge mode, and many swore they would take no more prisoners.

Concerned that his little slice of an ugly war was about to get uglier, Butler instructed his company commanders to inform their men that fighting with a vengeance was not the best way to get the job done, that information from prisoners of war could save American lives, that not all Germans were so radical, and that he did not want his men to kill any German prisoners. But the men of the Second Battalion never rescued another wounded German beyond their lines.

From Civita Castellana the Thirty-fourth Division moved swiftly up the coastal plain on the west side of the Italian boot to the Arno River Line, which ran generally east to west through Florence and Pisa. Casualties had been relatively light. In early September 1944, shortly after Butler had been promoted to major and made regimental S-3, he called Colonel Hine on the field phone and told him that Colonel Bourne, the Second Battalion commander, had been wounded and evacuated. Hine said, "Who can we get to replace him?" As a captain, Butler had commanded a battalion three times for brief periods, only to lose out to a senior officer or a regimental commander's buddy. He felt that he had earned the right to command, and he wanted the job. He said, "Sir, I'm right here with the battalion." Hine chuckled, and said, "You are it." Butler could hardly conceal his joy and excitement.

By the end of August 1944 the Allies were applying pressure on the German Gothic Line, running generally east to west across the narrow neck of Italy. The strongly fortified line cut Highway 65 between Florence and Bologna at the famous Futa Pass about 170 miles north of Rome.

One day Hine said to Butler, "I hate to tell you, but you are going to have to break the Gothic Line." Early the next morning, September 21, 1944, Butler and two of his staff officers lay on a hogback southwest of Futa Pass. Through his binoculars Butler observed a line cleared of bushes for fields of fire, a belt of barbed wire entanglements, and numerous fortified bunkers. Butler shook his head as he studied the menacing obstacles and fortifications. Suddenly, a German shepherd dog appeared, coming from the direction of the Gothic Line. He stopped and looked at the Americans, flashed his teeth, and raised the hair on his back. Alarmed, Butler said, "Be careful, that dog might be trained to attack Americans." Nevertheless, on the chance that the dog might have a common German name for dogs, Butler called out in German, "Kommen sie hier, Fritz." To everyone's surprise the dog trotted over and licked Butler's hand. A smile spread across Butler's face when he read "Fritz" on the dog's nametag. Butler offered him a C ration biscuit. After Fritz licked the last crumb out of Butler's hand, he started back toward the Gothic Line, now and then looking back over his shoulder as if to say to his new friend, "Come on." An inner light clicked in Butler's mind, and on an impulse he decided to take a chance. He called Fritz back, held onto his collar, turned to Capt. Harold Bishop, his S-3, and ordered him to move the battalion forward.

Making the risky decision to follow Fritz through that dangerous terrain strewn with mines and covered by enemy weapons took what the military theorist Karl von Clausewitz called "a special kind of courage." "War is the province of chance," he wrote. "From this uncertainty, . . . this continued interposition of chance, the actor of war constantly finds things different from his expectations. . . . To get safely through this perpetual conflict with the unexpected, two qualities are indispensable: in the first place an intellect which, even in the midst of this intense obscurity, is not without some trace of inner-light which leads to the truth, and then courage to follow this faint light. The first is figuratively expressed by the French phrase coup d'oeil.

The other is resolution. . . . Resolution is an act of courage in a single instance. . . . But here we do not mean courage in face of bodily danger, but in face of responsibility, therefore to a certain extent against moral danger."

Butler had demonstrated courage to face bodily danger; now his courage to face moral danger was about to be tested. His decision caused him to face the responsibility of exposing his battalion to destruction. He called Hine on the phone and got his approval to cancel the planned artillery preparation and told him he was going on radio silence while he tried to sneak through the line. Low-hanging clouds settled down on the valley floor. Butler canceled the artillery smoke screen.

Following Fritz, this twenty-seven-year-old farmer from Milton, Kentucky, took off for the Gothic Line. His 800-man battalion stretched out single file behind him across the narrow valley. At the barbed wire entanglement Butler paused to see whether Fritz knew the secret pathway through the minefield. Satisfied that he did, Butler quickly followed the dog. As he zigzagged through the barbed wire obstacle, as if walking through a maze, Butler glanced down at the partially decomposed bodies of Italian civilians lying across the barbed wire on both sides of the crooked path. Seeing them heightened his tension and sharpened his alertness to the danger of mines. But he concentrated mostly on keeping up with Fritz.

Knowing that if the Germans were alerted and caught his battalion in a nonfighting formation in the minefield and barbed wire lanes revealed by Fritz, his troops would suffer heavy causalities, Butler kicked into a faster gait. His men had to hustle to keep up with him. Fully alert, with long legs churning, he watched for signs that the Americans might have been discovered. He listened for enemy guns booming in the distance, signaling an artillery barrage on its way. His ears searched for the "slush" sound of a mortar tube being loaded or the clicking of an automatic weapon. But he heard nothing.

Once through the barbed wire, he changed his plan. Instead of attacking the two smaller hills butting up against the barbed wire, he led his battalion through the gap between the hills and aimed for the mountain peak about a mile beyond. Just as he cleared the gap Fritz turned left and trotted away toward a nearby German bunker, never to be seen again. Butler thought, "This is bound to alert them." His heart pounded faster. Glancing back at the single file he saw soldiers still snaking their way through the minefield and the barbed wire maze. The men just approaching those obstacles were hidden in the fog, but most were dangerously exposed. There was nothing Butler could do; the silent men were weaving their way through as fast as they could. No one dared not keep up.

Near the base of the 3,000-foot mountain covered with fog, Butler instructed Capt. H.K. "Doc" Johnson, Company E's commander, to head straight for the top and establish a defensive position the moment he got there. Butler and his command group fell in behind Company E. Just beneath the summit Johnson deployed his company and stormed over the crown. German command-center personnel scurried out of their bunker and disappeared, leaving the biggest field switchboard the Americans had ever seen as well as radios and other equipment.

On top of the high ground where a ridge ran east to west, Butler hastily reconnoitered the area. As companies arrived, he carefully positioned them so that the battalion could defend against counterattacks from any direction and instructed them to dig in quickly. Seven hours after he fell in behind Fritz, Butler controlled the high ground about a mile behind the Gothic Line. The first part of a desperate gamble had succeeded. Being out of the danger zone of the mines and barbed wire, Butler felt safer. But the fate of the World War I "Lost Battalion" flickered through his mind. His hunch that the dog could lead them through the barbed wire and minefield obstacles had been correct. Nevertheless, he was surprised to be on top of the mountain and behind the German line without a casualty.

A little past 3:00 P.M., some fifteen minutes after the battalion had arrived on the mountaintop, enemy machine gun fire crisscrossed its position, and soon elements of the German attacking force overran part of Company E. Butler led Company G to their aid and drove the Germans out. Still, sporadic machine gun tracers continued to streak across from the front, rear, left, and right. By their expressions, Butler knew the men were nervous about being cut off and fearful about their fate. He put out the word that they were going to stay; the Germans had a bigger problem, and the Americans were not to worry. Then he ended radio silence and reported his position. Over the radio he heard the regimental staff cheering in the background and someone shouting excitedly, "Butler is on top of the mountain beyond the Gothic Line."

Soon he received a coded message: "Fifth Army aware of your situation. Hold. Have twenty-eight battalions of artillery in place to fire in support." Encouraged, Butler called his four company commanders together and shared the good news. He instructed them to have their artillery forward observers adjust defensive artillery fire concentrations so that "we can bring down a ring of steel around our position in short order." Before long, friendly artillery rounds whistled in and exploded all around the Second Battalion's position. When the forward observers adjusted the artillery to hit a specific desired spot, they called that spot a concentration and gave the concentration a number.

The artillerymen in about eighty-four batteries, all in different locations on the other side of the Gothic Line, had the data set on their howitzers ready to fire at their assigned concentrations on notice. That night, any unusual noise, even the crack of a broken stick, triggered the order to fire on the defensive fire concentrations. The orders went out over the radio. On several occasions through the night Butler and his men heard American artillery thundering in the distance, followed by roaring noises in the valleys that turned into a whistling sound just before the converging shells splashed down on their assigned concentrations. The ring of explosions just outside the Americans' perimeter rattled the ground like an earthquake. Men inside the circle who had feared being cut off and captured spoke in more assured tones.

The next morning Butler got a message from the regimental S-3 asking how they could best cut his battalion out from behind the German line. Butler, not wanting to climb that mountain again, told the S-3 that he didn't want to go backward but forward. After some delay he was granted permission to attack forward.

That night, September 22, 1944, Butler attacked to the northeast toward Highway 65, steadily advancing from dusk to dawn in the face of light opposition. The next morning he observed in the distance a convoy of German trucks loaded with troops speeding to the north on Highway 65. Later that day other units in the division caught up with him and helped evacuate his wounded, only three of whom were litter cases. Butler did not destroy the Gothic Line, one of the two most formidable defenses in Italy, with one battalion; the line was already coming unglued at Il Giogo Pass, about six miles to the east of Futa Pass, when he made his bold move. But in accordance with Clausewitz he had had his inner light (coup d'oeil) and the courage to follow it, and the daring chance he took paid off.

Still, the Allied forces did not break out into the Po Valley in northern Italy, as planned and as expected by Butler. Instead, the Germans fell back to yet another defensive line. The fighting continued. Near Tazzoli, a town south of Bologna, the Thirty-fourth Division had tried all morning to breach the German lines. Finally, about 2:00 P.M., Butler found a gap and sent one company through. Soon he had another company following. Pleased with their progress, he was watching with his binoculars when the sudden firing of a nearby company of American tanks startled him; then, horrified, he saw the tank shells exploding in the midst of his lead company, which was just then entering the town. He grabbed the radio mike and screamed, "Cease fire! cease fire!" over the tanker's radio net. The firing stopped, but the damage had been done. Butler and his command group fell in behind the second company and followed them into the town.

In Tazzoli a surprised Butler came upon an SS doctor and his medics giving medical aid to the Americans who had been wounded by their own tanks. The SS doctor told Butler in good English that he had seen the tanks fire on their own troops and that his commander had given him permission to help the wounded Americans. Butler thanked the doctor and told him, "You and your men can stay and be our prisoners of war, where you will be treated well and be out of danger—or you can return to your unit." The doctor tightened his lips, thought for a moment, and then said, "We must go back."

He must have sensed that Butler was puzzled by his heroic act of compassion, though, because he said, "Most Germans don't want to serve in the SS—they are too mean—but we have no choice." Soon the doctor and all but one of his medics departed for their own lines with their pockets full of American cigarettes. The one SS medic who chose to stay remained for a couple of days with the company that had been hit by the American tanks, and wanted to continue working as its medic, but Butler thought it best to send him back through the prisoner of war channels.

The Second Batallion was still fighting in northern Italy when Butler got orders in March 1945 to rotate back to the States. He had earned enough points, based on his twenty-four months overseas and military decorations which, besides the Distinguished Service Cross, included the Silver Star for valor and the Purple Heart for wounds in battle at Monte Pantano.

With orders in hand, he visited each of his five companies to say goodbye. By the time he reached the last, he had mixed feelings, for he had developed a deep respect for his men. Leaving them with the job unfinished saddened him, yet the lifting of the heavy weight of responsibility for their young lives gave him a sense of relief. For a long time he had endured the physical exertion and suffering demanded in war; he was extremely weary in both body and soul. But he also knew that his very being had been tested and that he had done well. All these things coupled with thoughts of the coming reunion with his wife, Ruth, and his parents, Mark and Minnie Butler, waiting for him in Kentucky, overpowered his sadness and left him with a sense of joy and well-being. He walked to his jeep with his head high, and though his eyes were moist, he departed with a smile.

FIVE

The Air War over Germany, and Stalag 17

Sergeant Bernell S. Heaton
B-17 Gunner, U.S. Army Air Force

In the wee hours of the morning on a summer day in 1943 in England, twenty-four-year-old Bernell S. Heaton climbed into his B-17 bomber, worked his way over to the left waist gunner's station, and prepared his gun for action. Soon the big four-engine Flying Fortress roared down the runway, tucked in close behind the plane in front and straining at full power to get off the ground.

Having realized his dream after volunteering, while stationed in England, to be a waist gunner and now embarking on his first combat mission, Heaton felt good but nervous. Most of his training had been on the ground. He had been in the air three or four times, but this was different. The seven big bombers in his squadron, the 427th, each loaded with aviation fuel and bombs, climbed dangerously close one behind the other toward their assembly point. From what little he could see and the limited conversation on the intercom, he felt the tension in the ten-man crew. The dark sky was full of flashing lights from the planes of the other three squadrons in his group, the 303d, and those out of other airfields now converging in the sky. Just as they reached their assigned altitude of 10,000 feet, the sun broke the horizon. As planned, the gathering planes jockeyed to form a gigantic formation, and soon Heaton's squadron was flying in an inverted V with squadrons above, below, in front, and behind. The boxlike formation stretched for miles in the sky. Heaton strained to take it all in.

He knew they were going to bomb the submarine pens near Bremen, Germany, and they had been told that the Germans had concentrated antiaircraft guns there. Still, Heaton was not sure what to expect; his anxiety increased, and the pilot did not have to tell him to be alert. He felt his grip on the machine gun tighten as he stared out the window, his eyes sweeping the blue sky above, below, to the front, and to the rear for the hostile fighter

Sergeant Bernell Heaton (standing) was a waist gunner on a B-17 bomber flying out of England in 1943. Courtesy of Bernell Heaton.

planes he expected to see at any moment. Meanwhile, the four-engine bombers droned on over the North Sea, reaching for more altitude as the column moved toward the German shoreline.

The conversation on the intercom between the pilot and the bombardier told him that they were nearing the target. Suddenly, a black puff of smoke appeared not far off, and soon Heaton's plane, now on its bomb run, was flying straight and level, boring right into puffs of smoke from the exploding antiaircraft shells that soon dotted the sky. Close-in explosions batted the plane around; Heaton felt it being driven downward, bounced upward, and hurled from side to side. He could not hear the explosions over the roar of the engines, but he did hear shell fragments banging against the plane's fuselage and it made him wonder, "What in the hell is going to happen to me?" He felt helpless. It was praying time. Although he had been taught how to use the parachute he was wearing, the thought of having to use it was not something he wanted to think about. Yet however torturous the stress, he did not forget why he was there. He felt compelled to maintain his vigilance for enemy fighters, and that sense of duty dampened the impulse to panic.

He did not see the bombs hit, nor did he know whether they had struck the target, but he felt great relief when the plane ended its bomb run and turned toward the sea. Back on the ground in England, Heaton thought, "That wasn't so bad. I can do it." Soon most of the gunners of the squadron gathered at the Black Swan Pub, just off the base, where they drank a few beers, told war stories, laughed, and let off steam. They could laugh because all planes in the squadron had returned from this mission.

Heaton soon learned that each mission was different and that danger lurked everywhere. Once, the number-three engine was hit. After landing back in England, Heaton and the rest of the crew rushed out of the plane to take a look at it. Just as they gathered around the engine, it came apart and fell to the ground in pieces. Later, over Germany, Heaton's bomber had two engines knocked out, and they had to jettison things to lighten the plane as it labored back to England.

Returning from one mission Heaton anxiously listened to the pilot advising the tower that he had to land through the fog because he did not have enough fuel to go to an alternate airfield. The tower warned the pilot that the ceiling was on the ground with a few little patches open now and then at treetop level. The grim news worried Heaton. He thought he could feel the plane descending, but all he could see was thick fog moving by. He strained, hoping to find a clear hole. Suddenly, an opening did appear, at treetop level, near the end of the runway. At that moment another B-17 roared right at them from the opposite direction. Instantly, the pilots flipped their planes over on opposite wings. Bouncing off the side of the fuselage, Heaton knew that the wing had just missed the ground. The roaring masses swishing through each other's sacred space and the violent slamming around of the crew terrorized him. On the ground it took him a moment to collect himself, before he could get off the plane.

On another mission, right over their target at Geisenkirchen, Germany, Heaton saw the biggest storm cloud he had ever seen. The tall, black cloud dwarfed the approaching column of B-17s. Heaton knew the bombers couldn't penetrate the threatening dark mass in a tight formation, so he wasn't surprised when the column started climbing and circling to get above it.

Soon the intercom bristled with fear-laden voices announcing the approach of enemy fighters from one o'clock high. Heaton swung his .50-caliber machine gun around and stared in the direction of the threat. At first, the ME 109 appeared to him like a speck in the sky; then it shot by him so fast that he could only snap off a poorly aimed burst before it zoomed out of view and back into the cloud. Heaton didn't see the tragedy, but he heard the pilot announce that one of the planes in the squadron had been hit and destroyed.

The German fighters had the American bomber formation where they wanted them. A fighter would dart out of the cloud above and in front of the bomber it was going to hit. The rapid closing speed of two planes flying in opposite directions plus the scant time it took the enemy to dart back into the sanctuary made it almost impossible for the bomber's gunners to hit the fighter planes.

Meanwhile, the bomber column continued climbing and circling the menacing cloud. Somehow, they had to find its top so they could make their bomb runs. Every fiber in Heaton's body was alert and poised to get off more rounds at the next predator. Again he heard the warning, but the best he could do was to snap off a burst. In the midst of the roaring engines, the nervous voices on the intercom, and the chattering of the machine guns at various locations on the plane, Heaton saw one of the squadron's planes blow up in the sky—just a big puff of smoke with pieces flying about. In an instant the puff was behind his plane and out of his view. The imminent danger facing him and his crew and the urgent need to fight for his own and their lives precluded any thoughts about the fate of his friends on the doomed plane.

As the bomber column continued climbing and circling the tall cloud, the fighters kept zooming down on their prey from the front and darting back into the black cloud. They knocked out another plane in the squadron. Heaton didn't know how many planes of the group had been lost, but he knew that three of the squadron's seven planes were gone. He knew also that the black cloud boiling with deadly German fighters posed a threat to the remaining bombers. He was nervous and anxious to get out of the trap.

Finally, the commander decided to abort the mission and return to England. As the column departed, Heaton watched the German fighters gather in the distance, out of range of the American machine guns. They continued to stalk the column at a safe distance for a while before they disappeared. Heaton helped to disarm the bombs before they landed in England. He had frequently seen the squadron return because of weather and land while still loaded with bombs, but this was the only time he had seen the squadron return with their bombs after they had reached Germany. Nevertheless, he was glad to be on the ground. For a brief moment the relief from extreme danger gave him a good feeling.

In the barracks that housed four enlisted crews, Heaton and the other five men in his own crew busied themselves around their bunks, stowing their gear and getting organized. The contrast between the activity around the bunks of the crew that had returned and the eloquent silence that surrounded the bunks of missing friends in the other three crews caught Heaton's attention. Soon, he and the others sat in silence on their bunks, staring at the empty beds and pictures of families and girlfriends in each missing man's space. The trauma he had suppressed out of necessity while he was fighting for his life rose up, and a state of extreme anxiety, helplessness, and fear seized him.

Later, Heaton helped others go through the personal belongings of the missing crewmen in order to remove things that his friends might not want their parents or next of kin to see, or things that belonged to the government. Handling a picture of a smiling friend with a girlfriend or a parent overwhelmed him. Grief, sadness, remorse, and anger converged to torment him, and he had to fight back the tears. Yet he continued with the depressing task until all the personal belongings of his departed friends had been packed for shipment to their next of kin. Soon, new crews occupied the empty bunks.

On still another mission, while flying at 20,000 feet, Heaton realized that his electrically heated, wool-lined leather flight suit was going bad. The heat went out first in a glove and then in a boot. He thought the temperature was about seventy degrees below zero, and he knew the danger of frostbite. Once, his eyes had frozen open. He had solved that problem by placing his heated glove over his eyes. But this was a more threatening situation, and he worked frantically with the plugs and the control knob. Nothing worked. The common heating source for both waist gunners was out, and he felt the cold creeping into his flight suit.

The pilot guided the plane to a lower and warmer altitude, but by the time they landed in England, both waist gunners had to be rushed to the hospital. Heaton's face, feet, and hands were frostbitten. In a few days all the skin on his face peeled off, and two little pouches hung down beneath his lower jaw. His ghastly appearance shocked his friends for a while, but he fully recovered and soon returned to flying.

In the last week of December 1943, Heaton's plane lifted off the end of the runway on its way to Kiel, Germany. Even though an enemy threat wasn't likely in the local area, he felt some tension at every liftoff. Consequently, his eyes fixed on the moving, flashing lights dotting the moonlit sky as planes converged on the assembly point. Standing at his gun station, Heaton was focused momentarily on the bomb-laden plane in front and to the side of his when suddenly a bomber from another group rammed into it. One gigantic explosion lit the sky, and odd-shaped flames flew in every direction. In a flash there was nothing left to see, but the image of the tragedy remained in Heaton's mind.

Stunned, he agonized over the abrupt and violent fate of the men in the two crews. While he pondered the lightning swift crossing of twenty men from this world into the unknown from one little spot in the sky, and his bomb-laden aircraft jockeyed to find its place in the formation, his clearer awareness of his own mortality as a bomber crewman weighed heavily on him. As the plane droned on toward the target, Heaton had to make a conscious effort again and again to control his thoughts, to keep his mind on finding and dealing with any enemy attacker.

Hours before daylight on January 11, 1944, airmen hustled about the well-lit American airfield, performing the numerous tasks that had to be done to get about sixty bombers of the 303d Bomb Group loaded and ready for their mission to bomb an aircraft factory at Oschersleben, Germany. Ground crewmen hurried around the airstrip in their vehicles, towing trailers loaded with bombs, while others hurried to their bombers to make last-minute preparations. Officer crew members rushed out of the briefing room to draw equipment and to take care of other matters. Enlisted air crewmen rushed out of the mess hall to draw their parachutes and other equipment. This was the normal busy traffic at the base before a bombing mission. But for Heaton, weaving his way through the crowd with his dog, Flack, this morning was different.

Heaton and Flack had become great friends. Flack liked to fly, and Heaton took him along whenever he flew rescue missions over the channel. At the supply room he said to their ground crew chief, "Milligan, take care of Flack, I don't think we're coming back." Milligan said, "Don't tell me that stuff." Heaton replied, "Well, that's the way I feel." Saddened by the thought of never seeing his dog again, Heaton handed the leash to Milligan, drew his parachute, and departed.

On his way out he ran into the pilot and asked him where the squadron would be in the formation. First Lieutenant McClovern told him they were flying the "low, low" position. Heaton understood the danger that lurked in the low, low position—below the lowest squadron at the tail end of the formation. The German fighter pilots knew that the low, low squadron had fewer machine guns to aim at them than the others; consequently, they would often gather to the rear and below the column of bombers like a pack of hungry wolves and make repeated attacks against this most vulnerable squadron in the formation, which had no squadrons flying below or behind them to offer support. Only a few days earlier, Heaton had replaced the tail gunner on a mission in which the squadron had flown in the low, low position. He had fired the twin-mounted .50-caliber machine guns so long and so fast that the barrels had glowed red hot before the guns jammed.

The bad news infuriated Heaton, and he reminded his boss that they had flown the low, low position more than any other squadron; he didn't think it was fair. Knowing they would surely have to withstand an onslaught of German fighter planes again confirmed his premonition and added weight to his sagging spirits. The gunners were volunteers and could quit flying any time they wanted to, yet despite his certainty that he was not coming back from this mission, Heaton boarded the jeep waiting to take the crew to their bomber.

In the air over Holland near the border with Germany, the short-range American fighters escorting the long bomber formation turned and headed back to England. On past missions, when the short-range fighter escort left the formation, the bombers were on their own. Recently, long-range fighters (P-51s) had arrived in England to provide fighter support to the bomber formation deep into Germany. Heaton peered out the waist gunner's open window, looking anxiously for the long-range fighters scheduled to join their formation when the short-range fighters turned back. But as his squadron flew on in the low, low position, the sky remained empty. Soon the pilot's voice crackled in his earphones with the news that the long-range fighter escort was not going to join them. The pilot said, "We are going to have to go in without them." "Ohhhhh," Heaton mumbled to himself, "I'll never live through this."

Suddenly, his earphones came alive with tense voices shouting out locations of enemy fighters coming from below and from the rear. Heaton heard the tail gun and ball turret gun chatter before he could see anything to fire at. The German fighters would make one pass and then another. He saw one of his squadron's bombers take a fatal hit. His own plane shook and an engine went out. He could hear machine guns rattling from all six stations. Firing his gun at the maximum rate and with all the concentration he could muster, Heaton saw two more bombers of his squadron take hits. He didn't know whether the crews had bailed out or not. Soon, a second engine of Heaton's plane was disabled by enemy fire. The pilot feathered the engine and put the plane in a dive until the fire was blown out.

Now, with the stricken aircraft out of formation and even more vulnerable, the hostile fighters pounced. While Heaton aimed and fired at one enemy plane, another came from the rear and slid along underneath the B-17. The tail gun fell silent, and Heaton had to assume that the tail gunner had been hit. Then the frantic voice of the pilot broke in over the other voices on the intercom: "Prepare to bail out, prepare to bail out." In an instant, a 20-mm round from the fighter beneath the bomber crashed through the fuselage and exploded by Heaton's left leg. Blood ran down into his boot, but the stunned gunner didn't realize it, nor was he aware of the tiny fragments lodged in his arm, neck, and elsewhere. With his ears ringing, the young Kentuckian collected himself from a stupor and whispered, "I've got to get out of here." He felt a compulsion to jump out the open window but remembered his training and started moving toward the door on the right side of the plane.

American Boeing B-17 bombers fly through vapor trails left by American fighter planes escorting the formation. The Eighth Air Force lost 5,000 heavy bombers in the air war over Europe and suffered 26,000 killed, 18,000 wounded, and 28,000 captured. Courtesy of the Kentucky Historical Society.

The other waist gunner was trying desperately to detach the door as they had been taught, but it wouldn't break loose. Instead, Heaton swung it open, and the other gunner motioned to him to jump. The wide shoulders that had served him so well when he played football for Centre College in Danville, Kentucky, made it hard for Heaton to squeeze through the narrow door, but he jumped—and to his horror a strap on his chute caught on the door handle. He had fallen only a few inches from the plane which was steadily losing altitude in a straight and level glide pattern. The wind from the propellers on the two good engines banged him against the fuselage in a rhythm like a beating heart. The other waist gunner worked desperately to get the strap off the handle, assuring Heaton with his eyes and body language that everything would be okay.

Suddenly the wind blast of the propellers hurled him toward the tail of the bomber. He ducked, as he had been taught to do, but the horizontal, winglike part of the tail clipped the top of his head. When he regained consciousness, he was tumbling head over heels. Then he was falling feet first, above him nothing but beautiful blue sky and thousands of feet below him a white cloud blanketing the earth. So far as he could see, he was the only speck in the blue sky. He felt nothing as his body accelerated, and he heard nothing, could not even sense that he was falling. The lack of sensation surprised him, and he was baffled by the contrast between this complete silence and the noise he had just left: voices cracking on his intercom, machine guns chattering, engines roaring, ear-splitting explosions. The sensation of being suspended in the blue sky, alone and in total silence, gave him an eerie feeling. He had to force himself to concentrate.

He worried about when to pull the rip cord on his parachute. If he pulled it too soon a German fighter might attack him. He had never seen that happen, but he had heard of such incidents. Without waiting, he pulled the rip cord. The chute did not open. Panic began to engulf him. To regain control, he said to himself, "Remember your training." This time he grasped the rip cord handle and jerked his right arm out straight, as he had been taught to do. The parachute opened.

Now he could feel the pull of his chute. The straps, too loose around his legs, made him worry about slipping out of his harness. He raised both hands above his head and held on tight to the two risers. He never gave his wounded leg a thought. Instead a host of things raced through his mind as he floated down alone. He wondered where he was and what was going to happen to him next. Surely Holland would be better than Germany, he thought.

In a little while the white cloud below him hurried upward toward him. He dropped into it and shortly afterward saw through the fog the tops of tall trees. He worked feverishly with the risers, trying to steer his parachute between two trees. The chute caught on a limb and gently stood him on the partially snow-covered ground. It didn't even jar him, but for the first time he became keenly aware of the sharp pain throbbing in his wounded leg. Still, obedient to his training, he hurried to get out of his parachute harness. Then he heard a stick break, and looking up he saw running right at him a wild-looking man wielding an upraised ax. Heaton's knees got so weak that he had to sit down. Nothing in his training had prepared him for this. Pretending that there was no threat from the charging assailant and that he was not afraid, Heaton pulled up his pants leg and exposed his bleeding wound. It worked. The woodsman stopped and lowered his ax.

Both men could see that the wound was a mess. Heaton pulled off his boot and poured out the blood. The woodsman spoke in German. Heaton thought the man was asking if he had a pistol and shook his head, "No, no." Two other civilians came over, a German farmer and a French laborer, and helped carry Heaton into a big U-shaped building that housed both the farm animals and the farmer's family. By then it was about 11:30 A.M. A woman in her thirties and a bunch of children gathered around and stared at the American. The woman took over and tried to communicate in a friendly German voice and with sign language. It took Heaton a while to make her understand that he wanted some water to wash his wound and a piece of cloth to make a tourniquet. While washing the wound, she struggled to help him understand her questions: what is your name, where are you from, are you married, what is your religion, and other inquiries about his personal life. She learned that he was Protestant and single, and he learned that she was Catholic. For the first time his fear subsided and he relaxed a little in spite of the throbbing pain in his leg. The tourniquet he had applied soon stopped the bleeding.

Anxious to learn where he was, Heaton pulled the map of Europe out of his escape kit and pointed to it. With some difficulty, he discovered that he was in Germany. For some reason the map fascinated the woman, and she wanted it. Gently and firmly, he let her know that he couldn't part with his map.

The oldest girl, about thirteen, kept smiling at Heaton, and the farmer's wife let him know that the teenager liked him. They gave him a little bowl of soup and a little piece of white bread, and offered him a drink of cognac from the bottle. Afraid that too much might make him drunk and dull his alertness, he took only a swig and thanked them for their kindness.

About 2:30 P.M. the men came and put him on a one-horse cart and took him out of the security of the kind lady and children to a big dairy barn. There, an old man Heaton took to be a veterinarian wrapped his wounded leg in paper bandages. The veterinarian was all business: there were no broken bones, and the other wounds were minor. When he was finished, he directed Heaton to a waiting car. En route to an SS camp, the old anxieties about the uncertainty of his future came back into his mind and pulled his spirits down again.

In a large room where the Germans had gathered about twenty-five downed American airmen, Heaton spotted four others of his crew. His bombardier, navigator, ball gunner, and tail gunner joyfully welcomed him into their little group. Not being alone in enemy country and knowing that others in his crew had survived made Heaton's spirits soar upward for a moment. Still, when the smiles receded the faces looked grim. Heaton saw that his close friend Charles Dugan, the tail gunner from Pittsburgh, had a serious wound. In a little while the Germans took Dugan to the hospital.

The faces became more downcast as they swapped information about the rest of the crew. For six months the close-knit team had fought together and stood on the threshold of death several times. Now they wanted desperately to know what had happened to the others. Someone said the radio operator had been killed in the plane. Someone else thought that Alfred Charles, the other waist gunner, had bailed out farther down the valley. Each added little pieces to the puzzle. Lieutenant Galliger, the navigator, told about asking the pilot if they could get back to England; Lieutenant McClovern had answered, "There's no way." Galliger told the pilot that he was going to get out. When he asked, "Mac, are you leaving?" Mac just sat there, staring ahead. According to Galliger, the pilot and copilot had gone down with the plane.

Heaton remembered his earlier concern about their pilot. He thought Lieutenant McClovern was a great pilot but even after a week of rest (following their twelfth mission) at a large manor in Oxford, he had still looked extremely stressed when they came back to their base. Heaton had thought that Mac might be suffering from combat fatigue and discussed the matter with other crew members, but he had chosen not to say anything about it to anyone in the chain of command. Now he wondered if he should have.

After a night in the basement of a large building, Heaton and about three freight cars full of prisoners of war were loaded onto a train destined for the interrogation center at Frankfurt, Germany. At Frankfurt, the Germans isolated the POWs in individual cells about three feet wide and six feet long. Heaton felt cramped and lonely. Only sleep could lighten his misery, but the painful throbbing of his wounded leg robbed him of sleep.

Heaton's contempt for the Nazis didn't help him during interrogation. At one session his interrogator told Heaton that according to his information, Heaton had not attended gunnery school in the States. The questioner wanted to know where he had gone to school. Heaton snarled out his name, rank, and serial number, the information he was authorized to tell. He said, "You can take me out and shoot me, but I'm not telling you any more." The captain shouted, "You can't talk to me like that!" and slapped him in the face. Heaton gritted his teeth and thought, "Go to hell," but he held his tongue.

By the end of the second week in his cramped cell he could not walk. Ugly blisters surrounded the wound, and a red streak ran up his swollen leg to the knee. The stench of infection fouled the air in his cell, and the excruciating pain now robbed him not only of sleep but of his appetite. Homesickness, pain, and misery converted his contempt for his captors into a deep-seated hatred.

After another session, while Heaton hobbled along on one foot and hung onto a guard, he ran into a lieutenant from his unit who asked, "Well, Heaton, did they do anything for your leg?" Heaton said, "No, and I wouldn't ask them sons of bitches for nothing." As the guards moved them along, the lieutenant said, "I'll see what I can do about it." Soon a German medic came to Heaton's cell. He took the paper bandage off and exposed the festering wound, then poured something over it. Heaton gritted his teeth and tightened every muscle in his body. The wound burned as if it had been hit with acid. But the treatment helped: by the time he was loaded on the train to

Stalag 17, Heaton could walk on the injured leg. It didn't heal completely, however; he had to endure the pain of an open wound until after the war ended.

Heaton and about twenty other slightly wounded POWs were put in the same boxcar. He couldn't see out, but he knew he was going somewhere in Austria. Soon after the train pulled out of Frankfurt, a German medic changed the bandage on his leg and told Heaton in perfect English that he had been a student at Northwestern University, near Chicago. Heaton asked him what he was doing in Germany. The medic told him he had come to Germany to visit some relatives and hadn't been allowed to leave. Heaton didn't believe the story. That the medic might be an American serving the enemy annoyed him.

Some three days later the train came to a stop. The guards slid the doors open, ordered the POWs out, and herded them into groups of about sixty. Heaton read "KREMS" on the railroad station and wondered where in Austria they might be. In the melee of forming up Heaton spotted his crewmate Dugan and limped over to get beside him in the formation. They greeted each other and soon learned they were not to talk. Still, it was nice to have someone you knew by your side in this cold, bleak setting.

Under an overcast sky the grim-faced column marched over a mile to the top of a small hill and looked down the valley at their new home, nearly another mile away. Struggling to keep up, Heaton surveyed the dreary-looking camp blanketed with snow. He saw about forty one-story barracks and other buildings, all surrounded by two barbed wire fences. Carefully spaced guard towers and the double fence spoke to him about the nature of his new life. Not a soul stirred in the compound.

Heaton had not had a bath since being shot down nearly a month before. Limping painfully in the quiet column snaking its way toward the prison camp, he felt grimy and cold and homesick. But the uncertainty of his future added most to his misery. The question "What is going to happen to me in this prison camp?" dominated his thoughts.

Inside the gate, things began to stir. The POWs were taken to a building where they had to strip naked, and their hair was cut off. Before a German guard started going through his clothes, Heaton wadded up the map of Europe that he had managed to hide in every search and threw it on the floor in a pile of other papers and trash. Dressed again and on his way out, he scooped up his map while the guards were not looking and stuffed it back into his pocket. For nearly an hour he stood in formation in the cold while the guards checked each POW's face against his picture, taken in Frankfurt, before assigning them to their barracks.

In the barracks, a delegation of American airmen who had been in the camp for some time greeted the new POWs with smiling faces and hand-shakes. They briefed them on the camp facilities and routine and offered to help the new arrivals in any way they could. Their friendliness boosted Heaton's spirits.

As the days and weeks wore on, Heaton didn't sit down and outline a strategy for surviving life in a prisoner of war camp, but he soon came face to face with its challenges: sustaining his health, keeping faith, maintaining hope, avoiding boredom, and preserving his sanity. One day he saw what the stress of imprisonment could do: one POW went berserk, ran through the camp in a shouting rage, and started climbing the fence. A shot rang out. He tumbled to the ground—dead. The incident cast a cloud over the camp.

Order and discipline helped the POWs deal with prison life. Each bar-racks elected a leader who reported to the American colonel (who was por-trayed in the 1953 movie *Stalag 17*). Fortunately for Heaton he formed what the POWs called a "combine" with Stanley Sadlow, a Polish-American pris-oner who spoke Polish, Russian, German, and English. The two to four mem-bers of each combine shared and shared alike and looked out for each other.

In about three months after his arrival at Stalag 17, Heaton got a letter and a packet from home. He shared both the good feeling and the "goodies" with Sadlow. His parents in Science Hill, Kentucky, had learned from the Red Cross only that he had been captured. In the limited number of words he was allowed in a censored letter to his parents, he had told them that he was a prisoner of war and that he had a slight leg wound. Apparently they had not yet received his letter when they mailed his package. Thereafter he would only get three of the many letters and packages mailed by his parents.

Daily at 5:30 A.M. Heaton rolled over in response to the wake-up call and placed his feet on the cold floor. At 6:30 he and the rest of the camp stood outside in formation for roll call; periodically, the guards would again match the faces to each POW's photograph. At about 4:00 P.M. the POWs filled the streets for the second roll call. Otherwise, the Germans demanded very little from them. Medics, barbers, cooks, and a few others had routine duties, but Heaton and the vast majority, who were mostly army air force noncommissioned officers, had nothing to do. Consequently, boredom lurked everywhere, continually threatening to devour the POWs' spirits.

Trying desperately to find something to help pass the time, Heaton put aside his hate for the Germans long enough to approach one old German officer who had lost a leg in Palestine during World War I. He tried to per-suade the officer to let him and three other POWs work for the local farm-ers. The officer said essentially, "We got the cream of the crop in here and we're going to keep you here. It'll take more folks to guard you out on a work detail than we can afford. You are staying right here." Disappointed, Heaton returned to his barracks. He had hoped to get some fresh produce while working as a farm laborer, since he didn't look forward to chow. Every morning the Germans issued him a slice of dark bread about an inch and a half thick with a little glob of synthetic butter. Sometimes at lunch the cooks would send a half-barrel of boiled potatoes to each barracks; each man got one little potato or half a larger one. On rare occasions they had horse meat. Heaton never ate it. He and the others mostly snacked in their barracks on canned and preserved food received once a week in Red Cross parcels from Switzerland.

Maintaining and cleaning the barracks and taking care of his personal needs absorbed some of his time. Every day he fought bedbugs, fleas, and lice. He washed his clothes and took a sponge bath with cold water in a metal sink located in a room in the middle of the barracks. Two or three times a week he shaved with a straight razor that he had bought with cigarettes. Still, the hours dragged. He decided to enroll in a French class, one of many offered by other POWs, but his open leg wound caused him to miss too many classes. His wound kept him out of the basketball, softball, and other outdoor games as well. Attempting to stay physically fit he walked, usually alone, around the camp two or three times a day. He also spent some time exposing his wound to the sun. That seemed to help but did not heal it.

On one occasion the medics sent Heaton to a hospital for French laborers in the French Foreign Workers Compound, up the hill from his camp. At the hospital the news from the French and Russian doctors that the Russians working on the farms were not guarded sparked Heaton's interest. He was puzzled by the knowledge that the Russians were afraid of going home. The friendly French doctors worked on him but still did not heal his wound. Nor did his stay in a POW ward in the American camp. His time there, however, turned out to be a good thing, for he met Lee Lewis from Piqua, Ohio, and they became great friends. Heaton moved to Lewis's barracks and added him to his combine, where Lewis's trading and language skills became very important.

In the new barracks Heaton never entered the big poker games going on all day and into the night (some gambled away their food and cigarettes); instead, he played pinochle hours on end. He read the books sent by the Red Cross and stored in the camp library. Translating French newspapers with his little French dictionary helped him while away more time.

The POWs learned that the Germans' nicotine addiction offered them a means of getting things they needed: the five packages of cigarettes received in each Red Cross parcel gave the POWs the resources to do business. Great traders were identified and put to good use. Heaton's contempt and hate for the Germans disqualified him, but Sadlow, a member of his combine, was one of the best. Because the camp craved information, always hoping for good news about the progress of the Allied war effort, the traders bribed corrupt guards with cigarettes for crystals, headphones, and other materials needed to make radios. The radio technicians built the radios, and the camp tuned in to the British Broadcasting Company. Heaton found a POW who could duplicate his cherished map, and he posted the copy in his barracks, using pins to show the current war situation. Passing German guards studied the situation map and tolerated its use, but whenever they found a crystal radio they confiscated it.

After Heaton arrived at Stalag 17, one more group came and filled the camp to its capacity of about 4,000 POWs. Now and then thereafter, one or two POWs were added, and one of the new arrivals was an American doctor who organized sanitation teams. Among other things, he declared war on the bedbugs and fleas and won. For days Heaton and the others dismantled their wooden bunks and ran each board through burning torches, and ran torches over cracks and crevices in the barracks walls and floors. Heaton tossed his burlap mattress stuffed with lumber shavings onto the bonfire. The absence of bed bugs and fleas more than made up for the discomfort of sleeping on a plank cot.

As time ticked by, Stanley Sadlow, who had established a clientele of corrupt guards, routinely bribed them with cigarettes to get out of camp and come back with vegetables that he had traded for in the Russian compound. His combine partners enjoyed both the food and the knowledge Sadlow gleaned of Russian life before and after capture. One day in the fall of 1944, Heaton's friend didn't return from the Russian compound. Days passed without word about Sadlow's whereabouts and condition. Finally, in about ten days, Sadlow returned under guard. Heaton eagerly listened as Sadlow told how a Nazi plant in the Czechoslovakian logging camp had turned him in. He also reported that the talk in the logging camp was about not letting the Russians capture you.

By January 1945 the Allies had the Germans on the run on both western and eastern fronts. Allied bombing had left most German cities in rubble. Guards would look at the POWs' situation map, shake their heads, and say, "Nix, nix" in either disbelief or denial. As the German situation worsened daily, the guards' attitude toward the POWs improved, and they broadened their tolerance of prisoners' misconduct. With but one exception, in fact, the guards had treated the POWs reasonably well, and the one who had bullied them had been sent to the Russian front. Some conduct by the prisoners, however, remained intolerable. Those that threatened to have a guard sent to the Russian front usually got a good cursing for their error.

The POWs felt the fuel and food shortage that distressed the German nation, and Red Cross parcels came less often. Allied bombing of communications and transportation might have been a factor, but Heaton thought the Germans were keeping most of the supplies that got through for themselves. Lewis and Sadlow exercised their trading skills to get extra food for the combine, but the food shortage brought some tension to the camp. Fights rarely occurred, however.

On a typical winter day early in 1945, someone from Heaton's barracks waded through the snow to draw the barracks' ration of coal bricks. Six small bricks made of compressed coal dust provided just enough heat to cook a little food. By bedtime no one huddled around the stove; it was cold. Before retiring for the night, Heaton, wearing every stitch of clothing he possessed, folded one blanket over the boards as a mattress and crawled under his other blanket. Still, in the frost-permeated barracks he felt miserably cold and restless except for the moments when he managed to drift off to sleep.

About the time the Russian army captured Warsaw on January 17, 1945, a small group of POWs decided they were going to escape. Heaton joined the group, as did Dugan. They made digging tools out of Red Cross cans, and in Dugan's barracks they cut a trapdoor in the floor that was imperceptible when closed. Late every night a flurry of activity began. Some POWs stood guard while the trapdoor near the washroom was lifted and carefully set aside. Some took turns digging, while others carried the dirt in Red Cross boxes to the clothes washing sink, where still others kneaded the hard clay under the running faucet until it dissolved and ran through the drain pipes. The escape team had a mission of hope that made their days go faster.

Weeks passed as the little tunnel snaked its way toward the fence. One day the Germans ordered the POWs out while they searched every barracks. A guard had inadvertently spotted muddy water running out of the pipe that drained the camp. The Germans knew, but they had not found the trapdoor. For days the amused POWs watched the "moles" probe for the tunnel under the barracks with sharp-pointed steel rods.

One night in the tunnel, about fifty feet from its entrance, Heaton started digging. The shortage of oxygen caused him to take deep breaths, and claustrophobia began playing with his mind in the darkness. He tried to turn around but couldn't. Frantically, he backed out of the tunnel. To solve the thin-air problem, they made a fan.

Three more times the POWs had to wait in the streets for hours while the guards searched. But finally the jig was up, and a line of indignant Germans paraded through the barracks directly over the trapdoor site and lifted the cover for all to see. Downcast eyes watched in quiet frustration. Only a few feet had separated the saddened escape team from their goal.

The POWs knew the Russian-German front was approaching and wondered restlessly whether the Germans were going to move them. Suddenly, thundering guns from the vicinity of Saint Poltin, Austria, startled the camp. Heads turned and conversations ceased. When word came that the prisoners would leave the next morning, the camp erupted into a beehive of activity. Heaton gathered materials and tools, made a rugged and comfortable backpack, and carefully filled it with food and equipment for a long march. Fortunately, he allocated a lot of space for cigarettes.

On April 8, 1945, with high hopes but much anxiety, the 4,000 POWs walked out of Stalag 17 under guard into a new and dangerous world filled with uncertainty. In eight groups of 500 each, they wound through the back roads up the Danube Valley. Patches of melting snow dotted the ground. Heaton, burdened with his heavy pack and still favoring his wounded leg, meandered along with the fourth group in the column. The guards, including one on a bicycle moving between groups, prodded the stragglers in Heaton's group to close the gap. Heaton didn't know what route they were taking. He knew only that they were moving westward and assumed they were heading for the distant American lines. The Austrian people in the little villages were friendly, sometimes giving individual prisoners a piece of bread. Sadlow and Lewis talked to them and traded cigarettes for food, while Heaton did any cooking to be done. One day, the best they could do was one onion and two slices of bread for each member. They hoarded their remaining Red Cross rations when they could. At night Heaton rolled out his two blankets on the cold, damp ground. Only once did they have the luxury of sleeping in a barn.

The weary POWs trudged on and on as the days passed. Drinking cold, untreated water from nearby streams, a few got dysentery and became so weak that they were left behind. Heaton had a mild case of dysentery, but he had already decided that he was not going to be left behind. He was determined to keep up with the group if it killed him. Every seventh day the German commandant allowed the POWs a day of rest. By then Heaton felt so filthy and grimy that he bathed in the ice cold streams fed by melting snow in the mountains. Even though he organized things so that he could bathe and dress in a hurry, the ice water always chilled him to the bone. He would lather up hurriedly and splash the soap off his body as if fighting a snake, but regardless of how fast he did it, he turned first blue and then purple before he got his clothes back on.

In a combine conference while on the move, Sadlow advised the others that they probably would have more influence on the guards if they could arrange to move to the group behind them; he had established a trading relationship with the German interpreter marching with that group. The combine agreed, so at the cost of a few cigarettes, Sadlow got permission, and the four members started dropping back. While they were between groups, at a little pub between two hills the combine met up with some young SS troops standing around their truck. Sadlow and Lewis started talking to them, and soon the Nazis were smoking American cigarettes. But while Sadlow tried to talk them into getting him a bottle of wine, from the pub, the Germans' leader came out, looked at the American POWs, and went into a fit of rage. He knocked the cigarettes out of his men's mouths and stomped on the butts with his shiny boots. His ranting and raving alarmed Heaton. There were no guards or other POWs in sight. When Heaton whispered to Sadlow, "What in the hell is wrong?" Sadlow said, "That son of a bitch is crazy." Heaton's heart was pounding. The fanatic marched the Americans over to the bridge and halted them. Heaton thought, "He's going to kill us," and decided to fight. He whispered to Sadlow, "If he pulls that gun let's jump him."

Suddenly, the guard patrolling between groups on a bicycle appeared and confronted the furious German. Tempers flared, and the cursing antagonists stood poised to draw their guns. Heaton said, "What the hell do you think?" Sadlow reported that the bicycle guard said, "They are my prisoners and they belong to me," and the fanatic said, "I'm going to do anything I want to do." But the German guard had his orders, and he was not going to relinquish control of his POWs; he stood his ground. Finally, the SS officer stomped off.

Days later, as Heaton's group approached the bridge at Linz, Austria, an air raid alarm sounded, Russian planes appeared overhead, and guards and POWs ran for their lives over the long bridge across the Danube. The planes did not bomb Linz or strafe the column, but the POWs ran a couple of miles before the breathless men felt safe again. It was near the end of April, and everyone knew the war in Europe was drawing to a close. But weariness, threats from the air and fanatics, and the danger of crossing the front lines kept Heaton from getting his hopes up. There weren't many jokes in the slow-moving column, either; the men were concentrating on keeping up and trying to stay healthy.

But then, on May 2, near the little Austrian border town of Braunau, an American tank column appeared at the POWs' roadside campsite, and a young American captain announced, "You are liberated." It was a beautiful sight. Spirits soared. The officer, with Patton's Third Army, said his unit had to move on, but the infantry would soon be there to take care of the POWs. He instructed them to stay put to avoid getting shelled by American artillery or strafed from the air.

On May 3, 1945, the infantry arrived. A corporal from New York told

Heaton, "Show me a guard that has mistreated you and I'll shoot him." Heaton thought the corporal meant it. He reflected for a moment and said, "Let's don't do that—it's over now."

Normandy, Holland, Bastogne, and Stalag 4B

Captain Willis P. McKee
Airborne Surgeon, U.S. Army

In a somber mood, Capt. Willis P. McKee and his ten medical corpsmen moved to an airfield with the paratroopers of the 506th Airborne Regiment. The time for the great invasion of France had come, and he was ready and eager to go.

For nine months this native of Lawrenceburg, Kentucky, had trained and experimented with packaging medical supplies in England. As a member of the 326th Glider Medical Company, he could have landed in France in a glider after the airborne troops had parachuted in, but he had requested and received permission to go to the short airborne school in England. Now he and his team would make a night jump with the others.

After they were locked in the barbed wire–enclosed compound, they learned that they were going to jump into Normandy behind the beachhead, named Utah, more than four hours before the infantry was to land. For the next few days the paratroopers worked diligently, making detailed plans, studying maps and sand models of the terrain in the landing zones, and checking equipment and supplies. Dr. McKee selected a farmhouse in the regiment's drop zone as his aid station, showed the team how and where they would assemble, and explained how the house would be cleared before they entered it.

Late in the evening on June 5, 1944, while the men were making final preparation before boarding their C-47 transport planes, General Dwight Eisenhower showed up in the compound. The men with their charcoal-blackened faces surged forward and gathered around him. Both the supreme commander and the paratroopers knew that some of the young men in that gathering were spending their last night on this earth. The presence of the general, bumming a cigarette and swapping barbs with them, evoked shared laughter and cut some of the anxiety that lay over the compound like a shroud. Both Ike's and the men's spirits rose.

Captain Willis McKee, an army airborne surgeon, took part in the landings on D-Day and the Battle of the Bulge. Courtesy of Willis McKee Jr.

Finally, engines started, propellers whirled, and small groups of men loaded down with weapons, ammunition, personal equipment, and parachutes moved toward their planes. It reminded McKee of a huge parking lot after a college football game, except that the mood and the faces were different. There was no joking, no laughing—just somber, serious, and reflective expressions. Still, the massive movement of planes and men reinforced McKee's confidence.

Once in the air, McKee reviewed in his mind the things he needed to do

General Dwight D. Eisenhower talks with men of the 101st Airborne Division in England just before these paratroopers took off to jump behind German lines in Normandy. Both the general and the men knew that many of them would be killed hours before the Allies landed on the beaches. Courtesy of the Kentucky Historical Society.

when he hit the ground. He was aware of the large armada of ships moving toward the landing beaches to the east of his flight path and of the long stream of hundreds of planes carrying his 101st Division and the 82d Airborne Division to their drop zones, but he couldn't see any of them. Cramped in a steel-bottomed seat, he dozed now and then in the darkness, despite the loud droning of the propeller-driven twin engines. He carried no weapon or ammunition, but he had blood plasma strapped to both legs, and about forty pounds of medical supplies filled his large pockets and packs. They had been told to expect flak from the German antiaircraft guns on their last leg, and between snoozes this thought nagged at him. He had to clear his mind before he could go back to sleep.

Suddenly, a cracking explosion jarred McKee awake. The flak bursting in the midst of the plane formation made him welcome the command "Stand up and hook up." The red light by the door came on. He felt his heart pounding as he hooked the parachute line to the overhead cable running down the center of the plane. Up to this point the notion of an invasion and a jump behind enemy lines had been like a dream. Now reality set in: "This is it," he said to himself, standing in the middle of the eighteen-man line. He checked the parachute of the man in front of him; the man behind him checked his. The green light came on, and the jump sergeant hit the first man on the butt to signal in no uncertain terms that he was to jump. The rest, in a tightly pressed line, were squeezed out like toothpaste by the men in the rear, each pushing the body in front of him with his chest.

In a flash McKee was tumbling and accelerating toward the ground. A sudden jerk jolted him, but the unpleasant feeling was immediately replaced by the good feeling of knowing the parachute had opened. Below in the dim moonlight he saw the outline of a house, but he also saw huge boulders coming up fast. In the split second he had left he tried desperately to maneuver away from them, but it was too late. Fortunately, the large "stones" turned out to be sheep, and they moved out from under him as he hit the ground in a little field fenced in by huge hedgerows. Two spooked horses, however, stampeded, and he listened for their pounding hoofs as he tried feverishly to get out of his parachute harness before they trampled him to death. He couldn't get unstrapped. Quickly, he reached for his parachute knife and cut the web straps.

Finally, able to survey his situation, McKee realized that unlike the many in the division who were scattered great distances from their planned drop zones, he had landed near the house he had chosen while in England. He could hear sporadic firing in the distance but nothing in his immediate area. Moving with apprehension toward the nearest hedgerow, he pressed the little handheld toy that made a cricketlike sound. When he heard the cricket answer, he knew he had found friends. Some of his ten-man medical team greeted him warmly. They laughed, shook hands, and slapped backs. It felt good. "It's working," he thought, as other team members joined them while they moved along the hedgerow to the assembly point at the gate in the corner. There, where the lane led to the house, the rest of the team joined them within ten or fifteen minutes. Some brought in drop-injured paratroopers. While waiting for the infantry to check the house for Germans, they set broken ankles and wrists and treated sprains. Feeling more secure with time, they began to tell stories and joke about funny things that had happened to them.

At 5:50 A.M. there was a sudden roar in the distance, and the joking stopped. The preinvasion naval gunfire panorama unfolded before their eyes. Incoming rounds exploded on the beach about five miles to their front and extended for fifty miles to their right to the other landing beaches. Guns boomed, shells cracked and the earth rumbled beneath them. For forty minutes they sat there quietly in the dark and watched the sky light up with continuous flashes over the hedgerows. It reminded McKee of the great northern lights. The sheer magnitude of it increased his confidence, but he wondered what the men waiting to come ashore were doing and thinking.

At daybreak, he decided not to wait any longer for the infantry to check the house for Germans. Unarmed, he and Sergeant Klutter moved cautiously down the lane toward the open end of the U-shaped house. A dog reared up against the end of his leash, growling and barking ferociously. McKee felt a little squeamish, but he kept going, glancing around sharply for snipers. At the house there were no sounds or movements. He opened the door to the living quarters opposite the barn side and entered. It was empty. He sent for the casualties.

Someone rounded up a donkey. They hitched him to a two-wheel cart and started bringing in casualties and the medical supplies that had been dropped from the belly loads. Meanwhile, the farmer, his wife, and two small children came out of hiding, and McKee, using sign language, showed them what part of the house they needed. The children stood around and watched the Americans treat casualties.

Soon the gliders silently floated down. Some of them plowed into the dirt embankment under the hedgerows and disintegrated, but miraculously, most of the injuries in the immediate area were minor. Throughout the day, however, other casualties increased. McKee and his medics did what they could for them: stopped the bleeding, administered plasma, cleaned and bandaged wounds, set broken bones with temporary splints, relieved pain, and treated patients for shock. Except for the knowledge that snipers were firing at his medics now and then, McKee knew nothing of the tactical situation, nor did he have time to think about it. The two rooms and springhouse soon overflowed with casualties. When the medics brought in a wounded German officer, McKee ignored the apprehensive expression on the captured man's face and started treating the wound. Soon the prisoner relaxed and spoke a few words of appreciation in English.

Next morning the medics joyfully greeted the medical company's motor officer, who had come ashore by sea with the rest of the company. The patients were soon evacuated, and McKee's group moved a short distance to join the rest of the medical company and a corps surgical team at Château Columbières in Hiesville. The team of three surgeons and an anesthetist with their equipment gave the medical company the capability to do emergency operations on patients with life-threatening wounds before evacuating them by ship.

The 101st Division (the "Screaming Eagles"), while fighting hard to take Carentan between Utah and Omaha Beaches, had suffered heavy casualties. McKee and the medics worked exhausting twelve-hour shifts trying to save the severely wounded being brought in ambulances from the division casualty collection points. At the triage area on the first floor, Major Crandall selected the next wounded paratrooper to go to one of three operating rooms set up on the second floor. Those with apparently fatal wounds were treated for pain.

On the night of D + 5, after three days of this demanding duty, McKee fell asleep the moment his head touched the pillow. Suddenly, a loud explosion jarred him awake in the midst of shattered glass crashing to the floor and crumbling plaster dropping over his bed. Ears ringing and heart pounding, McKee reached for his glasses, which he'd placed in his combat boots. Relieved that they weren't broken, he slipped them on, hurriedly dressed, and rushed down to help with the new casualties. One bomb from the lone plane had destroyed part of the building; the other dug a crater in the yard in the middle of the medical company men's tent. Luckily, most of those wounded in the yard had minor injuries.

Confusion reigned in the area and in the part of the building not destroyed. Fortunately, however, with the continuing troop buildup on the Utah beachhead, an evacuation hospital had opened nearby. Captured German medical corpsmen hustled around in the dark and helped the American medics bandage wounds and evacuate the previously and newly injured.

The next day the medical company moved into tents, but with the normal processing of casualties taken over by the evac hospital, they were practically out of business. The seriously wounded moved from the battalion aid stations to the regimental aid stations to the evacuation hospital and then on to a general hospital in England. For the first time since parachuting in, McKee had too little to do. Tired of field rations, he and a friend decided to pay the big tent hospital complex a visit. In the large mess tent there, for the first time since landing in Normandy, they enjoyed a meal of fresh food. Sitting across the table from them, they met Lt. Margaret Hornback, a nurse from Shelbyville, Kentucky.

After fighting hard to take and hold Carentan, the 101st Airborne left its equipment in France and returned to England. The Screaming Eagles had accomplished their mission. Now the still proud and cocky paratroopers had to replace their heavy losses and get ready for their next mission.

Back in England, not knowing when they would be called on again, the Screaming Eagles frantically drew new equipment, incorporated replacements, and trained vigorously. McKee and twenty other doctors and medical officers loved their new quarters in a beautiful twenty-room estate home near a little village called Kentbury. The big buildup of Americans for the invasions had emptied into France, so the paratroopers had England almost to themselves and got warm receptions as returning heroes. They received invitations to dinner and in turn invited farm families to dine with them. McKee went about making lifetime friends.

In August, Gen. Maxwell D. Taylor, the division commander, assembled the division at nearby Hungerford Commons and told them that Gen. George Patton had beaten them to the next place they had been scheduled to jump. McKee sensed Taylor's disappointment and his eagerness to get the paratroopers back into action. When Patton did the same thing again, General Taylor assembled the division and expressed regrets once more. McKee and friends wanted to boo him. They were glad that Patton got there first. They were having the time of their lives, and now they knew what to expect the next time they jumped.

At midmorning on September 18, 1944, McKee, sitting in the copilot's seat of a large glider over the North Sea, watched the Belgian coastline come into view. The good life in England was over. Already three airborne divisions, including the 101st, had jumped into the Netherlands the day before to open up a sixty-five-mile corridor by seizing and securing bridges over three main rivers. McKee was in the lead glider of sixty, all carrying newly attached field hospital doctors, other medical personnel, and equipment. He saw one glider break loose and float gently downward into the sea. Once they were overland an occasional German antiaircraft gun fired at the tow planes, but usually the Allied fighter plane escorts quickly knocked out the guns.

Unlike the newly attached doctors, who had heard about previous disastrous glider landings into the Normandy hedgerows, McKee was confident that there would be no problems landing on the level, open fields near Zon, Holland. When the pilot cut the tow rope, McKee enjoyed the silent slow glide to the ground; the glider rolled up to within ten feet of the gate where the pilot had bragged he would put it. The division's medical company met them and helped move the field hospital into an already prepared building.

On the other end of the corridor, deep in enemy territory, the British First Airborne Division was being wiped out by furious German counterattacks. In the 101st's sector the British ground linkup force had passed through, but there was still sporadic fighting in the area. One day while McKee stood over a patient in the middle of an operation, an enemy machine gun bullet smashed into the operating room, shattering glass over the floor. The medics ducked, recovered, and continued their work.

Later, when things slackened, McKee and friends rode in a jeep to nearby Eindhoven. A twelve-year-old Dutch boy greeted them with, "Hello Yanks." McKee said, "What do you know about Yanks?" The little boy responded, "Chicago, New York, Los Angeles, and Kentucky." McKee felt a pleasant smile stretch his face.

At noon on a Sunday McKee's roommate, Lt. Lou Shaddig, woke him in the middle of his off-duty twelve-hour shift to say he had found a place to take a hot shower. McKee, though exhausted, agreed to meet him at company headquarters. When he got there, his all-time favorite program, Sammy Kaye's Sunday Serenade, was playing on the Armed Forces Radio network. McKee, still drowsy, stretched out on a cot and listened to the relaxing music. When Shaddig appeared and announced that they were ready to go. McKee said, "I'm not going. I am going to stay here and listen to this program." Even though he needed and wanted a shower, he resisted Shaddig's persuasive arguments. Shaddig and Lieutenant Vogt turned and walked out the back door to their jeep. And then disaster struck: a German plane zoomed in and dropped one small bomb right beside the jeep. The earth-shattering explosion splashed burning gas all around the vehicle, killing Shaddig instantly. McKee and others hurriedly moved Vogt inside and worked frantically to keep him alive, but in thirty minutes he too was dead. Sammy Kaye's music had saved McKee's life.

About six weeks after the beginning of the Netherlands operation, the Canadians relieved the Screaming Eagles. Despite the failure of the combined airborne and ground linkup force operation, designed to penetrate the Germans' heavily fortified west wall and then turn the German right flank, the men of the 101st knew that they had done their duty. They loaded onto trucks to leave the area for Camp Mormelon near Rheims, France.

The battle-weary and grimy paratroopers' morale soared when they first saw the army barracks at Camp Mormelon. Here in the heart of the champagne country, with hot showers available, they would prepare for their next airborne mission. Captain McKee and friends made plans for celebrating Christmas and went to work stockpiling goodies. In a relaxed and festive mood they shopped for the best champagne. The contrast between life at camp and life on a battlefield kept their spirits high.

Since the Germans were mostly licking their wounds behind the concrete fortified west wall on the German border, the party planners thought that it might be spring before they were called on again. McKee worried now and then about his wife and children and when he would see them again, but he never worried about what might lie ahead. Neither he nor the rest of the world—except for a few top German generals—knew that Hitler was massing three German armies loaded with tank divisions behind the German lines opposite the Ardennes Forest.

"We had our Christmas party planned. We had our champagne stocked. We were really having a great time." Then orders came: "Get ready to roll." Hundreds of trucks roared into the troop barracks areas. In the midst of shouting and sleepy troops running in all directions, McKee and his medical company worked desperately to load their equipment, tents, and supplies. On December 18, 1944, with lights blazing, the long convoy raced toward the collapsing Allied front in the Ardennes about a hundred miles away. The Battle of the Bulge awaited them. Men shivered in the open trucks, and after traveling most of the night the cold, weary, hungry paratroopers arrived at Bastogne, Belgium, just ahead of the Germans who were fighting hard to capture the most important road and railroad center in the Ardennes Forest.

At a crossroads about five miles out of Bastogne, the medics hurried to get their tents up and the medical unit operating. Casualties began to trickle in about four in the afternoon. As they worked, McKee and his colleagues watched long lines of panic-stricken civilians crowding the road moving westward. They carried their belongings on their backs or pulled handcarts or pushed baby carriages. Alarmed, McKee and Capt. Curt Yeary tossed a coin to see who would go into Bastogne and get permission to move. McKee lost. In the war room, McKee explained, "These civilians are all passing us. Something is pushing them. If we are captured, the medical care for the division is gone." Brig. Gen. Anthony McAuliffe said, "You will be all right, Captain; go on back and stay where you are." The medics, though fearing the town would soon be surrounded, continued treating their casualties.

Late that night, with the operating tent hidden in a sea of fog, McKee and the exhausted medics labored over their patients, unaware that a German armored column was approaching in American vehicles. Suddenly, the lead tank blasted the American antitank gun near the operating tent. The explosion destroyed the gun and killed every crewman. McKee saw holes appear as machine gun fire stitched its way across the tent. Captain Van Gorder shouted over the noise in German, "Cease fire! Cease fire! We are unarmed medics!" The firing stopped. Fortunately, only one soldier in the tents, already a casualty lying on an operating stretcher, was slightly wounded.

The fact that McKee had proved General McAuliffe wrong did not console him for his capture. The Germans gave their prisoners forty-five minutes to load their casualties and equipment on the medical company's trucks. The doctors and dentists climbed on a truck loaded with five-gallon cans of gasoline, and all during the night, as they moved toward Germany, they emptied the cans. McKee and two others each had a bottle of rum that they passed around. By daylight the bottles were also empty.

Early the next morning the convoy stopped in a German city and offloaded the twenty-five American casualties at a German field hospital. On the road again, the doctors wondered why the Germans had taken the American wounded, "going to the trouble of loading up all of our casualties and taking them with them and adding that to the burden of their own medical personnel."

This photo, taken from captured Nazi film, was made while the Germans were sweeping around Bastogne during the Battle of the Bulge. Robert Haney and other Americans were surrounded in the town, and Dr. Willis McKee, along with his division's field hospital staff and patients, was captured near Bastogne. The burning vehicle is an American halftrack.

Sol Dworkin, the anesthetist of the surgical team, declared that he was going to throw away his dogtags before the Germans discovered he was a Jew. "You're crazy," the others said, arguing and pleading with him not to do it. They weren't aware of the German concentration camps, but though they knew the Germans were mistreating the Jews, they also knew that if he threw his tags away, he would lose his status as a prisoner of war and perhaps be classified as a spy. Besides, they told him, they will know you are a Jew anyway. Reluctantly, Dworkin slipped the dogtag chain back over his head.

The roads were crowded with German tanks and infantrymen moving toward the front. Horse-drawn artillery and supply wagons created traffic problems. Seeing all that armor depressed a few of the men, but McKee noticed that they were using charcoal to fuel their trucks, and he figured that if they had to use horses and charcoal burners they were in bad shape.

That first night the exhausted and hungry medics huddled in bunches in a stable and buried themselves in straw trying to ward off the cold. When morning came, they found that the Germans had taken their trucks. Wherever they were going, they were going on foot.

After walking in the bitter cold weather for three days, they came to a village railroad station where about a thousand POWs from other units had been gathered around railroad boxcars. The strong smell of animal manure mixed in the wet straw and the thought of riding on that mess depressed the medics. Again the German-speaking Captain Van Gorder stepped forward and in an outraged voice demanded that their captors do something about it: "We don't treat your prisoners like that. We feed them well. We house them well. We wouldn't think of putting them in boxcars like that." As a result, the POWs cleaned out the cars, and the Germans brought them new straw. McKee was amazed that Van Gorder's tactics had worked.

It was Christmas Eve when they were loaded on the train, and they just sat there in the straw and shivered all night.

On Christmas morning the sun broke the snow-covered horizon, but although McKee had not seen the sun since his capture, his spirits did not rise with it. Like the others in his boxcar, he sat silently in the straw. All around him, sad, motionless faces were propped up on a hand or bent over on knees. The great champagne party they had planned at Rheims never entered his mind. Mostly he thought about his future. How long would it take to win the war? What was going to happen to them? When would he see his wife, Mary Evelyn, and his baby girl and son again? He thought, "God, I miss them." His thoughts soon turned to food, since the Germans hadn't fed them a thing. To ease his hunger he reached into one of his many large pockets and pinched off a little piece of the cheese that Mary Evelyn had sent him. Cold added to his misery.

In the distance they heard the roar of approaching airplanes but recognized them as friendly. Then the realization struck: in an enemy train, they were targets. Suddenly, bullets burst through the roof of the boxcar and jarred them out of their gloom. McKee saw a soldier near the front of the boxcar cut in two at the waistline. Amid noise and confusion the prisoners burst out of the boxcar like a flushed covey of birds. The medics raced to unlock the other cars, and men poured out of the deadly traps. Van Gorder or someone shouted, "To the hilltop!" and in one mass they rushed up the slope through the snow. Word rippled through the crowd, and like cheerleaders at a basketball game they spelled out with their bodies, "USA POWS." The American fighter escorts moved on with the large formation of B-24 bombers, but the men refused to get back on the cars.

At noon, the numb POWs each received a thick slice of black bread. McKee and the others marched by a row of ten-gallon cans of molasses and scooped some up with their bread. They ate the molasses-soaked slices and licked their sticky fingers as they moved on foot along the road.

The days ran together for McKee. At dusk, after about four days on the road, with no place in sight for the large group, Van Gorder talked the guards into letting fifteen feverish and weak men stay with a farm family. The medical team bedded the sick down in the hay on the barn side of the house. Then the farmer invited McKee and the other two doctors into the family side, where they saw a big bowl of fresh milk on the stove and lots of bread and butter on the table. When the farmer told them to help themselves, the doctors ate as if they might never eat again and enjoyed every morsel. Through Van Gorder's interpreting, they engaged in a friendly conversation with their hosts and learned that the grandson's deformed arm had been caused by a bullet from an American fighter plane. Even so, the German family showed no resentment toward their American guests. After that visit in such an odd setting, McKee pondered the meaning of the ravages of war and all the strange things going on around them.

At Stalag 4B, on the Elbe River, McKee finally got off the second train. He saw thousands of exhausted and cold prisoners who had also been captured recently at the Battle of the Bulge, being herded into a new section of the huge camp where POWs from Russia and many other nationalities lived in wooden barracks in their own segregated areas. The Germans stripped them naked and ran their clothes on revolving hooks through a gas chamber to delouse them; they sent the men through a cold shower. Some of the men were in bad shape. In their compound of about fifty barracks, McKee and Capt. Curt Yeary took over one and established a makeshift hospital. By collecting all the soldiers' individual first aid kits—which, among other things, contained sulfanilamide tablets—they established their own pharmacy and were soon treating pneumonia and frostbite patients.

McKee knew the old army saying, "Never volunteer," but he and Yeary did volunteer to stay and continue to run their makeshift hospital when the rest of the officers and their friends in the medical company shipped out to an officers' POW camp in Poland. McKee had no way of knowing what his friends would later suffer at the hands of their Russian liberators: not only did they take their watches and personal belongings but they also physically beat some of the Americans. One Russian soldier hit Major Crandall in the stomach with his rifle butt, and after he returned to the States Crandall died from the injury to his pancreas.

Sometime around mid-March 1945, while the Allies squeezed Hitler's armies from the east and west into a narrow strip of German soil centered on Berlin, McKee, Yeary, and their patients were loaded on a train and moved to Leipzig. Again the German mentality mystified McKee. Why would a disintegrating army, near total defeat, tie up a badly needed train to move them?

At Leipzig-Wahren the train pulled into a large railroad yard and almost up to the door of a 400-bed POW hospital that had once been a choco-late factory. Sergeant Shrike, a POW from India, met McKee and Yeary and announced that Major Mateaschevitz, who ran the hospital, sent greetings and wished to see them at once. McKee told the sergeant that they needed to attend to the offloading of the American patients. Sergeant Shrike replied, "The major says that will be taken care of. He wants you to join him for coffee."

When they saw Major Mateaschevitz, a doctor from Yugoslavia and a POW himself, they had to hide their shock and disbelief. With a command-ing air, the major welcomed them dressed in sparkling shined boots, a red-lined gray tunic with a high collar and one side thrown over his shoulder, and a fancy hat. He reminded McKee of Napoleon. At the gate leading through the barbed wire enclosure, the major tapped the inattentive, slumped-over German guard on the shoulder and rattled off something to him in Ger-man. The guard popped his heels together and saluted. McKee and Yeary got the message. This Yugoslavian POW had power.

McKee liked what he saw—beds, sheets, showers, and better medical supplies than he had had. Obviously, Mateaschevitz had used the influence he had created to improve conditions for the hospital and living conditions for the POW hospital staff. McKee learned that he could even visit the se-verely bombed city.

As he approached his room, the sound of a guitar and an English voice singing the Woody Woodpecker song amused McKee, and when he met the source of the snappy tune, he and Sergeant Lerant became close friends. Lerant, from Marseilles, translated medical records into German for the major, a Russian, an Italian, and two Polish doctors, plus the two Americans. McKee asked him, "How come there are no English-speaking doctors here? Don't you have a lot of English-speaking patients?" Lerant said, "Oh, there have been British doctors here several times before, but they would come in and try to take charge and order everybody around. First thing you know, they were assigned out to a work camp somewhere."

It didn't take McKee long to size up the overall advantages of living at Leipzeg. With the massive bombing of German cities and especially the rail-road networks, conditions at Stalag 4B had gotten bad. The POWs' Red Cross food parcels had stopped coming, and medical supplies had decreased. The Germans complied with the Geneva Convention's requirements of one hot meal a day, but the one slice of bread and boiled rutabaga lacked pro-tein; the turniplike plant, normally fed to cattle, didn't taste too good either. Two or three times a week they received one or two little potatoes, and once a week they got a small pat of butter. In the two and a half months he was there, McKee's weight dropped from 165 to 130 pounds. Still, there was no active mistreatment; Stalag 4B even had a full orchestra and staged great shows.

Seeing the beneficial results of Mateaschevitz's influence, McKee told Yeary, "We ought to tread easy and not upset the environment or try to act officious, because we want to stay here." To improve their relationship with the boss, McKee, Yeary, and Dr. Lenisch, from Poland, would soon start playing bridge with Mateaschevitz.

On his first day on the ward McKee observed with interest while Dr. Mateaschevitz used the ancient method of "cupping" to treat a pneumonia patient. McKee watched him light an alcohol sponge on a wire and twirl it around in a flask to create a vacuum. The opened end of the flask was then stuck on the patient's chest to suck out the infection.

McKee worked with a Polish surgeon, Captain Dimanski, who looked like General Patton. Dimanski and the others knew about Patton's increasing fame through the BBC reports over the radio they listened to openly, so every time McKee called him General Patton, Dimanski's face would light up.

Many American pneumonia patients came to the hospital in bad shape, with fluid seeping out of their lungs into their chest cavity (pleural effusion); if the men were left untreated, it could fill the cavity and suffocate them. Dimanski, using a long-discarded technique, took a rib out, inserted a tube, and drained the fluid into a bottle; he knew that everything would be cross-infected, but had he not done it, more of them would have died.

Then suddenly, like manna from heaven, a near-miracle occurred. From the Red Cross McKee got a shipment of penicillin. He had known from the medical journals that it was being developed, but he had never seen it before. With Dimanski's permission, he used the new drug to treat the next patient who came in with pleural effusion. He stuck a needle into the chest cavity and drew the fluid out, allowing the lung to expand against the chest wall. Then, leaving the needle in, he squirted a penicillin solution into the cavity. The next day this very sick young soldier, who had had a high fever, felt a lot better, and his temperature was normal.

From then on, McKee treated the pneumonia patients, and word soon spread around the city about the new miracle drug. A Scottish doctor who was a POW working in the German general hospital in downtown Leipzig called McKee on the phone and asked him to come treat an American with bilateral pneumonia and pleural effusion. Mateaschevitz arranged for McKee to go. When a German doctor saw the American's response to the drug, he called McKee and asked him to come and treat a German pneumonia patient. McKee refused to do it.

In mid-April 1945 the American bombers came. In the past they had flown over Leipzig on their way to targets elsewhere, but this time McKee watched from the second floor of the hospital as they bombed the city. He and Yeary knew from the BBC broadcast that the American ground forces were approaching and that the war was about over. Their German guards were good to them. McKee and Yeary nicknamed one old master sergeant "Grandma," and when he got mad at them, they would laugh at him. Mateaschevitz scolded them for their behavior. He said, "We have never had any problem with him. He has taken good care of us, and he doesn't like for you to laugh at him."

The next night the British bombers appeared. One plane dropped flares and lit up the hospital area. The staff hustled the patients to the basement. McKee heard one plane approach. Bombs whistled down and exploded; the shock wave rattled the building, and broken glass hit the floors. For thirty minutes the doctors, staff, and patients huddled on the basement floor while the British, using one plane at a time, bombed a circle around the building. They destroyed the railroad marshaling yard and the nearby Japanese embassy, and left the hospital without lights and water.

The next day the German guards surrendered to the prisoners on the hospital staff and turned in their weapons. Two American infantry divisions, the Second and Sixty-ninth, fought their way around Leipzig, captured a lot of antiaircraft guns, and surrounded the city. Then they turned the antiaircraft guns on the city, set the fuses timed to go off a thousand feet or more in the air, and fired thousands of rounds in a few seconds. The booming guns and bursting shells left hot shell fragments raining down over the city, fragments of different sizes making different sounds as they accelerated and fluttered to the ground.

Resistance was light. The next morning the Scottish doctor at the POW convalescent unit downtown said over the phone, "Hey Mac, the first Yank just walked in." A lieutenant from the Sixty-ninth Division asked McKee over the phone if he needed anything. McKee told him that they had no water and lights and that someone needed to make arrangements to evacuate the patients. A chaplain drove through light, sporadic fighting in the city and took McKee and Yeary to see the corps medical officer in a headquarters downtown where the medical corps colonel promptly set a bottle of Kentucky bourbon, a bottle of champagne, and food on the table and told them to help themselves. They thanked the colonel and listened with furrowed brows as he told them his plan to send them to a POW outprocessing camp. At the camp they would be debriefed, deloused, immunized, and issued new clothing, draw back pay, and undergo other time-consuming procedures. McKee told the colonel he really didn't want to go through that damn routine; he had a car spotted, and he and several others wanted to turn themselves in, in Paris.

Fortunately, the key was in the little four-door Opel. With a pocketful of francs that they commandeered from the abandoned office of the German commandant, four free and happy POWs headed for Paris. The Military Police checkpoint at the city limits frightened them. If they weren't technically AWOL, two of them were out of uniform: McKee and Yeary wore British battle dress with their United States rank and medical corps brass. McKee, remembering his mentor Major Mateaschevitz, pulled his shoulders back, stopped the car, and scolded the MP before he could ask any questions. While the MP was still wondering what it was that he ought to be saluting, McKee drove on.

They were speeding merrily along and struggling to negotiate a sharp curve when a loud noise startled them. McKee thought an airplane had fired at them. They discovered instead that they had lost their exhaust system, but they pressed on at full speed. Near Buchenwald they stopped at an American army ordnance garage to get water for the overheated engine. The cold water cracked the block. Still they pressed on, barely noticing a number of gaunt-looking people in striped clothing.

When they limped into an army airfield, knowing that the car was on its last legs, McKee offered it to a sergeant in exchange for an airplane ride. Before the day ended, they were in Paris. Their war had ended at last.

New Guinea and the Philippines

Technician Fourth Class Thomas W. Murphy
Combat Medic, U.S. Army

Loaded down with plasma and other medical supplies, Thomas W. "Jack" Murphy from Springfield, Kentucky, strained to keep up with the platoon-sized patrol. It moved westward along the beach of Maffin Bay, New Guinea, heading for the hill that jutted out into the ocean. He wasn't overly concerned about leaving the friendly lines to go into enemy territory to see how many were there. He had done that before, and this hot and humid day was little different from the others he had experienced since landing in New Guinea with the Sixth Infantry Division in March 1944. As they started to climb the steep hill, Murphy chose his footing with care to avoid the loose coral, shredded logs, and jagged stumps created by the pounding the hill had taken from friendly artillery and aerial bombs. In the heat and high humidity, sweat dripped from his face and soaked his clothing.

His anxiety level increased when he noticed that the coral rock face of the hill was honeycombed with big and little caves. Still, Murphy and his comrades trudged upward. Then a shot rang out, and a soldier crumpled to the ground. The others also dropped to the ground and combed the area with their eyes but saw nothing. Murphy crawled over to the wounded man and pressed a bandage to the shoulder wound to stop the bleeding. He sprinkled sulfanilamide powder over the wound and bandaged it. Litter-bearers gently placed the wounded soldier on the stretcher and, struggling to maintain their footing, moved down toward the aid station just beyond the foot of the hill, where the rest of their Third Battalion of the Twentieth Infantry Regiment waited.

The patrol continued to climb with an even greater degree of alertness and readiness. Someone tossed a grenade into a cave. Instantly, it was hurled back into the midst of the patrol. Terrified, Murphy watched an American

Technician Fourth Class Thomas "Jack" Murphy, a combat medic in the Pacific Theater. Courtesy of John Murphy.

grab it and, in one quick motion, sling it back into the cave just before it exploded. Shock waves and debris shot out through the opening.

On top of the hill Murphy took in the unusual terrain, noting that it was essentially one big, flat, chalk-colored coral rock about half a mile long with its nose jutting into the bay. Except for one old hardwood on the northern end, the shelling and bombing had cut down the few trees that had been there. Murphy and the other men didn't know that the Japanese had built an elaborate and cleverly camouflaged observation post about a hundred feet above the ground in the branches of that lone tree and that the enemy observer's eyes were following the patrol's movements. Nor were they aware, as they completed their mission and reported back to their unit, that about 850 Japanese soldiers were hidden in the caves.

The next morning, Jack watched eighteen American P-47 fighter planes strafe, bomb, and release their belly tanks full of gas on the hill. As the planes raced out of the area, volleys of artillery rounds roared over his head and splashed down on the northeast side of the hill to his immediate front. For ten minutes Jack and the men of the Third Battalion, wearing their helmets and loaded down with rifles and other combat gear, waited in the heat near the base of the hill for the artillery preparation to end. At 8:30 A.M. the Twentieth Infantry Regiment crossed the line of departure and launched their attack to capture what historians later called "Lone Tree Hill."

Heavily loaded with medical supplies but no weapon, Jack moved out with Company K, the lead unit. Only scattered rifle fire marked the first part of their ascent. A little anxious but not really scared, Jack concentrated mostly on getting his equipment up the steep, rocky hill. Suddenly, Japanese machine guns sprayed the two leading platoons and mortars pounded them. Everyone dropped to the ground and crawled or rolled around seeking cover in crevices. The fire appeared to come from the cave openings and crevices. Company I maneuvered up, and the combined fire of the two companies drove the Japanese back into the caves. By 12:40 P.M. Murphy and the men of Company K, dripping with sweat, moved over the crown of the hill onto the flat coral top. In the one big hardwood tree, a Japanese artilleryman peered down on the Americans.

Dusk was approaching when the Second Battalion joined Murphy's unit on top the hill. Both battalions worked feverishly to organize their defensive perimeter against an expected counterattack. Not being able to dig foxholes in the flat rock caused some concern, and the suspicion of some that the Japanese might have deliberately allowed the Americans to take the hill without offering serious battle added to the tension. At dusk the first shot rang out. Murphy saw the bullet clip the radio antenna off and thought, "That bugger can shoot." He wouldn't learn until later that the Japanese had cut their telephone lines to the rear at the same time.

With darkness, all hell broke loose. Screaming "banzai" and firing as they came, the enemy charged the Third Battalion's perimeter with suicidal fury. Instantly, U.S. machine guns and Browning automatic rifles (BAR) started chattering, adding their characteristic sounds to the familiar crack of American M-1 rifles. Incoming and outgoing mortars exploding on the rock added to the battle noises. Tony, a BAR man, worked his way out in front of the perimeter and down the hill a little to get a better field of fire and got himself wounded. Someone shouted, "Tony's wounded." The Japanese picked it up and shouted, "Tony's wounded, hold your fire—Tony's coming in!" Pretty soon they shouted out other names, but the Americans didn't fall for the ruse.

Rain poured out of the sky in sheets, and glowing outgoing machine gun tracers, crisscrossing incoming tracers that burned a different color, did little or nothing to light the pitch-black sky. Some tracers swept across the rock just above the defenders; others plunged into the rock at an angle and ricocheted upward. Some tracers and bullets slammed into the defenders. Blood and water ran over the rock. Murphy, hugging the rock, had squirmed behind a small log. He couldn't see the carnage, but he knew that agony and suffering surrounded him from the moans and groans and shouts for "Medic!"

A soldier almost within reach was his first patient. He said, "Doc, I'm hit." Murphy said, "Lie still just a minute." His own stomach stung like hell. Said Murphy, "I ain't so sure that I'm not hit. And I'll see you in just a second." Murphy rolled over and ran his hand over his stomach expecting to feel warm blood, but there was none. Instead, he felt a welt where a hot bullet, plowing through the rock, had barely touched the skin pressed so tightly against the ground. He breathed a sigh of relief and went to work. He gently rubbed his hand over the patient's face and felt a bleeding scratch across the nose. Murphy said, "Is that the only place you are hurt?" "Yes," came the answer. In the midst of all the noise Murphy reassured the soldier and then crawled away under the tracers.

He soon got too busy to pay attention to his burning belly. Filtering out the danger to his own life from the battle raging around him, Murphy felt no fear, just an urge to get to the next casualty. His confidence in the men of the Third Battalion, who were fighting desperately to hold on, helped him stay calm. He paid little attention to the details of the noise and the confusion, but he sensed that his friends were stacking up Japanese bodies where the main charges were hitting the perimeter. Coping might have been harder for him had he been able to see the American wounded and the dead scattered over the hilltop.

Suddenly volleys of heavy shells rained down on Company L, maiming and killing men bunched together not more than seventy feet from Murphy. The big rock shook under him, and the deafening explosions made his ears ring, but he heard agonizing screams between volleys. Mercifully, the barrage soon ended. Given the size of the incoming volleys, Murphy thought the shelling came from friendly forces.

Sometimes the intensity of the battle would slacken, and then the Japanese would strike again. At other times men were locked in hand-to-hand fighting. A few Japanese crawled out of caves inside the perimeter and added to the turmoil. Now and then a flare would drift down through the rain and dimly light the raging battle for a few seconds. In the midst of it all, pressed against the rock as close as he could get, Murphy crawled from one bleeding man to another. Many of the wounded suffered in silence, but some begged for help, some just moaned, and those in excruciating pain filled the air with their screams. The voices crying out above the roar of battle in the rain-filled night etched themselves into Murphy's permanent memory. He didn't know then that those agonized voices would cry out to him again and again in nightmares long after he returned to his home in Springfield, Kentucky, voices he could recognize. For now, though, he hastened to stop each man's bleeding, then sprinkled sulfanilamide over the wound and dressed it. Usually he administered a shot of morphine. Before departing he always offered words of encouragement. The pain in other pleading voices pressured him to hurry.

Someone crawled to Murphy and told him that Lieutenant Feron needed help. Feron was not in Company K, but Murphy and others who knew him well not only respected Feron as a leader but also admired and liked the friendly lieutenant. Murphy agreed to go to his aid. To keep from getting lost in the darkness, Murphy kept one hand touching the guide as they crawled along under the tracers, the guide navigating by checking in with those he had passed en route to Murphy. Now and then a bolt of lightning would freeze a view of the violence for a microsecond and give the guide a bearing. The loud thunder that followed each bolt of lightning added its voice to the sounds of battle.

When Murphy reached the lieutenant's side, Feron told him that he didn't have any pain. In the darkness Murphy searched for the wound with his hand. Rain pelted his hand as he moved it gently down Feron's back. Below the shoulder blades he felt a warm, open hole. To gauge its size he doubled his fist and discovered that enough flesh had been torn out of Feron's back to allow him to put in both fists. Saddened, Murphy knew that the lieutenant would not live long. He had seen pictures of Feron's young wife and two children. Still, he continued with his treatment. He filled the gaping hole full of compressed bandages, wrapped it up, and administered a shot of morphine. Feron thanked Murphy, said some nice things about him. As Murphy departed, Feron said, "I'll never forget you."

Murphy's bruised and scratched elbows and knees hurt, but he crawled on, searching for Company K's position in the perimeter. A lull came over the battlefield. When a bolt of lightning flashed across the sky, he saw men of Company L dragging their wounded and dead over the crown of the hill in the area where the battalion had approached the crest that afternoon. They were collecting the casualties behind stumps and the roots of a big overturned tree, and Murphy figured the casualties would soon be evacuated to the regimental casualty collection point and aid station located over the creek just beyond the bottom of the hill. He did not know that the Japanese were maneuvering to cut off the two U.S. battalions from the rest of the Sixth Division.

The suicidal Japanese attacks against the perimeter continued well into the night; by midnight the enemy had worked around behind the Americans and had cut off their supply lines. As morning dawned, the hard fighting that had slowed down as the night wore on came to a halt—unless the

Americans moved; then they would draw fire. As the sun began to break the horizon, Murphy saw Japanese bodies scattered over an incline that rose toward the American perimeter. The color of the dead men's uniforms made the incline look like an off-green carpet. At another point he saw Japanese bodies stacked up like feed sacks—the work mostly of one American machine gunner. It was the regiment's first intense combat action, and the men had measured up to the task, reinforcing the confidence that Murphy had had in them all along. But there was no time to dwell on these things.

During the night, 30 Americans had been killed and 100 wounded, mostly in the Third Battalion. Early in the fighting some casualties had been evacuated down the hill, but that soon became impossible. At daylight Murphy discovered to his consternation that he was the only medic left in his battalion. He learned that one medic had been wounded and evacuated; the other two had helped a group of wounded get off the hill and then couldn't get back. No wonder the wounded in the other companies had called on him for help during the night. The news soon spread that the regiment was cut off, but word came to hold on; help was on the way. Murphy believed it.

The wounded now depended on him for their medical aid. It was an awesome task made worse because he knew them all. All day he labored in the heat, rendering whatever aid he could and trying to make the wounded as comfortable as possible. Water ran low. The loss of blood and the heat increased the wounded men's thirst and added to their discomfort. All day sporadic Japanese rifle and mortar fire harassed the weary soldiers. The nature of the situation and the demands for Murphy's help made even a catnap impossible.

By late afternoon the Second Battalion had moved around the 400-yard enemy-occupied gap that had existed between the two battalions and then reorganized the perimeter. Small volunteer groups worked their way through the Japanese lines and delivered some ammunition to the beleaguered Americans; only their heroic efforts enabled the units to carry on the fight. In the midst of all this activity, time moved fast for Murphy, and before he realized it the sun had dropped below the horizon.

With darkness the rain came again, but this time Murphy and the thirsty men welcomed the water pouring out of the sky. They removed their helmets, caught the precious gift, quenched their thirst, and filled their canteens. But there was no rest for the exhausted men. The Japanese struck with fury again, this time on the northeast side of the hill, their initial assault ending in a bayonet charge. The Americans beat off the attackers and inflicted heavy losses, yet the Japanese kept coming. There were fewer now, but all night small groups made suicidal attacks against the perimeter, adding to Murphy's workload.

At dawn a terrible, inescapable odor hung over the hill like a cloud, the worst Murphy had ever endured. Decaying bodies lay everywhere inside and around the perimeter, and some Japanese bodies remained stacked in piles where they had fallen. Although exhausted, sleepy, numb, and weakened from not having eaten a bite since the battle began, Murphy continued to minister to the suffering. He could look down the hill to the creek where they had started and see the regimental aid station working in comparative safety. He overheard some say, "Why in the hell can't they get up here?"

As the morning wore on, the infantry began clearing the Japanese from the crevices and caves on the hilltop plateau with flame throwers and grenades. The regiment was still taking a few casualties, but more men were moving inside the U.S. lines. American bodies were being collected in the vicinity of the lone tree, just over the crown of the hill. Murphy tried not to look at the dead, especially those he recognized. He didn't want the vision of a decaying corpse to register on his memory, but it did. And so did the noxious odor.

Sometime during the night of June 24, what were left of the Japanese defenders of Lone Tree Hill withdrew, leaving behind more than 700 swollen enemy corpses. On Sunday, June 25, the First Regiment started replacing the Twentieth.

"Jack, is that you?" asked Paul Riney in a concerned voice, standing over his hometown friend at the bottom of Lone Tree Hill. Murphy glanced up and said, "What's left of me, Paul." Despite his exhaustion and numbness, he pondered the meaning of Riney's startled and frightened expression. Riney said, "If that is what it does to you, I don't know whether I want to go up there or not." Murphy thought, "I must really look like hell."

It was not the three-and-a-half-day growth of beard, the bloody and muddy clothes, the weariness, or the general disheveled appearance and stench that put that disturbed expression on Riney's face; it was a look revealing the condition of Murphy's soul. It was the look of a combatant who had been on the threshold of death in the midst of the dying and the dead. Ernie Pyle described it best: "It's a look of dullness, eyes that look without seeing, eyes that see without transferring any response to the mind. It is the display room for thoughts that lie behind it—exhaustion, lack of sleep, tension for too long, weariness that is too great, fear beyond fear, misery to the point of numbness, a look of surpassing indifference to anything anybody can do to you. It's a look I dread to see on men. And yet it's one of the perpetual astonishments of war life to me that humans recover as quickly as they do."

Murphy had no knowledge of how the capture of Lone Tree Hill fit into the plans to control the Maffin Bay area so that the Wakde-Sarmi region could be used as a staging base for future operations. But he did know that he and his outfit had taken a terrible beating and suffered heavy casualties: about 140 killed and 850 wounded or evacuated for sickness, heat exhaustion, or psychoneurotic disorders. He also knew the men in his regiment had fought gallantly, and he was proud of how they had done their job. But when he saw the writeup in the newspapers about the great victory won in the battle for Lone Tree Hill, he and his peers agreed that the "great victory" was an exaggeration.

Later, after participating mostly in jungle patrol actions, Murphy and his unit reached the northwest corner of New Guinea at Sansapor. Here the Sixth Division drew supplies and equipment, filled its depleted ranks with replacements, and began a rigorous training program for an amphibious landing. In the Sansapor area, which nearly touches the equator, the sand on the beaches was so hot by 10:00 A.M. that it would burn your feet. When they loaded on ships on Christmas Day of 1944, after eating their holiday dinner, Murphy looked forward to leaving New Guinea and going wherever the navy might be taking him.

On January 9, 1945, at Lingayen Gulf in the Philippine Islands, Murphy waded ashore near San Fabian on Luzon with the first wave, in the general area where the Japanese had landed on December 22, 1941. With no opposition, his unit moved inward for about three miles to their objective and dug in. For a while they took a pounding from enemy air and artillery. When the smoke cleared the next day, Murphy looked up a little dirt road and saw happy Filipinos coming toward them, jubilant civilians who welcomed them with open arms and whose joyful faces and cheerful words in fluent English nearly overwhelmed Murphy with delight. In the midst of the celebration, however, the infantrymen queried their new friends about the location of Japanese strong points, and soon they were back to the business of war.

Shortly after the landing, Murphy's truck lumbered along in a stream of army trucks loaded with armed men of the Sixth Division. Word came back that the old abandoned tanks that had belonged to the Harrodsburg National Guardsmen had been sighted. Near Bayambang, Murphy craned his neck to see them. He didn't know that the Harrodsburg men of Company D, 192d Tank Battalion, had had to abandon their tanks because the Americans had blown the bridge over the Agno River before they could cross. He did know, however, about the Guardsmen's capture on Bataan and the brutal treatment they had endured on the Death March. Since they were from a neighboring county of his own Washington County, his curiosity peaked and adrenalin poured into his veins. As he passed by the seven or so burned-out tanks lined bumper to bumper in a semicircle beside the road, he wondered what had been going on in the minds of the tankers the moment they left them. The silent tank hulls and other rusted-out wreckage spoke to his soul, and the scene made a lasting impression on his mind.

His truck traveled down the steep embankment onto the pontoon bridge, across the Agno River and up the steep bank on the other side. Engrossed in his thoughts about the meaning of it all, Murphy hardly noted the remains of the old blown-out bridge. In his mind's eye he was seeing a tank battle and the brutal treatment of the captured men. He didn't know then that some of the Harrodsburg Guardsmen had swum the river and that those who couldn't swim had crossed on logs and boards about where he had just crossed. Nor did he know that the Harrodsburg men had walked several miles to friendly lines and fought again. The trucks lumbered on for a distance before he could clear his mind of the images.

Days later, word flashed across the American front lines that the Rangers had rescued the American prisoners of war from the Japanese prison camp at Cabanatuan. Murphy's unit was deployed in the vicinity of Guimba when the Rangers made their daring raid behind the enemy's line and liberated about 500 emaciated POWs. Although Murphy didn't see them when they arrived at Guimba at noon on January 30, 1945, he heard the good news, thought about what the POWs new freedom must mean to them, and felt the great sense of joy that spread through the ranks.

The next day Murphy marched all day with the Twentieth Regiment in the blazing hot sun. At dusk they pitched their tents on the outskirts of Munoz, a small fortified village where nearly 2,000 Japanese soldiers with tanks and artillery were all dug in and hidden. Murphy and the men bedded down in the hot, humid night, knowing they were going to attack the village the next morning but believing they would take it in a couple of days at the most. They didn't know the strength or determination of the enemy, or that the tanks were dug in as pillboxes. Neither he nor his commanders knew that the Japanese had no withdrawal plans.

On the morning of February 1, Murphy, now leader of the litter-bearer squad, made last-minute preparations. Southwest of Munoz the infantry moved into position to launch the assault. For fifteen minutes Murphy watched American artillery and mortars pound the town into rubble. At 8:00 A.M., his Third Battalion led the attack. Their goal was the capture of Route 99, which ran north and south on the western edge of Munoz. Intense shelling and rifle fire greeted the American attackers from Japanese gunners and infantrymen operating out of strong points. Dug-in enemy tanks, their turrets barely above ground and hidden in the debris, hurled 47-mm shells at them; artillery in earthen-walled emplacements boomed and sent shells roaring into their midst. The heavy fire stalled the attackers some 500 yards short of Highway 99.

In the broiling tropical sun Murphy moved on his belly under the withering fire to reach the wounded and the dead. He and his helpers gave first aid, placed immobile casualties on stretchers, and dragged their charges to the collection point behind a large stack of rice hulls. Sometimes there would be a little slack, and Murphy could move around more easily. Sometimes he could get a friendly infantryman to engage the enemy position that was firing nearest the wounded soldier he was trying to reach. But mostly he just worked his way around or through the enemy fire as best he could.

He took pride in his ability to find cover and to reach it in a flash. He could recognize enemy fire aimed at him by the sound of bullets whizzing past, by a popping sound over his head, or by rocks and dirt spattering over him; then he would quickly roll over or slide into a position that offered some protection: in a depression or a ditch, behind a rice-paddy wall or a tree stump. But the flat and open ground around Munoz made his task of staying alive difficult.

The next day was essentially the same as the first. Major General Patrick, the division commander, got so upset over the slow progress that he relieved Colonel Ives, commander of the regiment. By the end of the third day the regiment had had 15 killed in action and 90 wounded. For the next three days the regiments used all the firepower they could get. Artillery pounded the enemy, the air force dropped napalm bombs, and the company of supporting tanks hurled shells at the Japanese positions. Still only minor gains were made.

During the day the Americans kept up the pressure; during the night they dug in deeper. Murphy and other medics had dug their detachment headquarters hole so deep that they needed steps to get in and out, and it was as big as an average room. For Murphy his dangerous work had become almost routine. Every day he got up and went about his business of treating casualties with all kinds of injuries and getting them to the collecting point.

But this one day was different. Murphy recognized Sgt. Joe Hoffman immediately. He cradled his friend from Iowa in his arms and had gently placed him on the litter when, to his consternation, he saw the back of Hoffman's brains just run out on the litter. Murphy paused a moment, looked down on his friend whose eyes were closed, and then said to the three other medics, "Let's just lay Joe off. No more we can do for him. Joe's dead." Joe opened his eyes and said, "No, Doc, I'm not, but I got a terrible headache." Devastated, Murphy said, "Ohhh, I'm sorry Joe," and gently tied a heavy compress bandage around his friend's head. Then they took him past the big rice mill and laid him behind the stack of rice hulls for the collectors. Murphy agonized over his friend as he went about his business. That afternoon Murphy asked the battalion surgeon, Capt. Lee Ed Shelton, "What about Joe?" The doctor said, "Well, Joe died. Good thing he did." Murphy knew the doctor was right, but it didn't help him with his grief. As hard as he tried to force that traumatic event out of his mind, he never could.

By nightfall on February 6 the Twentieth Regiment and its supporting forces had knocked out some 35 of the 60 Japanese tanks at Munoz, but the enemy still held about half the town. The Twentieth had suffered 40 men killed in action and 175 wounded; others had been evacuated for heat exhaustion or combat fatigue.

That night when Murphy joined Captain Shelton and others in the Third Battalion medics' dugout, he didn't know that the Japanese and American division commanders directing the battle for Munoz each had plans of their own. The Sixth Division's Sixty-third Infantry Regiment, on the San Jose road northeast of Munoz, was making preparations to join the Twentieth in an attack on the town the next morning. Meanwhile, the Japanese were preparing to launch a diversionary attack that night to cover the withdrawal of their forces in the darkness. For a week the battle had raged only during the day, and in his dugout at night Murphy had felt relatively safe. But in the wee hours of the morning the battlefield suddenly came to life as the Japanese tanks started firing and rumbling out of their dugouts toward the American perimeter. Sleep-dazed Americans hurriedly manned their weapons.

At the first sound of danger Murphy bolted into a sitting position and assessed the situation. He heard American engines roar as the company started their Sherman tanks. He heard them clank and roar out of the coconut grove and rumble toward the threat. Soon, he realized that two opposing tanks were converging on his dugout, and the notion that one of them might come crashing in petrified him. Then, only yards apart, they opened fire in the darkness, casting eerie, flickering lights over the little group huddling in the dugout. Shells whizzed by just over their heads. The noise made their ears ring, and dirt particles cascaded down the walls of the dugout.

Murphy knew that the Japanese tank had breached the perimeter, and in the midst of the noise and confusion he tried to figure out what the enemy infantry might be doing and what other dangers might come his way. The uncertainty and the noises, lights, vibrations, sent his fear level skyrocketing. His instincts told him to bolt out of the dugout, but his head told him to stay put. It took every ounce of discipline he could muster to resist the urge to run for it. The wit and training that had served him so well in the past now offered him no help; all he could do was hunker down and wait on fate for the outcome. He began to shake, and some chemical change in his body fouled the taste in his dry mouth. Dr. Shelton had told them that deep breaths would dampen the shakes, but that didn't help. Murphy's arms, legs, and body had gone into uncontrollable tremors.

In seconds that seemed like an eternity the tank duel was over; the American tank knocked out the enemy tank just a few feet from Murphy's dugout. The Japanese withdrawing up Highway 5 toward San Jose ran into the Sixty-third Infantry and an artillery battalion. There they lost the rest of their tanks, guns, and vehicles to the Americans' fire. A few Japanese soldiers got out on foot into the mountains to the northeast, where the Americans would see them again. From that night on, the medics would, in good-natured jest, tease Shelton for having had the "dry" shakes in the dugout.

One day soon after the Battle of Munoz, Murphy approached Camp Cabanatuan with curiosity and mixed emotions. He had experienced the joy and celebration of the Rangers' rescue of the camp's American POWs a few days earlier, and ever since landing at Lingayen Gulf he had been getting the history of the brutal treatment of the POWs by the Japanese. Even little children had horror stories they eagerly shared with their American friends as the troops fought their way southward toward Manila.

Now, as he and his unit approached the large camp in columns of twos, carrying their combat gear and medical supplies on their backs, Murphy, looked at the long rows of thatched-roof, open barracks behind the fence and pondered what had gone on in there. He knew from the Filipinos that the prisoners had suffered persecution and lived in misery, and that many had died. But he didn't know the extent of the calamity: that at Cabanatuan more than 2,700 young American corpses, naked or near naked, lay rotting in a shallow and water-soaked mass grave; that of the sixty-six Harrodsburg Guardsmen who served in the Philippines, eight of the twenty-eight who perished at the hands of their captors lay moldering in this unmarked graveyard. He only knew that the abandoned camp had been a wretched place for the POWs, and he was glad to get past it and get it out of his mind.

In the last week of March, in the mountains just a few miles northeast of Manila, the exhausted division engaged the enemy in a seesaw battle for Mount Mataba. The Americans came under intense small arms, machine gun, and mortar fire and sporadic but accurate artillery fire as they took ground and gave ground.

One day just before sundown, while Murphy was walking with two others, the soldier next to him stepped on a mine. The ear-piercing explosion slammed Murphy into the ground as if, he remembered, "a ten-story building had fallen on me." Stupefied, he lay there with bleeding ears. On their way to the field hospital in an ambulance, the soldier who had stepped on the mine began to talk and talk and talk. Murphy, though still groggy, listened and, although he couldn't believe it, began to realize that the wounded soldier strapped to the litter didn't know that all four of his limbs had been blown off at the sockets. Murphy carried on a conversation. He wasn't about to tell the poor soul that his arms and legs were missing.

At the hospital, a big old school building overflowing with the hurt and dying, Murphy saw wounded men lying unattended everywhere, waiting their turn. As far as he could see down the long, dimly lit hall, men lay on litters with blood-reddened bandages on wounds of every description. He had been around the wounded and dying for months, but this sight demoralized him. By now his head had cleared. Realizing they would have a long wait before they could hope to see a doctor, Murphy and the sergeant, both of whom had only minor wounds, decided to catch a ride back to their unit and see their own doctor.

For nearly eleven weeks since the landing at Lingayen Gulf, the Sixth Division had been in continual contact with the enemy. The division had suffered heavy casualties and had lost even more from noncombat injuries, sickness, and psychoneurotic causes. Lack of replacements and of timely rotation of units had taken their toll. Some of the companies in the Twentieth Regiment were down to platoon size. Murphy was worn out from the constant stress of combat and the physical exertion required of a medic in combat. Like the rest of the men, he found his morale sagging. Not until April 3 was the regiment relieved, taken out of action, and moved to Manila for rest and recuperation. It was a welcome contrast for him, even though the city lay in ruins. Not having the awesome responsibility of rescuing and treating the wounded while in harm's way made him feel like a new man.

Like the rest of the nation, on April 12, 1945, Murphy was saddened by the news of the death of President Roosevelt. The thought that the president would not see the end of the war in Europe, then winding down, added to servicemen's grief around the world. In spite of the gloom hanging over the regiment, Murphy decided to carry out his plan and look up his old hometown friend, Maurice Wheatley. There were four Springfield, Kentucky, men in the Sixth Division in different units, and they made it a point to visit one another whenever they could. Jack was close to "Doc" Cameron but even closer to Maurice "Chuck" Wheatley, a tall, well-built, redheaded, friendly young man with whom he had grown up. The last time he had seen Chuck was just before they left New Guinea. Murphy looked forward to seeing him again.

On his way out of the regiment's area around Rizal Stadium in Manila, Murphy ran into the mail clerk, who had a handful of letters for him. It had been several days since they had received any mail, and the letters from home lifted his spirits. Standing on the lawn, he read the oldest one first. When he got to the part where his mother wrote, "Mr. Watt (Wheatley) got a letter that Maurice had been wounded," his brow furrowed, and he read it again. In the third or fourth letter his mother wrote, "Maurice died." Murphy just dropped to the ground and sat there with his head down, grief-stricken, recalling their last encounter in New Guinea. He had said to Chuck, "Well, we are leaving this damn hellhole. Wonder what it will be like where we go now." Chuck had said, "Oh, I ain't worried as long as I've got this old Browning automatic. That will be the difference between me and Tojo." Murphy later learned that a mortar round had hit the jeep Wheatley was riding in.

After several days in Manila, the Sixth Division went back into action. The rest had restored Murphy's body, but his spirits were still low. He dreaded the thought of combat; each time he came out of a fight, it was becoming more difficult to go back. But the division had its orders, and Murphy had no choice.

Gen. Tomoyuki Yamashita, the Japanese commander, fought a skillful and successful delaying action. By the end of June 1945 he had gathered the remnants of his divisions into a circular formation with a diameter of about fifteen miles. The area he chose for his last stand, called the Kiangan Pocket, was located in the rugged, mountainous terrain near Baguio in northern Luzon. Yamashita's army was out of medical supplies and clothing; food was scarce, and his men were running low on ammunition. Their distressing condition was similar to that of the American army on Bataan in April 1942.

Murphy, now working at the Twentieth Regiment's aid station, was aware of the enemy's pitiful condition, for now and then at regimental headquarters he would see a Japanese prisoner of war. One day he saw soldiers leading a little skinny POW, his hands tied behind his back with a tent rope, much as if they were leading a dog. The little man, clearly scared to death, was clad in rags, and when a dressed snake wrapped in a palm leaf fell out of his clothing, Murphy almost gagged. Before the POW was evacuated, it took gentle persuasion by the Americans to calm him down and to get the hungry prisoner to eat their food and smoke their cigarettes.

Beginning in the first week of July the division's main attack toward Kiangan on Route 4 only inched forward because of the incessant torrential rain. By the third week, landslides and impassable quagmires on the steep and crooked mountain road marooned the troops at Kiangan. Parties carrying supplies by hand struggled to keep the division supplied at least at a subsistence level.

On August 15, 1945, after experiencing the roughest mountain fighting ever on Luzon and having advanced only about three miles in two weeks, the Twentieth Regiment bedded down in the rain on a high plateau just beneath a mountain peak covered with Japanese forces. Murphy and his partner had settled down in their damp, shallow foxhole under their pup tent when word quickly spread that the war was over.

No one shouted, no lights went on, and no fireworks went off. Some moved in the rain and darkness toward the big medical tent, and someone broke out a bottle of whiskey and passed it around. Murphy took his turn, and his spirits rose some, but like the others he did not know whether to believe the news and chose to guard his feelings. No one dared to celebrate wildly, as the rear area troops were doing—partly because they felt the presence of the Japanese just above them on the mountain peaks. Murphy did not allow himself to believe the good news the next morning, either, until the infantry guards brought fifty well fed and well groomed Japanese nurses down from their hospital on the mountaintop. The nurses would take cigarettes and candy bars that the medics pitched to them, but there were no flirtations.

Once Murphy did realize that the war was really over, he became paranoid about stepping on a mine. Not until he got out of the mountains days later did his fears leave him. But his bad memories never left him. Years after he returned home he continued to have combat nightmares in which the voices of the wounded—voices he often recognized—pleaded for help.

EIGHT

Normandy and Lorraine

Staff Sergeant Paul Mudd
Infantryman, U.S. Army

In a long line of infantrymen, Paul Mudd crossed over Omaha Beach. Behind him a ship disgorged more men of the Thirty-fifth Infantry Division. The nineteen-year-old soldier anxiously surveyed the scars from the hard-fought battle that had occurred there a month earlier, on June 6, 1944, when the Americans landed in Normandy. With a furrowed brow, the farm boy from Springfield, Kentucky, tried hard to take it all in, looking to left and right at the mangled vehicles and destroyed equipment strewn over the battle area.

He climbed the cliff that had caused the Americans so many problems on D-Day. Near the top he noted the Germans' abandoned concrete bunkers with their big, silent guns pointing out to sea. On top the cliff he approached a wire enclosure filled with German POWs. Near the compound his eyes met the eyes of a young German prisoner. Their heads turned while their eyes remained fixed as Mudd walked by. He tried to comprehend the meaning of these scenes and the meaning of war, but mostly he wondered what dangers lay ahead.

Farther along he heard the sounds of war for the first time, in the distance beyond the beaches. Out there the Germans were fighting tenaciously in the hedgerows, determined to keep the growing Allied armies from breaking out of Normandy. Finally, the head of Mudd's 137th Infantry Regiment reached the assembly areas. Exhausted and wet with sweat, Mudd took off his heavy pack and tossed it on the ground in Company A's assembly area. Soon, planning and preparation for their first attack against a real enemy created a beehive of activity. Mudd would be a company runner, a dangerous assignment.

Mudd started digging his foxhole near a road winding through the hedgerows. He had never seen anything like these thick hedgerows on mounds of earth which fenced the small, rectangular fields. He could not see either

Staff Sergeant Paul Mudd, an infantryman in the First Army, which suffered 40,000 casualties in Normandy. Courtesy of Elizabeth Mudd Johnson.

through or over them—but the Germans, more often than not, could see the Americans from tunnels dug under the hedges or little holes cleared through them in front of concealed foxholes.

While digging, Mudd looked up at an approaching jeep in time to see the regimental commander and his driver go by and out of sight behind the hedgerow. Just as Mudd was thinking, "Gee whiz, what is he doing up here? He should be way back," he heard a German machine gun rattle, and the jeep raced back around the hedgerow. Mudd stopped digging and looked up. He saw blood gushing out of the colonel's mouth. It was the first wounded man he had ever seen in war, and the reality of the danger and his nearness to it made his heart race. The sight made a lasting impression on his memory. He stopped digging and went beyond the hedgerow to join the others of his platoon, who were preparing for their first attack.

At 6:00 A.M. American artillery thundered in the distance, and in seconds Mudd heard the shells roaring through the air over his head. The roar turned into a whistling sound just before the rounds hit the ground and exploded in front of him. He lay on the ground for several minutes while the American artillery preparation continued.

On the signal to attack, Mudd's platoon went over the mound and through holes they had hacked out of the hedge. They had barely reached the next open field when German artillery whistled in and exploded in their midst, forcing them to withdraw behind the hedgerow where they had started. The regiment's first battle had failed. In the scramble to get out from under the shelling, Mudd got separated from his platoon. Among the American casualties strewn over the field, his close friend Hunt, the other Kentuckian in the platoon, lay mortally wounded.

Mudd dashed across the field to the next hedgerow and dived to the ground. He looked around, but saw no one in the little field. He crawled along a hedgerow and still saw no one. He thought, "Well I'll go back." He came upon Americans scattered over the field, all dead. From the enemy side of the hedgerow he heard a moan. He climbed on top of the hedge and looked for Germans on the other side, but apparently they had left. He crawled cautiously toward the moans coming from a ditch and found an American soldier lying face down. The American had been hit in the head. Mudd gently removed the steel helmet, which was partially filled with blood, and recognized the sergeant of the company that had been attacking to the right of his platoon. Mudd said, "I'm going to help you." The sergeant had tried to open his first aid kit; Mudd finished opening it and sprinkled disinfectant powder on the head wound and on the big cut on the sergeant's left shoulder. Mudd said, "You know, I can't move you out. I'm afraid to move you. I'm gonna mark you here and I'm gonna tell the medics to come up here and get you." The sergeant replied, "Well all right, if you think it best." Mudd took the sergeant's rifle, fixed the bayonet to it, rammed the bayonet into the ground, and tied a piece of toilet paper to the rifle butt.

Crouched down, Mudd moved up the ditch a short way, then jumped out and started across the field to his left. Suddenly, the Germans started firing at him. He dived to the ground. Bullets whizzed by. He had no doubt about who the Germans were after. He rolled over and crawled for a bit, then jumped up and ran a short distance before diving for the ground again. Repeating the sequence until he was out of the enemy's sights, he went to the medics and told them about the wounded man. Later, Mudd learned that his effort to save the sergeant's life had been in vain.

The green troops of his unit, in their baptism of fire, had taken heavy casualties without accomplishing anything. They were back where they had started. It bothered Mudd to think they had gotten off to a bad start. His new world gave him a lot to think about, all unpleasant.

After failing in their first attack across an open field, Mudd's unit changed tactics: they would crawl along the ditch running beside the hedgerow to an opening; then a few men would run through the hole to lay down a base of fire so that others could maneuver against the enemy. The hedgerows, however, made a natural fortress for the defender and created an obstacle for the attacking Americans. Having carefully selected their positions, the Germans usually had good fields of fire and observation, but Mudd rarely saw a German. Forward progress was slow, casualties were high. No two situations were ever the same. Mudd thought that nothing in his training seemed to be working. He felt frustrated and threatened.

Mudd realized that a runner's job was more dangerous than even the usual infantryman's high-risk job. Still, he intended to do his duty. One day while moving between units with a message, Mudd heard German artillery shells and hit the ground. Several rounds exploded near him, and shell fragments shot through the air. Mudd waited a moment, picked out a crater made by one of the shells, sprang to his feet, dashed to it, and dived in just before the next volley came crashing down. Again fragments whisked by overhead, and dirt from the explosion rained down. He waited until the next volley exploded, then instantly bounded out of the crater and ran full speed for a new crater, thinking always that the next move might be his last. Finally, after traveling about 400 yards from crater to crater, he delivered the oral message.

One dark night Mudd had to take a message to his company commander, Captain O'Connell. The company was deployed on line close to the enemy. Half of the men slept while the other half remained alert on guard in their foxholes. Mudd started from his Second Platoon's position, deployed farthest from Company A's headquarters. Aware that men moving at night were often shot by their own nervous troops, he feared the unit's guards in this situation more than he did the enemy, so he moved with caution while straining to hear any sound of a friendly guard. Suddenly, the point of a bayonet glared at Mudd's throat. He blurted out the password in a low voice, but the guard did not acknowledge it. Mudd feared that he might be facing a new replacement, maybe serving his first night at the front line. He stood frozen in place until finally the guard let him pass. Mudd moved on, a little more alert and a little tighter. Still, the next guard surprised him. Hoping the man was not trigger-happy from having been in combat too long, Mudd sputtered out the password and was ordered to pass.

No matter how alertly and quietly Mudd moved, the silent and motionless guards always surprised him. By the time he reached company headquarters, his nerves were frayed. He dreaded the return trip, but he went back to his platoon, going through the same nerve-racking ordeal in reverse.

The hedgerows continued to baffle Mudd and his peers. They never knew what trick the Germans might try next. Sometimes only the hedgerow with its mound of dirt separated the Americans from the Germans. When the Americans attacked, the enemy might have either withdrawn or reinforced its defenders. The Germans constantly counterattacked, sometimes taking back territory that the Americans had paid for dearly in blood. Replacements did not keep up with losses. On occasion word would come down, "Don't stop to help the wounded."

In the small fields surrounded by hedgerows, Mudd saw few Americans and rarely a German. He knew nothing about the division's mission to take Hill 122, a key terrain feature for the battle of Saint-Lô, nor did he know that Saint-Lô with all its roads was the key to the planned breakout into Brittany. He lived in a small world, knowing only what went on around an under-strength squad of eight or fewer men. Around the middle of July 1944, moving along with his squad, Mudd heard German machine guns burst into action. He dived to the ground. Deadly accurate 88-mm artillery shells roared in and exploded in the midst of the squad. Mudd slithered like a snake looking for a little dip in the ground as glowing-hot machine gun tracers zipped by just above his head. Exploding shells shook the ground, and the pounding went on and on. He dared not lift his head to see what was happening around him. For all he knew the others were dead. The longer he lay there face down, pinned to the ground, unaware of the fate of the others, the lonelier he felt. More time passed. He felt like he was all alone, surrounded by the dead. He had experienced loneliness before but nothing like this terrible feeling, intensified by fear of capture.

When things quieted down and the unit resumed the attack, only a precious few of his squad were left. The platoon sergeant lay bleeding on the ground and called for Mudd to come back and help him. So did two wounded men in the hedgerow and another man named Wilson. He knew it would be safer to stay and help them, and he had a passionate yearning to give aid and comfort to his suffering friends. But he had his orders, so he kept moving forward, fighting to help the company take its objective, knowing all the time that the platoon sergeant was mad as hell at him.

Days later, on top the hill overlooking Saint-Lô after a five-day fight to

Infantrymen scurry along one of the ancient hedgerows that enclosed the rectangular fields of Normandy. Courtesy of the National Archives.

take it, Mudd looked down the valley where the Vire River twisted around the town. The river, the houses with red tile roofs, and the green countryside looked so peaceful and beautiful that Mudd just stood there and marveled at the beauty and tranquillity. A wonderful feeling came over him. "The Lord has spared me," he thought. Just then, two German soldiers popped up from the other side of a stone fence and threw up their hands. Mudd motioned to them to come, but they just stood there as if they did not know what to do. He went and searched them to see if they had any weapons. They seemed so confused that he had to give them a brisk shove to get them moving toward the rear.

Mudd got his friend Harvey Hardwick, from Michigan, to help him take his prisoners over a mile to First Battalion headquarters. Mudd held his head high as they marched the two POWs to the rear. It felt good to have taken two enemy soldiers out of the war. At the battalion's POW collection point he proudly turned over his prisoners. Someone invited Mudd and Hardwick to spend the night at headquarters for a hot meal and a good night's sleep. Since he hadn't had either for days, Mudd really wanted to stay, but he felt compelled to return to his unit. When he got there, the sergeant told him it would have been all right to stay overnight at headquarters. Mudd thought, "Dumb me."

The days continued to pass in one hedgerow fight after another. In one such action Mudd helped a soldier bandage his wounded arm. Meanwhile, his platoon had moved out of sight, so he attached himself to a squad in a different platoon, as he often did after delivering a message while the company was on the move. Since a Frenchman had told them that the Germans had moved back, Mudd relaxed a little as he walked behind two soldiers along a sunken road. Suddenly, a German machine gun hidden around a curve burst into action and cut the two soldiers down. Mudd sprang up and out of the road like a frightened animal. Following his instinct saved his life. Had he dived to the ground on the road as he was trained to do, he probably would have been killed.

The next day, Mudd and Hardwick were moving along a hedgerow, crouched below the supporting mound of dirt, when Hardwick lifted his head to look across the field on the German side. He said, "Look over there." Mudd saw a white flag on a stick waving vigorously back and forth. Mudd said, "Damn." Hardwick said, "I'm going to wave him in." Mudd replied, "Don't do anything—that's a trick. That guy is too ambitious. He's waving it too much." "No, I'm going to wave him in," said Hardwick. Pushing his helmet back so that its rim was just above his forehead, he got up on the mound and reached through the hedgerow to motion with his hand. A shot rang out. The bullet pinged into the forward edge of Hardwick's helmet cutting the rim halfway around and leaving it hanging on the side. A fraction of an inch lower, and the well-aimed bullet would have hit him between the eyes. He coiled around and looked toward Mudd. Startled, Mudd stared at him in disbelief. His friend had turned white as a sheet and was staring into space as if his eyes were disconnected from his mind. Said Mudd, "I told you not to fool with that." Sitting there with a blank expression, Hardwick said nothing. Mudd continued, "We have got to get on up here with the rest of 'em." Hardwick just stared into space. Reluctantly, Mudd left his friend.

Bent over to keep his head below the top of the mound, Mudd swiftly moved along the hedgerow and caught up with his platoon, found a medic, and asked him to take care of Hardwick. Mudd never learned whether his friend's psychiatric symptoms were temporary or permanent. He had seen others suffer combat neurosis, and this new episode filled him with anxiety. Mudd wanted desperately to survive the war, but he decided that he would rather lose his life than lose his mind.

Battling the hidden enemy in the hedgerows was a tense, exhausting, and seemingly endless affair for Mudd and his peers. The skillful positioning of German forces in the hedgerows and the rectangular compartments

American infantrymen huddle in a foxhole under German artillery fire at Saint-Lô. Courtesy of the Kentucky Historical Society.

they enclosed created a continuous band of strong points in great depth all across the front. A day's progress, if any, was measured in yards, often a single hedgerow per day. Generally, the procedure was to take one hedgerow at a time and clean it up before moving to the next one. It appeared to the troops that the war might drag on for years. On July 18, 1944, however, after days of bitter fighting and heavy casualties, Saint-Lô finally fell. The feeling of despair that had enveloped Mudd and his understrength company would soon change.

Near the end of July the rapid Allied buildup of combat troops and war machines was poised on the Normandy beachhead, about twenty miles deep and seventy-five miles wide, ready to strike and strike hard. On July 25, 1944, after Allied bombers dropped a carpet of bombs on the Germans (and unfortunately on some Americans), Gen. Omar Bradley launched Operation Cobra, code name for the Normandy breakout. Soon, infantry broke through the German lines near Saint-Lô and held the shoulders of the penetration while armored and motorized infantry poured through the gap and southward toward Avranches, France, the gateway to the Brittany peninsula to the southwest and Mortain to the southeast.

The ruined city of Saint-Lô was the site of the Normandy breakout that ended the slow and costly hedgerow fighting. Courtesy of the Kentucky Historical Society.

Hitler ordered Field Marshal Hans Günther von Kluge to drive through the Americans' necklike corridor to the sea and cut off the southernmost U.S. forces, now wheeling westward into Brittany and eastward toward Paris. On August 7 Kluge launched the counteroffensive, and by the next day the Germans had made a seven-mile penetration into the American lines. The Americans, however, fought doggedly and stopped the German drive. On August 11 Mudd's Thirty-fifth Division fought to help retake Mortain, which had been the center of the bloodiest fighting.

On August 12 Mudd saw a German soldier with his hands up standing to his left front. Mudd asked Lieutenant Strong, a native of California, to yell to the captain, who was closer to the German soldier, to bring him in. Strong said, "He says he can't do it." "Then it falls on you to do it," answered Mudd. Strong said, "I don't know if I can or not." Mudd declared, "Well, you two guys are the closest to him." Again Strong balked: "The captain says he can't do it, and I can't do it." Mudd replied, "Well, hell."

Mudd moved up to within 300 feet of the enemy soldier and motioned him to come forward. But the German did not move. Mudd hollered, "Kommen sie hier." Still no movement. The prisoner stood in a depression that hid his legs from the knees down. Mudd looked him over carefully. He saw no signs of stress or fear on the German's face, and he was too well groomed and clean to have been in combat. Mudd began to expect a trick. Mudd thought, perhaps someone could wake him up by aiming a shot near his head close enough to part his hair. But, he discarded that idea. Although the battle that raged all around them had slackened off in their immediate area, Mudd feared that someone in hiding might shoot or capture him if he moved to the prisoner. Rather than risk his own life, Mudd could have killed the man. He had never seen an American shoot a prisoner, but he had seen Americans kill German soldiers when there was risk involved in taking them prisoner. Mudd, however, could not bring himself to do that. Instead, he moved cautiously toward the German, with his heart pounding.

By the prisoner's side, Mudd frisked him and removed a little horse-shoe-like item from his pocket and put it in his own pocket. The POW asked, in good English, to see Mudd's commanding officer. Mudd said, "Right now I'm the commanding officer" and shoved him toward the American lines. Behind the lines a bit, Mudd told him, "I've got to leave you here and you just keep walking with your hands up and nobody is gonna hurt you." The POW replied, "Well, you are supposed to take me back." Mudd answered, "I cannot take you back under these circumstances. It's a life or death situation here, and I'm leaving you. You go on back." Mudd gave him another shove and left. He looked over his shoulder and saw the German moving to the rear with his hands up. It would not, however, be the last time he would see this POW.

This was just one event in a day that Mudd would never forget. Later on, as battle noises raged all around, Mudd heard a strange, gentle voice above the moans and screams and weapons firing. Startled, he listened. Three times he heard this consoling voice coming out of and all across a rainbow-shaped arc in the sky. The voice said, "ARMO'DAEOoooo—ARMO'DAEOoooo—ARMO'DAEOoo." From that moment on, Mudd thought the voice was from God and that it was saying in Latin something like "God in battle." The strange feeling that came over him left him in no doubt about where the voice came from, but he told no one; he thought they might think he had lost his mind.

It remained his secret until he attended a division reunion in Kansas years later, where another veteran inquired, "Who was in the battle of Mortain?" Mudd acknowledged that he had been present on the first day. "Did you hear anything odd there that day?" the veteran asked. Mudd finally replied "Odd for a battle situation. I heard a voice." The questioner's face lit up: "Tell me about that voice, what did it say?" Mudd said, "It was the same voice three different times, and it came not straight overhead but out from high in the sky." With his face aglow, the other man asked, "Well, what do you figure it was?" Mudd answered hesitantly. "To me that was a voice from—from the heavens, and I never heard of anybody else who heard it. That's the reason I've never mentioned it." "Well, I heard it," said the man, "and it's been bothering me ever since, wondering why I heard it and nobody else." Mudd said, "I'm glad. What you said helps me a whole lot."

At Mortain in 1944, however, Mudd did not have time to think about the voice-from-heaven incident. Lieutenant Strong ordered him to go and administer first aid to Sergeant Caddy, who had been severely wounded. Just as Mudd reached down to bandage Caddy's wound, a German artillery shell roared in, and a shell fragment ripped into his neck. The blood gushing out frightened him. Soon, a medic arrived and sent him to the casualty collecting point, where Mudd waited his turn among the wounded lying on the ground. Fearful that he might lose too much blood, he decided to strike out for the aid station on his own, but in his confusion he wandered off in the wrong direction. He spotted an American tank and headed for it. A tanker, thinking Mudd was a German, tightened the trigger on his machine gun until Mudd said, "No, I'm hurt—where's the damn aid station?" The tanker gave him a drink of water and sent him in the right direction.

Mudd stumbled into the aid station tent at last and promptly vomited. The doctor said, "I've got some more ahead of you. I'll get to you in a little while." Mudd answered, "Well, okay," and stepped outside. He walked over to an army ambulance and told the driver that he wanted to ride back to the hospital. The driver said, "It's filled up." Mudd responded, "I'll ride in the cab with you." "I'm not allowed to let you ride in the cab," answered the driver. Then, two GIs without wounds climbed into the cab. Irritated, Mudd climbed onto the hood and announced, "I'll ride the hood back." The driver ordered Mudd to get off, but Mudd declared, "I'm going to ride it." Lying on the hood on his back, he reached over his head, gripped the tiny rain gutter above the windshields, and hung on.

Entering a little town, Mudd watched throngs of French people lining the streets watching American army vehicles go through. Suddenly, the ambulance driver made a sharp turn and Mudd nearly slid off. Angry French women swarmed in front of the ambulance, staring at the driver, pointing to Mudd lying on the hood covered with blood, and sending a clear message. Mudd appreciated the compassion they poured out to him; the driver surely had not shown any. Afraid for his life, alone on the hood of the ambulance and thousands of miles from home, Mudd had felt a need for some sincere compassion. It made a meaningful and lasting impression on him. Finally, at the tent city's field hospital, Mudd had his wound treated and the fear of death left him.

He had been in the hospital a couple of weeks when a group of men from Company A came to see Mudd. They told him they wanted him back on the front lines. To be needed made him feel good, so even though he still had trouble turning his neck, he got his release from the hospital and rejoined his unit. The company commander made him assistant squad leader and promoted him to sergeant. A few days later the squad leader was killed in action; Mudd became squad leader and was promoted to staff sergeant.

The battlefield had become more fluid. Instead of measuring a day's progress in yards, as they had done in Normandy, now they often measured their advance in miles. Still, there was difficult fighting ahead for the infantrymen.

Somewhere beyond Orléans, France, using every bit of the mental prowess and physical agility he possessed, Mudd moved his squad along in the attack. He had energized his senses to a state of full alert to deal with the dual task of controlling the squad and staying alive. Keeping the squad together was a constant struggle. Maintaining the proper distance between members by visual contact and arm and hand signals required minute-to-minute adjustments. Those squad members born with a little more courage tended to get too far ahead of those with less, who tended to lag behind. Even more distracting to maintaining the integrity of a squad on the move were the constant individual combat actions of the squad members—hitting the ground, engaging a target, getting up and running.

In order to fight when required to *and* stay alive, Mudd constantly panned the immediate landscape for hidden threats. The instant he caught a suspicious spot where an enemy rifleman or machine gunner might be hiding, he visually zoomed in on it, often firing a shot. Between battle noises, he listened attentively for any sound that might alert him to danger. Indescribable tension gripped him as they continued in this way. He saw a tall clump of grass move and instantly swung his rifle around to aim at the spot. But just as he started to squeeze the trigger, something inside him told him to stop. Mudd relaxed his grip on the trigger and kept moving toward the clump of grass. It moved again, and only twelve feet away from him, a small form bounded out. Mudd stood unbelieving for an instant until he realized the threat to his life had ended: what he saw was a beautiful little girl.

Elated because he had not killed her, he started toward the black-haired child, who appeared to be about twelve years old. She began to cry. Mudd patted her on the head and gave her a piece of candy. Then a tall, dark-haired woman hurried toward them from a building off to his left. She took the little girl's hand and scurried back to the building. Meanwhile, his squad members, scattered to his front, were looking back at him as if to say, "Come on, you're getting behind." He moved on, pleased that he would not have to live the rest of his life knowing that he had killed a little girl.

About September 11, 1944, on the west side of the Moselle River a few miles south of Nancy, France, Mudd's company leaders asked him if he could get his men to cross the 150-foot-wide river on a rope. Company A would follow and secure the bridgehead, so that the First Battalion could cross the river barrier. Angered that they would give his squad yet another high-risk mission, Mudd answered, "No, I don't think we could do that." The officers responded, "But on maneuvers in West Virginia you were the best man we had on the ropes." Mudd inquired further, "Well, what's going on across there?" After an explanation of the plan, he reluctantly consented.

The assembled squad too thought it an unreasonably high-risk mission and unfair, since they had been on more patrols than the other squads. Mudd explained they were to cross the river into enemy-held ground on a rope that was already in place. Then they would cross a little strip of bottom land, climb the cliff, occupy empty German foxholes at the top, and wait there while the rest of the company crossed. The company would secure a bridgehead while engineers bridged the river so that tanks and the rest of the battalion could follow. Angry voices objected. "You are crazy. They're picking on us again, getting us to do something no one else would do. It's suicidal. And impossible." Seeing a strong possibility of death, the men rebelled and said they were not going to do it.

Their hostile reaction did not make Mudd mad, but it made his stomach churn and rattle. He said, "Somebody has to do it." They replied that they had had enough: "Let somebody else do the dangerous part—We've done more than our share." Mudd said, "You can't win a war like that." Besides, he argued, he had been in the front lines longer than any of them. At last, reluctantly, they agreed to go if he would go first.

In the pitch-dark night, while friendly artillery roared overhead, the squad unbuckled and loosened their web equipment so that if they got hit and dropped into the water, they might be able to get out of their heavy gear and swim ashore. Mudd instructed each man to give the one ahead time to get halfway across before the next in line climbed onto the rope. In a swinging hand-over-hand rhythm he began the long torturous river crossing, every second expecting an enemy bullet to rip him off into the water. But soon he had all his squad safely over.

Being the only friendly unit in enemy territory created an extreme state of fear and anxiety in the little squad of nine men. One said to Mudd, "We can't go any further. This is as far as we go." Mudd declared, "We have got to go up there on top of that damn cliff." They answered, "No we can't go." The hassle from his rebellious troops added to the anguish he already felt in the dangerous setting. Vexed by their mood, Mudd said, "Yeah, we've got to," and headed for the cliff, hoping they would follow. They did.

On September 22, 1944, Paul Mudd's 137th Infantry regiment entered the Forêt de Champenoux during the Lorraine campaign. The battlefield was a lonely place for the wounded and dead left behind. Courtesy of the National Archives.

Mudd turned to the left, as instructed, and found the trail leading to the cliff. Cold rain dripped off his helmet. Near the foot of the cliff, someone popped up right in front of him and called out, "Who are you?" Mudd, barely able to see the man's outline in the darkness, answered, "We are American soldiers." The stranger told him, "You can't go this way." Mudd explained, "Yeah, we are going up that cliff. We're under orders and we are on the attack—I've got my finger on this trigger. You'll have to step aside." The stranger said, "There is no way you can live to get to the top of the cliff this way"; he said that if Mudd would turn to the right and go about 300 yards, he would find a road leading up the cliff.

Mudd did not know whether the stranger was a friendly Frenchman trying to protect him from a machine gun nest or some other danger or someone trying to trick him into a trap. He didn't even know the man's nationality. Perplexed, he went back to the squad and explained what had happened. Someone suggested they capture the man. Mudd said, "What are we going to do with him?" The nervous squad members pleaded with Mudd to go back across the river. Mudd took a deep breath and made a decision: "We are going to the right and I'll find the road." He moved out. Again, the men followed him.

He found the road where the stranger had told him he would and climbed to the top of the cliff. Dripping wet, he stumbled around in the darkness, hoping the German foxholes would be empty as promised. Finally, he found them. He placed the assistant squad leader and another man in the one closest to the cliff and two other men in each of three foxholes strung out away from the cliff. He occupied the last one alone, about 400 feet east of the assistant squad leader's foxhole.

Time elapsed, but no company messenger appeared. Filled with anxiety, Mudd stood with his upper body above the rim of his foxhole on full alert, scanning for outlines of enemy troops in the darkness and listening for any signs of an enemy attack. Friendly artillery continued to roar overhead through the rain. More time elapsed. No messenger. Mudd worried that his company might not get across the river. He knew his little squad stuck out like a finger in enemy territory and might well be cut off and captured. He had no radio to ask for help if there was trouble. There was no way for him to redirect the artillery roaring overhead and splashing down beyond his position. If the Germans hit him, all he had to fight with was nine rifles. He felt dangerously exposed, and his body tensed in response.

Preparing him to fight or run, his sympathetic nervous system dilated the blood vessels in his muscles and brain at the expense of the outer vessels. That and the cold rain chilled him down. Soon some of the men came over and told him they were freezing to death. He directed them to get some straw from the haystack and fill their foxholes. It did not help. Someone suggested they take their clothes off and wring out the water. Mudd took his off, and another soldier helped him wring them out. Still his teeth chattered. He put on his raincoat, laid his wet clothes on the edge of his foxhole, and set his senses back on full alert.

Standing in his foxhole dripping wet, wearing only his helmet, raincoat, and shoes, Mudd suddenly heard a dreaded pop overhead, and enemy parachute flares opened high above him, illuminating his position. Mudd did not know if they had been seen or if an attack was coming. Their only defense was to remain motionless. All night the flares popped and hissed. Anxious to hear if the company had crossed the river, Mudd remained in a prolonged state of fear. All night he braced himself to ward off death or capture. The drain on his nerves left him physically exhausted and mentally shaken.

Cold and still extremely anxious, Mudd watched the day dawn from his foxhole. Suddenly, rifle fire alerted him to the enemy attack he had been fearing. A German soldier crawled toward him. A squad member aimed at the intruder, squeezed the trigger, and killed him, but Mudd knew none of this at the time. The attackers soon withdrew, and tension eased a little— but only for a brief moment, for suddenly an American P-47 fighter roared out of the sky, aiming for Mudd's position. He thought the pilot was going to attack them, and his heart pumped even faster. At the last moment the P-47 pulled up and left.

The terrible night—the squad's rebellion, the stranger blocking the path to the cliff, the cold rain, the flares, the missing messenger, the threat of capture, the dawn attack, and the P-47 —all had plunged Mudd into a mixture of exhaustion, chronic fear, and anguish. Finally, the company messenger arrived with congratulations for a job well done. But to Mudd's disappointment, the orders were to hold his position. He wanted so badly to get off that cliff and back with the rest of the company.

Meanwhile, things began to unfold at the base of the cliff near the crossing site, and out of Mudd's vision. He heard the crescendo of battle noises: rifles cracking, machine guns chattering, mortars thumping, artillery thundering, tanks firing. Now he had to worry that the Americans might be defeated and driven back across the river. If they lost the battle at the bridgehead, his squad would be cut off and probably captured or killed. The battle raged on for hours. All he could do was wait for the outcome—and it did nothing for his mood to see fifteen or twenty captured Americans being marched under German guards across a ridge.

Eventually, things quieted down a little, and a second messenger arrived with orders for Mudd to stay on top the cliff and move to the north, paralleling the rest of the battalion and supporting units moving now along the valley. Before the squad left, one member told Mudd about taking care of the German soldier they had seen sneaking up on him early that morning. Another said that Mudd should go over there and take a look. Mudd said, "No, I don't want to see nothing. I've seen too much. I don't look at nothing except what I have to since the first day I've been in this damn mess."

With nerves frayed from the long night's trauma and the day's anxieties, Mudd moved his squad out. About half a mile from the foxholes he heard music and the popular American song "Pistol Packin' Mama," blaring up from the base of the cliff. He listened in disbelief. He thought, "I'm bound to be crazy this time. I've lost my mind for sure." Having seen traumatized men lose their sanity, he often worried that it might happen to him, and he dreaded it more than death. Compelled to investigate, he went down the cliff. In an orchard, he found the source: tankers had rigged an antenna across their tank and tuned their radio to the BBC station. As Mudd, relieved and amused, stood and listened for a moment, another American soldier emerged from the other side of the tank. Mudd asked, "Did you come here for the same reason I did?" "Probably," answered the stranger. Mudd said, "Did you think you'd lost your mind?" "Yeah, I did," he answered.

    . Just then a German shell roared in and exploded. The stranger flipped his right hand up over his heart and moaned, "I'm killed! I'm dying! I'm dead!" Mudd pleaded, "You don't look dead. You're still standing up." The soldier lowered his arm. There was a hot, two-inch shell fragment in his hand; it had not even ripped his jacket. Mudd said, "I've got to go." The stranger, his face as white as a sheet of snow, turned and walked off, his legs as stiff as boards. Mudd hollered, "You're walking real good for a dead man." The traumatized soldier never looked back, and Mudd could only wonder if he would eventually be all right. He turned and hurried off to catch up with his squad.

About the first week in November, Mudd occupied his last foxhole of the war in the Jallaucourt area between Nancy and Strasbourg, and he stayed in it longer than any other since he had arrived in France in July. One night shots rang out in the dark in the squad area. Mudd thought perhaps someone in the squad was just trigger-happy. He wanted to check it out but decided the risk of getting shot by his own men was too high, so he spent the night in his foxhole, alone.

    The next morning the assistant squad leader reported to Mudd that a recently arrived replacement had "dropped two people." Mudd said, "I can't believe that—he never shoots at anything." He decided to investigate. Near the edge of the woods and behind their barbed wire entanglement barrier, Mudd looked out into the well-defined no-man's-land beyond which, out of sight in the forest on the opposite hill, German defenders manned their positions. Sure enough Mudd saw two bodies lying motionless on the ground between the lines, face down with arms and legs spread. They wore strange caps, trousers tied down at the tops of their shoes, and old coats with the large letters USSR written on them. Mudd reported this to his superiors and went about his business.

    About 2:00 P.M. the company commander appeared and asked, "Do you know for sure those two stiffs out there are dead?" Mudd replied, "No—I do know they haven't moved, and they have been lying there all day." The commander returned and told Mudd to find out if they were dead. Mudd said,

"How am I going to do that?" The officer said, "We can't let darkness come without knowing for sure." Mudd invited the commander to come and judge for himself. He said, "No, I'm leaving it up to you. If you don't find out before it gets dark, we are going to make sure that they're both dead." Mudd said, "Can't someone else come up here and do it?" "No," said the commander.

At the edge of the forest, someone lifted the barbed wire and Mudd crawled under it, out into the open. To reach the two bodies about 200 yards away, he first crawled on his hands and knees, then dropped down and crawled flat on his belly, laboring to pull his rifle along. Every second he imagined enemy eyes were watching. Every inch of the way he anticipated getting shot. Near the first body Mudd knew that if they were alive and armed, he was in trouble. They never moved a muscle. What if they were booby-trapped?

With his rifle in his left hand and still flat on his belly, his heart pumping, Mudd reached out and grabbed the first one by the shoulder and jerked him up a little to look at his face. He saw a bullet hole in his throat. Relieved, he let the stiffening body down and crawled ten feet to the next one, expecting the same. But this time when he touched the shoulder, the man sprang to his knees. It startled Mudd until he realized that the man did not have a pistol or knife. On his feet and bent over, Mudd hurried him back to the barbed wire at the edge of the forest. Out of sight in the woods, the Russian, still trembling, made signs asking for a cigarette. Mudd gave him one. Feeling a glint of euphoria because he had saved the man's life at the risk of losing his own, he sent him back to company headquarters.

Later, word came back that the Russian soldier was one of three who had made their escape from a German POW camp. One had been killed earlier while crossing the German lines. The survivor did not know the name of the dead Russian soldier in front of the squad's position. Mudd argued in vain with his boss that the grave registration people should bury the dead man. Finally, he said, "Well, okay, if that's the way it has to be. You realize I'm taking a big risk on my life by going out there again." Nevertheless, he and two of his men went out and dragged the dead Russian in and gently placed him in a newly dug grave. Standing motionless, Mudd looked down on the corpse. The dead Russian's shoes were both for the same foot. His round face was red. Mudd thought, "That poor old boy. He is the most unknown soldier I've ever known in my life." With his helmet under his arm, Mudd said a prayer. Then they covered the unknown Russian soldier with dirt and drove a stake in the ground to mark the grave. The scene fastened itself in Mudd's memory.

About midnight on November 8, acting platoon leader Paul Mudd gathered the understrength Second Platoon around him in the dark to brief them on his orders from the company commander. They had been on the defense for days in their muddy foxholes. Standing in mud over his shoes, he organized the platoon into two squads rather than the normal three. He told them that at midnight, with one tank attached, they would leave the woods, cross the bridge over Osson Creek in no-man's-land, and take the small woods on the hill opposite their woods near Jallaucourt. They would not stop to help the wounded until they took their objective. They were not to take any prisoners; they were to take and hold the objective at all costs; and they were definitely not to go beyond the woods.

Just then a messenger appeared with orders for them to wait; a six-hour artillery preparation would be fired on the objective before they started the attack. As Mudd sent the men back to their puddled foxholes, a cold rain poured down in sheets. For six hours Mudd and his men huddled in their muddy foxholes while artillery thundered in from different locations in the distance, roared through the wet atmosphere, converged over Mudd's head, and splashed down on the objective. Even in the rain, it helped morale to see the enemy they were about to face take a shellacking.

Near 6:00 A.M. Mudd led his men toward the line of departure. Earlier, he had lost his argument that the lead unit should be the company closest to the bridge. It did not help matters when they told him that since he had been on patrol on the enemy side, he was more familiar with the area; in fact, it made him madder because he felt they had assigned him more patrol duties than his share. While walking through another company to get to the line of departure, Mudd felt irritated and put upon.

Events, however, quickly took his mind off himself. Near the bridge, they had to stop and wait in the open while the engineers finished repairing it. A German machine gun chattered, and dead and wounded engineers fell off the bridge. The remaining engineers persisted with their work, though taking many casualties, and eventually the machine gun fell silent. Word came to Mudd that the bridge was repaired, cleared, and ready to cross. Mudd told his leader, "I don't want to go across the bridge." The commander said, "You've got to cross the bridge." "I'm going to cross off the bridge," said Mudd. But knowing he had to do what he was told whether he liked it or not, Mudd led his two-squad platoon across the bridge. The big tank appeared as promised and followed them.

Having the tank with its big gun lumbering along with them pleased Mudd, especially since they had to cross an open field to get to the woods. But then, peering over his shoulder, Mudd saw to his horror the right track coming off the tank, which spun out of control into the ditch and off the road. Mudd wondered if the track had been shot off. He noted that no one came out of the tank. Dejected, he plodded on. Soon, a messenger arrived with word for Mudd to hold up until another tank arrived. While he waited, Mudd lay in the open field on his belly, his platoon dispersed face down on the ground behind him, while he scanned the woods for enemy activity.

Time dragged by, and neither tank nor messenger showed up. A soldier crawled up beside Mudd and said, "Remmler is sick." Mudd crawled back to Remmler, who was trembling so hard that his teeth chattered. Mudd said, "Well, you've got to get up and go when this next tank comes up." "I can't," he declared. Mudd asked, "Are you faking this? Are you playing possum— just getting out of this?" Shivering violently, Remmler said, "No." Mudd covered the trembling soldier with his only blanket and stuck Remmler's rifle in the ground. "This will mark your position for the medics in the event you pass out," he said.

Still they waited. Mudd noticed a soldier to his rear crawling from man to man. Finally, he crawled up to Mudd and offered him some chocolate candy that he had received from home. It amused Mudd that the soldier would make such an effort to pass the candy around in such a strange setting. Perhaps he thought they should enjoy the candy before the battle resumed and while they were still alive.

While Mudd savored the taste of the sweet chocolate, the new tank lumbered across the bridge and pulled up beside them. Since the tankers wouldn't stick their head out to man the mounted .50-caliber machine gun, Mudd put a couple of his infantry volunteers on the tank with instructions to fire over the foot soldiers' heads and give them covering fire as they entered the woods. The tank was to operate on the right side of the road with the infantry. Mudd gave the signal and the group started moving.

The tank lunged forward, off to the left and on the wrong side of the road. Like a loose cannon, it ran around firing its big gun helter-skelter. Galled, Mudd knew he would not be able to employ this tank to the best advantage for his infantry, but he could not dwell on the problem. Enemy artillery rounds roared in and exploded high in the air over them. White puffs peppered the sky, and white-hot globs of white phosphorus rained down. Like frightened animals one jump ahead of the jaws of their predator, the men darted to the right and avoided the most painful burns on the battlefield, because the white phosphorus burns its way into the flesh and continues to burn until one gets it out or cuts off the glob's oxygen with water. Relieved, Mudd reorganized and led his men into the woods, swinging off to the left as planned. Those following were to swing to the right. For a while things went well. As twilight approached, his men maneuvered and fired and moved along in the forest. Up front, Mudd set a fast pace, shooting here and there.

About halfway through the woods, he looked back—and saw no one.

He thought, "Damn, I'm out here all by myself." To compensate, he increased his rate of fire, pulling the trigger at a faster clip, aiming here and there to discourage any German from sticking his head up. Suddenly, his rifle would not fire. Quickly, he rammed the ejector arm against a sapling and ejected the empty cartridge, jammed a cartridge in the chamber, and fired. Again, the rifle failed to eject the empty cartridge. Desperately, he slammed the butt of the rifle to the ground and raised his foot to stomp the ejector arm down. A shot rang out and struck him, sending him sprawling in the air. He crashed to the ground, hollering "Medic!"

Darkness began to seep into the woods. Mudd continued shouting, "Medic! medic! medic!" No medic appeared. Breathing hard, he pulled down his pants and his long underwear below the nasty wound in his right hip and looked at it. It was bloody but not bleeding profusely, burning but not real bad. He opened his first aid kit and took the tablets, as he was trained to do. He ripped the bandage out of its container and hastily bandaged his wound. Unable to walk or crawl, he lay there and hollered louder and louder, "Medic! medic!" Still, no one came to his rescue.

Darkness shrouded the damp, cold woods. Mudd condemned himself for not having kept better observation. He pleaded for help, but no one appeared or answered. Time dragged by. The night chill penetrated his damp clothing. He had given his blanket to Remmler, and there was nothing he could do to ward off the cold air. Fearing he might die from exposure, he cried out more desperately. He thought he might be captured. Worse yet, he thought the Germans might find his hidden German pistol and stomp him to death with their hobnailed boots, as he had heard they had done in the past. Weakened, chilled to the bone, and afraid he would go into shock and die, Mudd could only do what wounded men often did when they found themselves isolated on the battlefield and at death's door: he hollered for help, pleaded for help, and finally whimpered and moaned—all to no avail.

At last, morning came, and with it the suffering and terror ended. Soon, he was in the good hands of the army's medics and out of harm's way. The contrast was indescribable. He went from the battalion aid station to the field evacuation hospital, and on to Normandy.

On the Normandy beach, lying on a stretcher and gazing up at the sky, Mudd waited to be picked up by German POW litter-bearers and loaded on the waiting hospital ship. Just four months earlier he had walked over the same beach taking in the destruction on the battlefield, searching for clues about combat and what lay ahead for him. Now, he had the answer. He had seen the face of battle firsthand and had experienced what historian John Keegan would later describe as what opposing armies do in war: namely, inflict human suffering through violence. For four months Mudd had lived in a world of fear and human destruction. But now he had the "million dollar wound," not bad enough to kill him but bad enough to take him out of the terrible combat setting, bad enough to send him home.

The POWs approached the wounded soldier lying next to Mudd. He shouted, "No! They shot me and I don't want the sons of bitches close to me!" One of the Germans said to Mudd, "You don't mind, do you?" Mudd answered, "No, I want to get on that ship and get out of here." As two POWs stepped up to pick him up, one moved to the head of the stretcher and his eyes met Mudd's. He paused. They stared. They recognized each other. It was the German that Mudd had captured on that terrible day of August 12, 1944, at Mortain. Neither he nor Mudd said anything or changed their expressions. The POWs carried the stretcher aboard the ship. For Mudd, the war was over. But many of his friends in Company A, still in combat, would be killed before the European war ended the following spring.

Depth-Charge Attacks in the Pacific

Torpedoman First Class Hanly Davis
Submariner, U.S. Navy

For days, Torpedoman First Class Hanly Davis, a farm boy from Paris, Kentucky, had plowed the waters of the Pacific in the submarine USS *Picuda*. Well into his first war patrol, he welcomed the excitement and tension. He wanted action. After all, that was why he had left the Bourbon County farm in August 1942 to join the navy.

In October 1943, after listening in awe to veteran submariners' war stories, he joined the submarine fleet. The nineteen-year-old sailor wanted the adventure of combat, but routine life on a cramped submarine had not offered much excitement so far. For weeks he had not seen the beautiful rays of the sun, for during daylight the submarine cruised underwater, looking for enemy ships. Only at night could it risk coming to the surface to recharge its batteries and catch a breath of fresh air.

In training Davis had already proved that he had the personality to tolerate the cramped living conditions on a submarine. Some of his fellow trainees could not and were eliminated from the elite program. But the duration and tension of inaction were having their effect. Day in and day out, night in and night out, he and three or four others just sat in this small compartment in the bow of the submarine with all those torpedoes and all that equipment.

At the end of his scheduled four-hour watch, Davis headed for the mess hall. In the narrow aisle he had to slide by oncoming sailors face to face, often touching. In the crowded mess hall, other sailors bumped into him, breathed on him, and sometimes pushed him out of the way. But Davis managed to keep calm, as did his crewmates. Only on rare occasions did Davis see an irritated sailor start an argument, and he never saw a fight.

When *Picuda* entered the South China Sea, where numerous Japanese ships sailed, excitement among the crew picked up, and when they reached

Torpedoman First Class Hanly Davis was a submariner in the Pacific Theater. Fifty-two U.S. submarine crews (almost one in five) were lost in the Pacific war. Courtesy of Hanly Davis.

the Formosa (Taiwan) Strait, they spotted a Japanese merchant ship convoy—easy prey for a submarine. The captain shouted orders. Sailors scurried to man their battle stations. Davis rapidly pulled each of the six levers that activated the hydraulic system and opened the outside doors to the six torpedo tubes in the bow. "Bow tubes, ready," he reported to the chief. Then he waited. His heart rate increased, but he was not scared. He heard "Up periscope" and knew that the captain, Commander Rayburn, before he gave the order to fire, wanted to take a look at the target that had been picked up by sonar and accurately plotted. Davis felt good. At last, he was going to help sink an enemy ship. He waited anxiously for the order to fire the torpedoes.

Suddenly, the captain shouted, "Down periscope, secure the boat for depth-charge attack." Davis hit each of the six levers in rapid succession, sealing the outer doors to the torpedo tubes. That ended his duties. Lieutenant Hall, manning the conning tower, barked out orders over the loudspeakers. Davis, accustomed to Hall's usual calm manner, noted with dismay the tension in the officer's voice.

Abruptly, Davis's attention moved topside to the sound of the Japanese destroyer charging full speed toward its prey, floating at periscope level, sixty-five feet beneath the surface of the water. The oncoming destroyer's propellers thrashed in the water, their rapid, rhythmic whump, whump, whump, whump getting louder and leaving no doubt in Davis's mind about the enemy ship's destination.

To Davis in the bow of the silent and motionless submarine, the loudest whump, whump seemed overhead and it battered his eardrums. He braced himself. The Japanese destroyer hurled its depth charges into the water above *Picuda,* now just a little deeper than periscope level and nearly touching bottom.

The sharp CLICK of a depth charge's detonator, just above the submarine, startled Davis. In an instant there was a loud, dull explosion that pierced his ears. The shock wave ripped the planking off the walkway on top of the superstructure and mangled the steel railing that held the boards. It also penetrated the pressure hull of the submarine, without damaging the hull, and slammed into Davis as if someone had thrown a hundred-pound sack of potatoes on top of him. The concussion buckled his knees, nearly knocking him to the floor.

Within seconds he heard a second CLICK and loud KA-BOOM. The explosion jolted him again. Still, he managed to stay on his feet. Lightbulbs exploded and shattered glass bounced around. Light in the torpedo room dimmed a shade. His heart pumped and he felt his pulse pounding in his hands as he held onto a torpedo-storage rack rail. Glancing over at the "old salts" who had been through this before, he saw faces white as sheets. That did not reassure him, and his fear level rose to new heights. Blood rushed toward the vital organs and muscles to enhance his ability to fight or flee—but there was no place to flee and no one to fight. Standing there in the torpedo room as pale as the others, he knew he was going to die. He moaned, "Lord have mercy on my soul."

Two ticks on a clock and another CLICK—KA-BOOM! The jolting pressure knocked the breath out of him, and that added to his fears. Soon he felt himself trembling. Another CLICK—KA-BOOM! His knees buckled again, and he strained to get his breath. His trembling was out of control now, but not wanting the others to see, he made a conscious effort to hold more firmly to the torpedo-rack railing. The distraction damped the rising fear that was about to drive him into a state of panic.

CLICK—KA-BOOM! More of the awesome pressure, more lightbulbs popping. In the dimly lit torpedo room, with no place to go, he peered into the eyes of death. In his mind he saw chunks blown out of the pressure hull and water gushing in, slinging him around. The idea of a watery grave, the thought that he might never be seen or heard from again, troubled him most.

Outside, debris blown off the mangled superstructure deck either floated toward the surface or sank to the bottom. Among the heavier-than-water items was a fuel-filling valve. Davis knew nothing about this, but the tearing noises and vibrations told him that the submarine was suffering damage. For all he knew water might be gushing into a compartment somewhere toward the rear of the 300-foot-long vessel. Depth charges continued to explode, and he continued to hang onto the rail in the torpedo room.

Finally, there were no more clicks and ka-booms, and Davis heard the beating whump, whump, whump fading away. Then absolute silence prevailed. Davis relaxed his grip on the rail. His breathing slowed. No one moved; all remained silent as they were trained to do, and all systems had been shut down as required in preparation for the depth-charge attack. Davis stood motionless, anticipating the Japanese destroyer's next run. It was about 3:30 P.M. He cocked his head toward the ceiling and listened. Time ticked by, and Davis puzzled over the enemy's inaction. He knew *Picuda* was a sitting duck in the shallow water waiting for the kill. "What are they waiting for?" he wondered. In the eerie silence eighty-five crewmen sat motionless in the darkened boat, still anticipating a fatal blow.

The air conditioner had stopped when the system was shut down. Heat continued to radiate from silent engines, from other heat sources, from the crew's bodies. Sweat ran down Davis's back and down his nose, dripped onto his soaking wet uniform. The mystery of the enemy's inaction continued to trouble him.

An hour passed, and another. The prolonged uncertainty drained Davis's energy and weighed heavily on his spirits. Thirst began to torment him. His focus shifted from death to his physical misery. Breathing became more difficult, and he worried about the dwindling oxygen supply. It occurred to him that following a plow behind a team of mules had not been so bad after all. It amused him that he would even think of such a thing at a time like this.

Finally, after darkness fell, the boat came to life once more. Orders blared over the public address system. Sailors hurried about their duties. Motors and engines began to hum, propellers turned, and the sub started plowing through the water. Davis breathed a great sigh of relief. His heart rate slowed. The torment and agony evaporated. Soon, activities returned to the normal routine. Sailors joked and began to laugh. Acting offensively one torpedoman said, "Davis, what were you doing so pale?" Irked, their boss shot back, "You didn't look so good yourself." That ended that conversation.

Although exhausted, Davis felt a great sense of joy at still possessing a life that he had been sure was going to end. A change came over him. Fully conscious of his mortality now, he vowed to heed, with more determination, his mother's advice: "Always be prepared to die." His Christian faith took on more meaning, and the feeling of being on a great adventure left him—forever. From now on he would serve only out of a sense of duty.

Later, conversations often turned to speculation about why the Japanese destroyer had not returned to finish off its cornered prey. Not until days after the attack did they get a clue: when the crew switched to a new fuel tank, instead of getting diesel fuel, as expected, salt water filled the pipes. Hearing that news, Davis saw in his imagination the filling valve on one of the large fuel tanks being blown off during the attack, oil spewing up and bubbling out on the surface around the floating debris. Now he could see that the Japanese captain probably left because he thought he had already destroyed the American submarine. Indeed, after five more war patrols and the war's end, Davis learned that a Japanese captain had reported sinking an enemy submarine on the day and at the place of their depth-charge attack. The charge that had blown away the fuel-filling valve had probably saved *Picuda,* its crew, and Hanly Davis.

T E N

Bastogne and Germany

Technician Third Class Robert Haney
Radio Operator, U.S. Army

"You had better wake them up," said Lieutenant Biggs. "There's no need to wake them up," came the answer from Robert Haney of Anchorage, Kentucky. "I'll volunteer for all of us right now."

On radio watch at Luxembourg city, Haney would not have volunteered his radio team without their consent had he known what lay ahead at Bastogne, Belgium. But his group had always worked with Combat Command B (CCB) of the Tenth Armored Division. He reasoned the five-man radio team of the 150th Armored Signal Company would want to go and provide additional radio communication support for the command headquarters that controlled a mix of tank and infantry battalions. Besides, it was midnight, and he thought his team would appreciate a few extra winks while he made some preparations for the forty-five-mile trip.

Although he sensed from his lieutenant's expression and tone that CCB must be in a fight at Bastogne, he still felt secure with his decision when he woke the team members. Despite the general aversion to volunteering in the army, they approved Haney's decision and went about drawing rations and ammunition for the .50-caliber machine gun mounted on the turret over the cab of their 2½-ton army truck and securing five-gallon cans of water and gas in their special mounts. The truck housed their high-powered radio and towed a trailer carrying their electric generator. Just before dawn on December 18, 1944, the radio team pulled out of the division rest area and headed for Bastogne.

A few miles north of Luxembourg, Haney suddenly realized that the long river of military vehicles was flowing southward, away from Bastogne. Only his lone truck traveled in the opposite direction. He began to worry. At the next stop he exchanged places with one of the men riding in the enclosed bed of the truck.

Technician Third Class Robert Haney, an army radio operator, was cut off and surrounded at Bastogne. Courtesy of Robert Haney.

An hour or so later the vehicle came to a grinding halt. Haney and the other two radio operators hurriedly opened the door and jumped out to see what was happening. When he saw army engineers frantically digging a ditch across the road, he knew they were placing land mines, and his anxiety rose. One engineer commented, "You fellows are going the wrong way." Haney answered, "We are headed for Bastogne." The engineer said, "Well, that's the way. But don't think you will get there." Haney wondered what on earth was happening. Since the Tenth Armored had first come in contact with the enemy in November, they had known only offensive action. Fighting with Gen. George Patton's Third Army, the "Tiger Division" had swung an arc across eastern France and rolled over the border of Belgium. Haney, who had thought the war was about over, did not know what to make of what he saw here—retreating Americans.

In a little while the engineers put a metal covering over the ditch, and the lone truck continued on its way. It carried five frightened men, but the thought of turning back never entered Haney's mind, and none of the others mentioned it.

From the truck cab, a few miles south of Bastogne, Haney anxiously scanned the countryside for signs of trouble. He was pleased that an American ambulance was now traveling in their direction, about 400 yards ahead. The ambulance rounded a curve and disappeared from sight. Suddenly, a thundering explosion jarred the ground. The driver, McKinley Boone, slammed on the brakes and managed to stop the truck short of the curve. Haney got out and peered timidly around the corner. He saw the battered ambulance in the ditch without a sign of life. He quickly scanned the tree line, a little distance from the ditch, for enemy tanks or mortars. He saw nothing, but he and his teammates all knew that the Germans had hit the ambulance with a tank or artillery shell. Alone and tense, they waited, not knowing what to do.

Then, fortunately, an American tank lumbered out of the woods behind them, and they told its crew what had happened. The tankers set up a mortar and lobbed a few rounds over the little ridge opposite the motionless ambulance. Haney listened and nervously waited for the German response, but there was none. A tanker said, "We are going to Bastogne, if we can get there, so why don't you follow us?" The truck fell in behind the tank. As they moved along, Haney remembered the ambulance and the stillness surrounding it. In his mind he was sure the Germans were going to fire at them too. He stayed uptight until they arrived in Bastogne about midafternoon.

In the small Belgian town sporadic incoming artillery shells flashed and exploded in the streets and on the buildings. The team found Combat Command B's headquarters and reported to the signal officer with whom they usually worked. The grim-looking lieutenant told them to find a house, run the occupants out if there were any, and set up to send the backlog of messages. "You had better locate in a basement, because we expect bombing and artillery shelling to be heavy," he said. Haney could tell they were in trouble, but he didn't know they were about to be involved in the largest pitched battle fought by American arms in World War II. Before it ended, about 19,000 of the 600,000 Americans involved would be killed on the snow-covered battlefield.

As Haney and his section leader, Sgt. James Pierce, turned to leave the quaint old three-story stone hotel, an artillery shell screamed overhead and smashed into the building. A jarring explosion, accompanied by a blinding flash, knocked men down, shattered glass, and scattered dust and debris over everything. Fortunately, no one was hurt. The CCB staff brushed themselves off and went back to work.

The signal officer said, "Now you know. They haven't got Bastogne completely surrounded yet, because you all made it in, but they are awfully close to surrounding us. If you don't find a basement, dig a deep foxhole." Haney and Pierce hastened to leave the grim scene. At the truck, Haney looked into the fear-filled eyes of his teammates and said, "I'm sorry I volunteered you guys for this. I'm afraid I've gotten us into some trouble." They kidded him about it. One said, "Next time, don't do it again."

About a block away from CCB's headquarters the team found an abandoned but fully furnished one-story stucco house with its front door ajar. Haney and the team scurried about and quickly set up their remote equipment on a heavy old table in the concrete basement and started sending the handful of coded messages given to them by the signal officer. The messages went out to division headquarters in Morse code.

The concrete floor to the house that covered the basement provided the team additional protection from the occasional artillery shell falling in their neighborhood. Haney felt fairly safe from artillery fire when he was in the basement, but out of curiosity they decoded some of the messages and learned that the Germans had launched a major attack in their area and that the front lines were collapsing. When Haney took his turn at manning the machine gun removed from their truck and placed in the back yard, he looked out over the railroad and across the open field, expecting to see a big German tank break out of the woods at any moment. He was scared.

Haney did not know that Hitler had massed three German armies comprising twenty-five divisions and unleashed them against four American divisions on an eighty-mile front, with the object of reaching the port city of Antwerp, about 140 miles behind the American front line. Nor did he know that Bastogne was a road center needed and wanted by the Germans. But he had already seen the dejected and worried expressions on the faces of stragglers filing into Bastogne from the battered divisions that had been overrun, and he knew his life was in jeopardy.

On December 18, 1944, their first night in Bastogne, Haney and teammate James Pierce responded to the call for two volunteers to operate a radio on CCB's radio net. They eased out of their concrete basement womb and hurried up the narrow street to CCB headquarters. Before they could report to the signal officer, a stunned colonel from the Ninth Armored Division entered the hotel and asked Haney, "Where is your commanding officer?" Col. William Roberts stepped out and asked the colonel, "How many tanks do you have?" The distraught officer mumbled, "I don't have any." "Well where are they?" demanded Roberts. The colonel in a nearly incoherent voice said, "The Germans have some of them." In a rage, Roberts said, "You know we are fighting our own tanks now manned by Germans."

For what seemed like forever, Haney watched Roberts give the colonel the worst dressing-down he had ever seen. To Haney the colonel appeared on the threshold of becoming a battle fatigue case, like the babbling straggler he had seen earlier whose words Haney could not make out. Understanding how easily he too could lose touch with reality, his sympathy went out to the poor colonel. He wondered what kind of enemy forces could have wiped out the tanks of an armored command and put its commander in a state of shock. But he could not dwell on that. He had to get on with his duties.

Outside, Haney and Pierce climbed into the bed of a halftrack parked beside CCB's headquarters and manned the radio mounted on the vehicle. In its steel, boxlike bed they had some protection from the artillery fragments of a near miss, but there was nothing over their heads to protect them from a direct hit. Haney felt exposed.

As the night wore on, enemy shells came more often and were soon falling like rain all over Bastogne. Without the concrete basement to muffle the noise, Haney heard German artillery thundering in the distance, shells roaring through the fog, and the whistling warning of those about to hit near the halftrack. The fog-dimmed flashes created an eerie sight for the radio operators, but it was the constant jarring explosions that filled Haney with fear. One artillery shell struck within a few yards of the halftrack. The ear-piercing explosion rocked the vehicle. Fluttering fragments banged into the side and bounced off in all directions. Pressed against the metal floor with racing heart and tight muscles, Haney trembled violently. In a quivering voice he mumbled, "God, help us." Pierce, too, prayed aloud. The incoming artillery would not let up. Haney thought, sooner or later a shell is bound to crash down on top of us and blow us into bits and pieces. Still, he managed to keep his fear below the panic level.

Within hearing range of Bastogne, three "task forces" out of CCB braced themselves to defend against the German tanks and infantry rapidly closing on their positions. A few American stragglers moving to the rear joined the teams. Soon desperate messages from Task Forces Desobry, Cherry, and O'Hara came in over the radio in the halftrack still shaking from exploding shells. Desobry, named after the battalion commander, operated a road block at Noville, less than five miles north of Bastogne. They reported contact with the German Second Panzer Division. Haney noted with dismay that the message had been sent in the clear; no doubt the situation was too critical to allow time to encode it. Now, someone had to deliver the message. Haney took the first turn.

The constantly exploding artillery rounds made Haney very aware that he would not have even the partial protection of the halftrack once he took to the street. Since the near misses came periodically, he waited until the next shell fragments bounced off the steel bed, then leaped from the vehicle, sprinted around the corner amid flashing explosions, and shot through the door of the stone-walled hotel. Out of breath, he delivered the message. The forlorn expression of the CCB staff officers increased his own nightmare.

Back in the halftrack, the artillery pounding continued and the incoming messages from Desobry to the north, Cherry to the northeast, and O'Hara to the southeast became more alarming as the night wore on. The visible shakes that had seized both Pierce and Haney would not let go. One task force, which had started out with about 500 men and 30 tanks, pleaded for help. Messages in the clear asked for more ammunition, more artillery support: "Without help we cannot hold out much longer." Then one task force went off the air. Alarmed, Haney tried to reach it, but he couldn't transmit a coherent message with his shaking hands; only by holding his right wrist with his left hand did he manage to key in a message. But there was no answer. Haney said to Pierce, "We're in trouble." If they were not blown to bits first, he thought, they were going to be overrun. He did not want to die. A shroud of gloom settled over the little radio team.

In about an hour, however, the silent task force came back on the air. Neither Haney nor Pierce queried what had happened; they were just glad it was still out there. As morning dawned, the enemy artillery tapered off, and the pressure on the task forces wound down. Haney and Pierce were relieved of their duties at the halftrack. Neither had slept a wink. Nor was Haney sleepy. Although he was glad to be alive and rid of the shakes, he still felt the gloom that hung heavy over Bastogne.

Back with the rest of the team, Haney and Pierce broke open a box of ten-in-one ration, fired up their little Coleman-style burner, and heated their breakfast. While Haney drank his hot coffee in silence, a company of men approached in a column of two files. Before they got in hearing range, Haney recognized the quick, confident step of paratroopers. The approaching infantrymen marching to an unknown destination and the radio team needed and desperately wanted information from each other. "Has there been much enemy artillery around here?" "Lots." "If you guys have any extra rifles or pistols, we sure would like to have them." "Sorry, we don't."

By the time the column passed, Haney had learned that the 101st Airborne had been scooped off the streets in Rheims, loaded on trucks in the division rest area and hurriedly transported through the night to Bastogne. Some were without their overcoats and helmets, and a few even lacked their rifles. Although Haney noted the paratroopers were serious and lacking their acclaimed cockiness, he felt reassured by their presence, their confidence in themselves and readiness to fight. For the first time since the beginning of the all-night artillery pounding and the incoming messages from task forces desperately pleading for help, a small ray of hope shone through the clouds, and Haney's spirits rose a little.

But the tone of the messages processed by the radio team soon dispelled any optimism. Air force messages told Brig. Gen. Anthony McAuliffe, commander of the Bastogne defenders, that it was useless to keep requesting close air support and bombing missions; the fliers promised, however, that the moment the fog lifted they would fill the sky with planes. But the fog continued to hang heavy over the snow-covered landscape. What if it did not lift in time?

Meanwhile, word of the Malmédy Massacre soon spread. Haney did not know the details about German SS troops capturing 100 Americans, herding them into a field, and then mowing them down with machine guns; a few feigned death and survived, but 86 were killed in cold blood. Haney did hear, however, that American prisoners of war had been murdered after they surrendered just a few miles north of Bastogne. This new threat added to his own woes—and his anger. The more he thought about it, the madder he got, and his bitterness turned to hate. Now if he had to, he could kill Germans without remorse.

On December 20, minutes after the event occurred, Haney learned that the Germans had encircled Bastogne. Being under siege came as no surprise to him, but his feelings did. Knowing that his radio team, the 101st Airborne, what was left of Combat Command B, and the remnants of other units were all in this predicament together caused him to feel a surge of comradeship with all the men now in mortal danger, surrounded and overwhelmingly outnumbered. "They'll never get us," he thought, and he felt a strange, unexpected uplifting of his spirits.

But gloom soon returned. Dense fog continued to hang over the snow-covered roofs and the streets pockmarked by artillery. Haney sensed the deterioration of the situation. He knew there could be no close air support until the fog lifted. Now and then a team member, out of curiosity, would decode a message given to them by the signal officer at the headquarters, and Haney knew before he read them that they contained fearful news. He saw the deteriorating situation reflected in the furrowed brow, tight lips, and grim expression on the decoder's face.

On December 21, while running toward CCB's headquarters at the hotel, Haney heard the friendly artillery outgoing from Bastogne booming at a faster tempo. Flames belched out of the angry muzzles of the gun barrels. A column of tanks roared past him, heading toward the sounds of fighting on the perimeter. It was not the first time he had seen CCB's reserve, a force of tanks and infantry, formed from tanks and men that had escaped destruction or capture in earlier fighting at the roadblocks with task forces Desobry, Cherry, or O'Hara. The reserve force had raced back and forth through town on several occasions on its way to aid paratroopers about to be overrun. Haney, hoping they would arrive in time, went on to deliver messages to the signal officer.

Later that day, a sudden burst of German machine pistol fire caught Haney's attention. "My God," he thought, "that's inside the town." Soon he heard American rifle fire over the sounds of the machine pistols. His heart began to race. Then, in seconds, the firing in the city grew quiet except for routine battle sounds—occasional friendly artillery fire, German artillery rounds periodically whistling in, sporadic machine gun fire out on the perimeter. Haney's pulse rate slowed down, and he decided to find out what had happened. About a block away he saw a German ambulance riddled with bullet holes. Haney learned that the Germans had appeared on the perimeter under a white flag and pleaded with the Americans to allow them to drive an ambulance through Bastogne to attend German casualties on the other side of the American perimeter. Once inside the town the ambulance had come to a screeching halt, and a dozen armed Germans had burst from it, firing machine pistols as they came. The American response left a bloody mess on the street. It was the ancient Trojan horse trick, and Haney wondered, "What in the hell will they try next?" He was not aware of Hitler's pressure on his commanders to capture Bastogne—the rail and highway center that was slowing the German effort to race to Antwerp and split the Allied armies—but he was feeling the effects of that pressure.

The next morning a driving snow blanketed the town, covering the black artillery pockmarks in the old snow and leaving a false appearance of serenity. Later that day, at CCB headquarters, Haney noticed that the grim look on the staff officers' faces had been replaced with laughter, something he had not seen since arriving in Bastogne. The signal officer shared the news with him about the one word uttered by General McAuliffe that would make the headlines and give the general lasting fame. Haney listened eagerly. A small German party under a white flag had appeared at an outpost manned by the paratroopers, demanded to see the commanding general, and presented McAuliffe a written message saying essentially that since Bastogne was encircled by strong German forces, the Americans could surrender or be annihilated. McAuliffe had said, "Nuts," and put it in writing.

Haney was not aware that the Germans were having trouble interpreting the meaning of the word, but McAuliffe's defiance boosted his morale, and he rushed to share the news with the rest of the team. They joked about it and enjoyed themselves—for a brief moment. As the day wore on, the news grew steadily worse. Haney did not know the width of the sixty-mile breach in the American line, or the depth of the German penetration. Through the message traffic, however, he felt the presence of German armies rolling westward above and below the surrounded town. He was not remotely aware that the great bulge forming around him would give the battle its name, but he was keenly aware of the deteriorating situation at Bastogne.

The thick fog continued to hang over the isolated town like a curse. Not a single ray of sunlight broke through the dreary, overcast sky, and the extended forecast did not predict clearing until December 26, 1944. Haney saw the request for close air support grow more urgent, and he wondered if the skies would clear in time to save them. Even more worrisome was the dwindling supply of ammunition. Once it was gone, the defenders would be overrun in minutes. General McAuliffe limited artillery firing to ten rounds per artillery tube per day. Desperate for ammunition, the tankers made a dash to the south with two tanks and three halftracks, trying to break through the German lines. In minutes, the Germans knocked the five vehicles out of action. The small amount of gasoline rationed out to the radio team to run their electrical generator required an armed guard. Haney's distress increased when he heard the infantry on the perimeter pleading to no avail for more artillery support. The radio team began to wonder aloud if the infantry could hold out until help came. They learned from decoded radio messages that General Patton's Third Army was coming up from the south to their rescue, but they knew nothing of its progress.

Haney began to feel abandoned. He did not want to think he had been forgotten by his countrymen, but the feeling lingered. In his little basement world, he saw only the damnable fog—no close air support, no resupply of ammunition by air, and no help from the ground forces on the other side of the Germans. Hopelessness crept in, and he felt his chances of survival slipping away. Thinking it unwise to be captured with any German souvenirs in his possession, Haney buried his huge German flag with its big swastika and his German Luger pistol. The other radiomen buried their souvenirs as well.

But the dawning of the morning of December 23, 1944, changed Haney's world. Bright sun rays reflecting off the snow-covered evergreens created a Christmas card setting, warmed his body, and soothed his spirits. About 10:00 A.M. he heard American planes droning in the distance, and soon the team saw planes diving on the German columns converging on Bastogne. They could not see the German vehicles, but smoke was rising from burning tanks and armored cars. Haney thought, "By God, we are getting help." A little twinkle returned to the sunken eyes of the dirty and unshaven team, but they knew they could still be killed or captured if the defenders of the embattled town ran out of ammunition.

Then, about noon, Haney craned his neck to watch the approaching two-engine transport planes. German antiaircraft opened up and threw a wall of tracers in front of the formation of American C-47s carrying their lifeline of ammunition and supplies. The low-flying planes never wavered. One exploded and disappeared in the air; another was hit and glided toward the ground. But the droning noise rose to a high-pitched sound as the remaining C-47s crossed the outer perimeter.

Suddenly, brightly colored parachutes blossomed pink, red, purple. American GIs cheered. Civilians poured out of their cellars to see what was happening. Pallets filled with boxes of ammunition, cans of gasoline, and other supplies swung beneath the multicolored parachutes drifting down inside the perimeter. Taking it all in—the snow-covered evergreens glistening in bright sunshine, the beautiful colors drifting down, the C-47s in formation droning on—Haney thought, "It's the most beautiful sight I have ever seen." Like little children, the joyful soldiers kicked up their heels while dashing through the snow to the crates landing all around. Haney's burden of hopelessness evaporated, and his spirits soared.

That night in their basement work station, Haney and the team grew silent and listened to airplanes droning in the distance. Since each type of plane had its unique sound, they soon discerned that the approaching planes were German. They slid under the heavy table that held their radio remote control equipment and lay face down. Falling bombs whistled, and gigantic explosions battered the outskirts of the town. Haney had never heard anything of this magnitude. The building vibrated, and Haney felt himself trembling against the cold concrete floor. The sounds of bombs slamming into the streets grew louder. So did the engines of the planes, and Haney knew the explosions were rolling his way. He felt his teeth chattering. He clamped his clammy hands around a leg of the heavy table and held on.

A great ball of fire flashed through the basement, followed immediately by an earth-shattering explosion. Shock waves shook Haney like a dog shaking a snake, lifted him a foot or so off the floor, and slammed him down as he held onto the table leg. The basement turned pitch dark. Sergeant Pierce shouted, "Is everybody all right?" All said, "I'm OK." Not another word was spoken. Through the door to the floor above them, Haney saw flames dancing and heard the crackling sound of burning wood. "My God," he thought, "I'm going to be burned alive." Without speaking a word, the team scooted out from under the table and dashed in unison to the concrete steps revealed by flashing flames. Haney felt crumbled plaster and debris under his feet as he shot up and out of their vaultlike basement.

The house was gone; only the concrete floor above the basement remained, looking as if a tornado had swept it clean. It didn't register on Haney's mind that the concrete basement was the best place to be. Instead, the men started crawling down the street while bombs continued to whistle and pound.

Haney heard moaning off to his right and crawled over to lend a hand. He saw a dying hog where he had expected to find a human being, and a little smile spread his lips. Eventually, the team took refuge in a bomb crater, still scared to death and now they were out of business. Their high-powered radio, the truck, and the generator had been blown to bits and pieces.

Finally, the terrifying night ended, and a bright sun rose over the horizon into a blue sky. Haney heard familiar airplane engines, and soon American aircraft of every kind filled the skies. Large and medium bombers struck German targets near the American perimeter and beyond as far as Haney could see. Fighters winged over, dived, and made their strafing runs. Wave after wave of planes came and left. Throughout the morning Haney and his teammates just stood and watched, so distracted by the awesome display of combat power that they almost forgot it was the day before Christmas. Still, a sky filled with American planes was a beautiful Christmas present. Thinking about all the German targets destroyed around their besieged town, Haney thought, "We just might make it." His spirits soared in striking contrast to his fear of the night before, and it felt good to be out of the gloomy mood.

About noon, hoping to salvage a radio, the signal officer loaded the team on a scout car and headed for the C-47 transport shot down by the Germans the day before. With the vehicles in four-wheel drive they plowed through deep snow in the open field beyond the railroad track, through the forest on a narrow trail, and across a little stream. Sensing the enemy's presence, Haney and his teammates grabbed their screwdrivers and pliers and hurried into the wrecked airplane. Finding the radio damaged beyond repair, they left just as quickly. Haney had barely cleared the plane when he heard the whisper of incoming mortar rounds. In rapid succession, about a dozen rounds exploded on and around the airplane. The radiomen made a wild dash to the scout car, jumped in and took off, their spinning wheels kicking up snow. Haney knew the Germans were aiming at them. Like their vehicle, his heart accelerated to full speed.

The scout car roared into the stream and came to a sudden stop in the mud and broken ice. Shifting gears back and forth, forward to reverse, the driver tried desperately to get the vehicle unstuck, but the wheels just spun in place. Knowing they were under enemy observation, everyone but the driver jumped into the icy water and pushed the vehicle up the bank. Even though they were disappointed that they did not get a radio, they were still glad to be back safely in Bastogne.

In their new headquarters, the basement of a bar, they made plans to salvage parts from damaged vehicles and equipment, and after much effort they had a working radio. But they had lost their high-power capability.

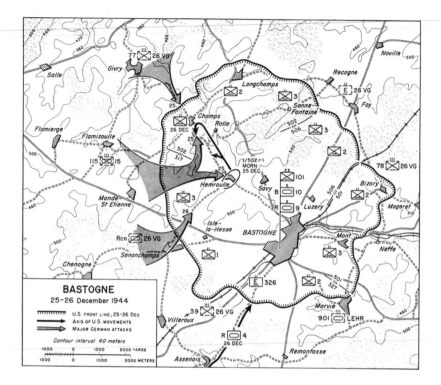

The Battle of Bastogne. Courtesy of the U.S. Army Center of Military History.

Even with an open keg of beer in the abandoned bar, the radio team was in no mood to celebrate Christmas Eve. Outside, a few soldiers were singing Christmas carols, but the radiomen just talked about home and their situation. Suddenly, planes drowned out their conversation, and whistling bombs again fell over the town. Many things had frightened Haney since his arrival in Bastogne, but nothing frightened him like the explosive power of the bombs. Once more he was convinced that they were headed specifically for him, and this time there was no overhead concrete floor. He was close to panic. But soon the last stick of bombs crashed down, and shook the ground around him. The noise ceased, and the planes faded into the distance. Haney and the team rushed out of the basement.

Down the street, six panic-stricken nuns, all holding hands tightly, hurried out of their bomb-damaged building. On the snow-covered streets under the flickering light of burning buildings, their faces caught Haney's attention. He saw mouths ajar, lips tensed, brows raised and drawn together, eyes reflecting pain and terror. Their expressions made a lasting imprint on his memory.

Farther along the street chaos reigned around a flaming inferno, a burning building that had been converted into a hospital. Wounded American soldiers trapped in the basement shouted and pleaded for help. Some screamed in pain. Others moaned. The scene was too much for Haney. Visibly shaken, knowing they could do nothing to relieve the suffering, he and the team turned and left by the light of flames reflected on the snow. His stomach felt queasy.

Christmas dawned cold. Fighting around the town increased in fury. More enemy shells fell in the streets. Haney heard the American machine guns firing and artillery shells exploding just a few blocks away. He knew from the messages that Patton's Third Army was getting closer, but would it arrive in time? At Bastogne the army did not have its usual gourmet Christmas meal. It didn't matter to Haney, who had lost his appetite anyway. Half-heartedly, the team exchanged Christmas greetings.

The next day both armies were fighting hard for the town. German divisions that had already passed by turned around to join other German units in a coordinated attack against all sides of the American perimeter. Patton's relief army pushing northward ran into the German divisions to the southeast, south and southwest of Bastogne. It was tough going. Besides the hard fighting, the American tanks slipped and slid on the slick roads, and the infantry waded in snow to their knees. Haney heard the battle noises south of Bastogne drawing closer. Filled with anxiety, he wondered if the Americans could penetrate the German lines. About 4:30 P.M. the Americans broke through. A chain of tanks roared down the street toward Haney and the radio team, and pandemonium broke out. Jubilant troops cheered and jumped for joy; the saviors of the Fourth Armored Division were as jubilant as the rescued. Good-natured shouting went back and forth between the two American forces. One tanker shouted, "Well, we pulled your chestnuts out of the fire again." Haney asked, "Where are our Christmas presents?" Soon, the tanks moved on past the radio team.

The siege was over, and the burden of fear of being overrun had been lifted from Haney's back. It felt good. But he knew he had to avoid taking unnecessary chances; he could be killed or maimed by the enemy artillery, still falling in the city. He vowed to be careful.

But about two days later, despite his vow, when Haney heard that hot food was being served down the street he yielded to temptation. After enjoying their first hot meal since arriving in Bastogne, Haney and two other team members, in good spirits, were heading back to their basement quarters at the bar when a German fighter plane swooped into a strafing run

Bodies of American soldiers killed during the German offensive drive in the Battle of the Bulge lie in the snow where they fell near Bastogne. General Patton's Third Army passed them during the fight to relieve the Americans in the besieged town.

down the street. As if he could outrun the plane, Haney took off at full speed. He could hear the pitch of the spinning propeller getting louder and bullets chipping the concrete. He was losing the race. At panic's door, he dived for a ditch, and like other combatants facing death, he felt suspended in the air. But he crashed to the ground as the clattering bullets on the pavement zipped past him. It all happened so quickly it made his head swim, and he had to collect his wits before he and his friends could laugh with relief.

On January 1, 1945, the radio team boarded a truck with orders to join their signal company at Metz, France. The stress of combat and loss of sleep had taken its toll. For two weeks Haney had not taken a shower or shaved and he felt grimy. Noting the sunken eyes of his bearded teammates, he assumed that he must have the same haggard look. Soon, the truck lumbered down the road away from Bastogne. Haney was wearing his only worldly possessions—he had lost his extra clothing and personal things when the bomb blew their house and truck away—but he had his life and the knowledge that he had participated in and survived a significant episode in American military history. He felt pride in having been there, in the manner in which his team and the American defenders had performed against overwhelming odds, and in the way the American military had come to the defenders' aid.

At Metz he drew new clothing, bought a razor, and headed for the shower. He shaved and then stepped into the hot shower and lathered himself from head to toe. The warm water running over his body, peeling off the dirt and grime in a safe haven—the contrast between his Bastogne world and the Metz world—filled him with joy. Soon, with rest and hot meals, his body and soul felt restored. He would learn later, however, that every time an enemy shell exploded nearby, his stomach would turn and he would come close to retching—something that had not happened at Bastogne.

In early March 1945 after the battle for Trier, a German city near the Luxembourg border, word spread back to the radio team that Patton had told the GIs the big winery in the city was theirs. He is supposed to have added, "Take it." Haney and his team jumped in their new radio truck and drove full speed for the winery. At the warehouse, GIs rushing toward the doors with empty five-gallon water cans met others coming out laden with full cans or boxes of bottled wine. Frolicking men shouted and giggled as they stashed their loot away in their vehicles.

In the basement of the huge building, Haney could not believe his eyes. Happy men stood in wine up to their ankles and held containers to catch wine spurting out under pressure from bullet holes shot into the large hogsheads. Rows of cylindrical storage tanks larger than a room spouted wine like a series of gigantic fountains. Americans drinking wine caught in their canteen cups laughed and shouted back and forth. Haney and his teammates filled three five-gallon cans and departed.

On March 11, Combat Command B made preparations to cross the north–south Moselle River running from France into Germany. Division engineers worked hard to lay a pontoon bridge across the 300-foot-wide river. The Germans allowed the engineers to get it about 90 percent completed and then bombarded the bridge with artillery, while the engineers sprinted or swam for their lives. When the firing ceased, the American engineers set about rebuilding the bridge. They made several similar attempts before they succeeded.

Meanwhile, Haney and his teammates followed orders and stripped down to their underwear—in case they had to swim. Haney worried less about the cold March wind than about artillery fire. As the end of the column approached the riverbank, Haney heard the roar of incoming enemy rounds. Muffled explosions sent gushers of water into the air. McKinley Boone, the driver, aimed the radio truck for the narrow pontoon bridge and sped through the geyser spouts. Finally, the truck with trailer in tow lumbered up the far bank and away from the exploding shells in the river, bringing up the rear of the column of tanks and armored vehicles. The tankers did not envy the radio team, who had only a layer of plywood to protect them from enemy shell fragments and bullets, but the tankers looked out for their radiomen by keeping them removed from the combat action as best they could.

Later, west of the Rhine near Kaiserslautern, Germany, the radio team's truck labored and strained to climb a steep hill. At the top, Boone drove into an abandoned fortified position encircled by barbed wire. Overhead three American planes circled, and the team hurriedly put the radio on the air and contacted the pilot leading the fighter bombers. The radio operators on the ground pointed out a patch of woods about 400 yards away where German tanks were supposedly hiding. After they waved their handkerchiefs to satisfy the pilot that he was talking to Americans, the planes dropped their bombs, made their strafing runs, and departed.

Haney still felt uneasy in their exposed position. He and his teammates quickly shut off the generator and stashed their gear. As he jumped into the cab, Haney anxiously scanned the woods. A German tank stuck its snout out of the foliage, rotated its turret, and lowered the gun barrel. Staring into its muzzle, Haney felt his neck muscles tighten. The gun barrel thundered and belched fire. The shell crashed near the truck, shaking the ground under it. Controlling his panic, Haney shouted, "Let's get the hell out of here!" Boone slammed the truck into reverse and rammed the foot pedal to the floor. The trailer jackknifed. Haney, knowing the second round was coming, thought his time was up. But Boone, still in control, shifted gears and crashed through the barbed wire at full speed. Like a race car, the truck and trailer dropped below the crown of the hill out of sight of the big German tank.

Before Haney could calm down and slow his heart rate, however, Boone announced he had no brakes. Haney looked down the big hill and decided to jump, hesitated, leaned forward again, and hesitated once more. Meanwhile, the truck continued to gain speed, and he had no choice; he had to take his chances on riding it out. He braced himself and held on. Finally, at the bottom of the hill, Boone geared the truck down and brought it to a standstill. Haney breathed a sigh of relief. The crew inspected the brake fluid hose that had been cut by the barbed wire, then limped into a military maintenance shop and had the hose replaced.

By the end of March 1945 seven Allied armies had crossed the Rhine, the last major barrier on the western front, and soon the Tenth Armored Division was on the move in southern Germany. Heidelberg, on the Neckar River, one of the few German cities to escape damage, was undefended. Haney marveled at the beautiful university town as his radio team, in the convoy behind CCB, whisked through. At Heilbronn, about forty miles southeast of Heidelberg, a fight broke out that lasted a week. A few miles farther east, at Crailsheim, a battalion in one of the other combat commands became cut off and lost many of its vehicles before the men fought their way out. Haney was glad to learn that two of his good friends with the radio team supporting the surrounded battalion had gotten out safely.

The division turned southward. Haney noticed white sheets and white flags hung out windows by the frightened civilians to communicate their peaceful intentions. By April 23 they had reached the blue Danube River at Ulm. Haney enjoyed the cleanliness of the German countryside and the beauty of the gently rolling green meadows. Soon he was on the Autobahn, heading southeast toward Munich. Hitler had built the four-lane roads that crisscrossed Germany in order to expedite military troop movement; now they were aiding the Allies in their victory sweep. Everywhere the eastward-advancing Allies met large numbers of German POWs moving westward. By now the German forces were incapable of forming a solid line; generally, only roadblocks and demolished bridges delayed the advancing armies. Yet, Americans were still being killed as isolated local commanders inspired their troops to fight a desperate battle for a day or two. But Haney could feel the end coming, and his morale was high.

Between Augsburg and Munich, CCB's convoy moved swiftly toward Dachau. Haney had heard rumors about Hitler's extermination camps, but he had no perception about the scope and degree of the merciless and unrelenting slaughter of human beings that occurred there. That would soon change. About four miles out of Dachau, a repugnant odor assaulted the team. Haney and Boone wrinkled their noses and looked at each other. Boone said, "That's a human smell."

Near the camp the lead vehicle came to a halt, and the rest of the convoy closed and stopped. GIs piled off their tanks and vehicles and walked toward a gate that had been blown off by the unit that had taken the camp a day or so earlier, on April 29. Haney moved along with the crowd converging on the gate. Some held handkerchiefs over their noses. Haney had never encountered a more noxious odor; it seared his nostrils and was never erased from his permanent memory.

Inside the fenced camp Haney stared in disbelief at human skeletons in zebra-striped prison uniforms. They had shaved heads and glazed eyes in deep sockets. This first of the Nazi labor camps established after Hitler came to power in 1933 still housed about 32,000 internees: Gypsies who, like the Jews, were classified as racially inferior; about a thousand Catholic priests and other clergymen who had resisted the Nazis' coercion of churches; political opponents; and Jews, most of whom had just been shipped in from extermination camps to keep the Allies from liberating them. Dachau was not one of the extermination camps designed to liquidate the Jewish race but a labor camp—though it did have a crematorium where thousands of cadavers were stuffed into ovens to disappear as particles in the smoke that roared out of the chimneys.

Haney did not get to see inside the crematorium as did his fellow Kentuckian Ralph Devine, one of the camp's liberators. Ovens had been red hot and blazing when Devine went into the crematorium where, he recalled, operations had come to a sudden standstill. Some emaciated bodies lay stacked on trailers that were hooked in tandem in the center of the big building; others lay on motionless conveyer belts at the doors of ovens; and some human forms were disappearing in the roaring flames. But Haney knew what had gone on inside the building as he stared at the tall, silent smokestacks.

American military police directed the GIs to the areas they were allowed to see. At one site, Haney listened in disbelief as the MP described how the guards used trained dogs to attack prisoners for entertainment. Later, he observed dead dogs that the liberators had shot in disgust. Standing over a long trench, Haney looked down on a huge pile of intertwined skin-and-bones corpses staring into space. White-faced and sickened GIs cursed Hitler and the Germans. The enormity of the suffering and the degradation of the dead and dying stunned Haney. This new knowledge that human beings could mistreat fellow human beings in this manner traumatized him more than the ungodly scene. His emotions nearly overwhelmed him and he felt intense rage and bitterness toward the Germans. Finally, he was glad to get out of there and back to war.

At about the same time, unknown to Haney, Hitler had committed suicide in Berlin, and his body, like those of his victims at Dachau, had gone up in smoke. Haney got the news while moving toward Garmisch-Partenkirchen through villages presenting a sea of white flags. Above Garmisch the famous snowcapped Zugspitze, highest mountain peak in Germany, glistened in the sun. The radio team found a hunting lodge and set up operations.

In the afternoon of May 7, 1945, Haney and the world got the word that German representatives had signed the unconditional surrender of all German armed forces at General Eisenhower's headquarters in Rheims. The GIs went wild. Haney and his teammates shouted and slapped each other on the back. They would have broken out the booze in celebration, but they had already drunk the world-famous resort village dry. Instead, they fired rifles, mortars, machine guns, tank guns, and artillery into the mountainside to create their own fireworks, which went on into the night.

For Haney the war was over. He was not sent to the fighting still raging in the Pacific, as he had anticipated. He went home to Anchorage, Kentucky, with a greater appreciation for the virtues of freedom and a sense of great pride in having fought for his country. He would cherish both.

Iwo Jima

Paul and Joe Simms
U.S. Marine Corps, and Hometown Friends

In January 1943 Paul Hubert Simms Jr., a Springfield, Kentucky, native, encountered a fast-talking recruiter who convinced him that he should meet his World War II obligations in the U.S. Marine Corps. Just out of high school, the young athlete wanted something with a lot of action. Consequently, when he finished boot camp at San Diego, California, he volunteered to take parachute training. Upon graduation, he joined the First Marine Parachute Battalion, one of only four such battalions in the Marine Corps of World War II.

In November 1943, after additional training in the Southwest Pacific, his battalion joined other American units already entrenched opposite 35,000 Japanese soldiers on Bougainville, the largest in the Solomon Islands chain. Located just below the equator, the hot, steaming, and jungle-invested island created a miserable setting for the combatants. In that environment, Simms went to work preparing his .30-caliber machine gun position for the defense. Dripping wet with sweat, he first dug his foxhole; then he and his crew built a bunker for the gun. If there were enemies out there, Paul could neither see nor hear them.

Grimy and sweaty, he decided to take a bath. Since drinking water was rationed and precious, he dug down to the water table as the old-timers had done. The cool water from the depths of the ground refreshed him as he lathered up. Suddenly, enemy machine gun bursts broke the jungle silence. Terrified, Simms dropped his soap, snatched up his helmet and cartridge belt, and dashed to his bunker to man his machine gun, wearing only the helmet and cartridge belt. He saw nothing but enemy machine gun tracers going by, ripping through the foliage. With his finger locked on the trigger and the assistant gunner feeding the belts of ammunition, Simms swung his gun down the line made by the enemy's machine gun tracers, hoping to reach the source.

U.S. Marine Corporal Paul Simms (left) joined his brother, Private First Class Joe Simms (right), and hometown friends in the battle for Iwo Jima. Both Simms brothers were wounded. Courtesy of Julia and Jeanne Simms.

The new marine gunners swept their shaking machine guns back and forth, firing at the maximum rate. Some began to run out of ammunition, but Simms and his crew had hoarded extra boxes. In three minutes, silence fell over the jungle. Simms looked and listened behind his hot machine gun but saw and heard nothing, not even a peep out of the birds. From his first fight, he had already learned that a gunner had to conserve his ammunition.

Soon, American Indians who had been selected and trained as scouts penetrated farther into the jungle to check it out. They found six dead Japanese soldiers. Either the Americans had wiped out the patrol or the remaining members had withdrawn. Simms had to see the results of his first combat action for himself. Shaded from the sunlight under the triple canopy of leaves, he looked down on the Japanese corpses with flies swarming around the bloody wounds. The silent bodies made him somber. There was no victory celebration; the vivid sight had revealed to him his own vulnerability.

Later, Simms's battalion was assigned a mission to conduct a raid behind enemy lines. Dressed in combat gear, he loaded onto a landing craft carrying a platoon of Marines. He had his .30-caliber air-cooled machine gun; the heavier water-cooled guns were left behind. The fleet of a dozen landing craft, escorted by destroyers and PT boats, moved along the coast to a beach about six miles behind the Japanese lines. As the rising sun approached the horizon, the craft nosed in for the landing.

In a state of anxiety, Simms hurried onto the beach. Light, sporadic enemy fire met the marines on a narrow beach that extended about twenty-five feet between the waterline and dense jungle. Frightened by the exposed, life-threatening situation, Simms and the others darted into the jungle, where the machine gun section chief quickly assigned defensive positions. While enemy rifle fire clipped twigs and leaves off the underbrush, Simms and Donaldson hastily set up their machine gun, loaded it with a belt of ammunition, and started digging frantically to get below ground level. A narrow footpath to his direct front created a small tunnel in the jungle foliage for a short distance up to a turn. It was the only open space they could see.

Now and then Simms would fire a few bursts into the jungle even though he saw nothing. As time wore on, enemy fire increased, but still he saw nothing. He began to fire longer and more frequent bursts. The shouting for medics, telling him that the Japanese were scoring hits, made him hug the ground even closer in his foxhole. Only frightened eyes under his helmet peered out above the ground, but he could still aim his weapon because he had had an extra sight mechanism welded on underneath the gun. In the dense steaming foliage he saw neither the marines to his right and left nor the enemy to the front. Except for the battle noises, it was as if he and Donaldson were fighting alone. Only by the vertical angle of the Japanese machine gun tracers' trajectory could Simms tell that the enemy was on a little hill. Paying close attention to the horizontal and vertical angles of the Japanese tracers ripping through the underbrush, he adjusted his gun mount to aim higher. He swung his machine gun up the path of the tracers and fired a few bursts, hoping to hit the enemy gunner he could not see.

By midmorning the intensity of fire on both sides had increased, and enemy mortar rounds began to burst in the treetops. Suddenly, Japanese bullets hit all around Simms's position, kicking sand into his face. As his heart beat faster and more calls for medics echoed through the jungle, he prayed. Then, glancing at his assistant gunner, he saw blood gushing out and pouring down Donaldson's face. He asked Simms, "How bad am I hurt?" Not wanting to alarm him, Simms answered, "Not bad," and told him to go to the first aid station. Simms's close friend crawled out and departed. Shaken, Simms ducked below ground level more often.

As the morning wore on, the firing would slacken for a while and then build up again. A prolonged fear of getting hurt or killed hounded him. No air stirred in the humid jungle, and sweat rolled down his back, causing his body to demand water. But Simms did not know how long his one canteen would have to last, so he just took sips—never enough to quench his thirst. His cramped muscles ached, but he dared not stand up to stretch. Between firing his weapon, he prayed and worried. With his eyes at near ground level, he could see only the jungle, machine gun tracers, and the short piece of the path tunnel. He did not know how the battalion was faring, how long they had to hold out, whether they would get help. He feared that he might run out of water or, worse, ammunition.

Then there were American airplanes overhead. He could not see what was happening, but he heard them roaring in on their strafing runs. Bombs exploded to his front and shook the ground. The knowledge that outside help was available reassured him, and his feeling of loneliness left him temporarily.

Time passed. A lull in the action came over the battlefield. Fortunately, Simms had the discipline to stay alert despite his weariness, cramps, and misery, for a Japanese soldier with a riffle suddenly appeared in the path tunnel. Instantly, Simms fired a burst, and the Japanese tumbled to the ground. Simms was startled by the speed with which the soldier's life was snuffed out in the remote jungle. Still, he maintained his alertness.

By late afternoon he felt exhausted. His water supply ran low, but he dared not quench his thirst, and he had not eaten all day. He could ignore his hunger pains, but thirst hounded him. He began to wonder whether they would ever get off the beach. Shadows crept into the naturally darkened jungle as the sun touched the horizon.

Finally, word came to head for the boats. Marines burst out of the foliage and onto the waiting crafts, which quickly headed out to sea. When Simms realized that his section chief had dropped his machine gun in the jungle in the mad rush to get on the boat, he tossed his machine gun mount overboard. He realized at last that his long day's ordeal under enemy fire behind enemy lines had come to an end. He felt a great sense of relief.

Two months later, in January 1944, an American army division replaced the marines on Bougainville, and Simms, now a combat veteran, joyfully returned to the United States for reassignment. In Springfield, Kentucky, relatives and friends greeted their hometown hero with pride and open arms. He looked sharp in his dress blues, decked out with his combat ribbons and parachute insignia. At that time in the small towns a combat veteran was a rare sight. Some teenagers anxiously awaiting their opportunity to serve plied him with questions. The contrast between the enemy-infested jungle and his hometown strengthened his appreciation for his country. But the partying and dates with pretty girls had to come to an end.

At Camp Pendleton, California, he joined the newly formed Fifth Marine Division's Twenty-sixth Regiment. The new division, comprising both combat veterans and recruits, embarked on a rigorous training program designed to get them ready for combat in the Pacific. Simms was promoted to corporal and made section chief in a machine gun squad of Company G. Every day they trained hard, and the training itself was dangerous. Simms's section with two machine guns concentrated on firing supporting fires for his platoon, often shooting over their heads. One day his section nearly killed some marines who were in the wrong place.

In a theater one night, Simms was enjoying his popcorn while waiting for the movie to start when his name flashed on the screen with a message for him to report to the lobby. Puzzled and concerned, he rushed out. There stood his younger brother Joe. Happily, the long-separated brothers reminisced about family matters and filled each other in about their own doings. Joe had joined the Fifth Division's Twenty-seventh Regiment, which was training day and night in a separate area. The brothers made it a point to get together as often as they could while they were in California. In September 1944, the division sailed for the island of Hawaii, where they trained further and practiced amphibious landings for about four months.

In January 1945, Paul Simms's ship eased into Pearl Harbor and anchored alongside three other ships. Hilo, the nearest town to the division on Hawaii, had not offered much to off-duty marines, so he looked forward to going ashore for a visit to Honolulu. His mother had written him to be on the lookout for their hometown doctor, Richard "Dicky" Hamilton, and had given him the number of the young navy doctor's ship.

On the deck of his vessel, Paul watched ships entering the harbor, some filled to the brim with marines, and strained to check their numbers. At last APA (transport attack ship) 156 crept into view: his hometown doctor had arrived in the harbor. After getting permission, he called on Lieutenant Hamilton. To celebrate the reunion, Hamilton brought out a bottle of bourbon and poured the drinks while they talked and laughed. After several drinks, Simms excused himself in a slurred voice and left. Until this special occasion, he had barely tasted liquor.

On the way back to his ship in a small boat he felt dizzy, and his warm glow became a feeling of anxiety. At his ship, to his consternation, he discovered that the crew had pulled up the gangplank and left only a Jacob's-ladder for the late arrivals. He staggered over to the long chain ladder with rigid rungs and struggled to get on it from the boat. Terrified by one glance to the top, three stories above him, he started the nearly impossible climb. He huffed and puffed, slipped, hung on. The higher he got the more alarmed he became. Still several rungs from the top, he thought, "I'm not going to make it," but finally he crawled onto the deck. Out of breath and barely coherent, he muttered to a waiting sailor, "Just let me head for my bunk."

Dr. Richard Hamilton (second from right) was on a medical support ship off Iwo Jima, where a torrent of casualties swamped the medical facilities. Courtesy of Dr. Richard Hamilton.

Shortly after his visit with Hamilton, Simms ran into a cousin, Ensign John "Skeets" Kelly. The young navy officer offered Simms a guided tour of his ship, which was undergoing massive repairs in dry dock. As they watched the busy repairmen on board the battleship USS *Maryland*, Kelly explained to Simms that on November 29, 1944, an enemy kamikaze plane had slammed into his ship and exploded in the sick bay compartment, killing thirty-one sailors. At the general quarters call, shortly before the kamikaze attack, Kelly had left the sick bay—against the doctor's advice—to con the ship. Simms listened attentively to the details of the tragedy, and the two men also discussed hometown news, their war experiences, and family matters. Simms left the *Maryland* in high spirits.

A day or so later Kelly was walking along a crowded street in Honolulu when a loud voice behind him cried out, "Sailor, where are you going?" He looked back and saw Joe Simms—Paul's brother—and Forest Grider, a soldier also from Springfield, and the Kentuckians had a happy little reunion right there on the street. Meeting up with friends in faraway places is an uplifting experience for servicemen, especially if they are about to go into battle. Pooling their information, they discovered that five other Springfield servicemen were in the area. Two of them, Joe "Tony" Cecconi and C.A. Milburn, had been football teammates of the Simms brothers and Grider. Why not hold a grand hometown reunion? After deciding where and when, and who would notify whom, the three went their separate ways, filled with excitement.

But the overflowing harbor and crowded Honolulu streets had made it obvious to most servicemen and civilians that something big was about to

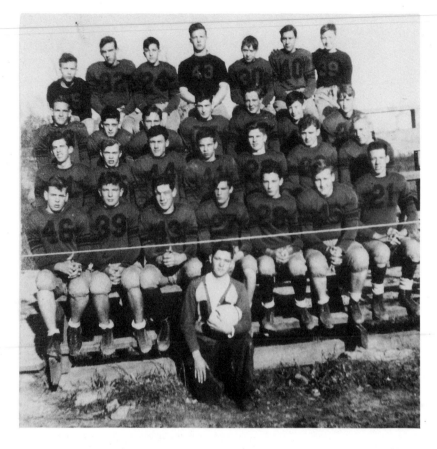

Five members of the 1942 Springfield, Kentucky, high school football team fought at Iwo Jima: Forest Grider (#46), C.A. Milburn (#28), Tony Cecconi (#11), Paul Simms (#33), and Joe Simms (not shown). Courtesy of Forest Grider.

happen. So after Kelly arrived at the appointed place, a nightclub, the time for the meeting came and went, but not a single other Kentuckian slated for the grand reunion showed up. Kelly kept looking at his watch. He was sure he was at the right place, but something was wrong. Finally, a sailor who had been watching him pace back and forth told him the fleet had pulled anchor and vanished. Disappointed, Kelly returned to his dry-docked ship. Fate, beyond their control, had canceled their great plans.

Most of the Springfield men, scattered in different ships of the long convoy steaming westward away from Pearl Harbor, had not even heard about those plans. Once on the high seas, they learned they were heading for Iwo Jima, a

small, ugly, volcanic island that they would help make famous. At their destination 22,000 unrelenting Japanese defenders awaited their arrival with
their rifles and guns in concrete bunkers, in pillboxes, and in a network of
interlocking tunnels and caves, all hidden under black volcanic sand.

About the second week in February the convoy of ships assembled and
dropped anchor off the island of Saipan in the Marianas. Soon the Springfield men, observing the activities around them from their own ships, saw
the reason they were there. Huge American B-29 bombers lifted off their
Mariana-based runways, climbed to their assigned altitudes, and headed for
Tokyo some 1,500 miles away. About halfway to their target the heavily burdened bombers had to get by the Japanese fighters and antiaircraft guns on
Iwo Jima, lying athwart their path. Moreover, the radar at Iwo Jima alerted
Japan of the bombers' pending arrival. For returning damaged planes, Iwo
Jima posed an even more serious threat. To provide the B-29s with fighter
escort over Japan and a safe haven for emergency landings, the Americans
had to take Iwo Jima.

Offshore in the Marianas, Paul Simms's hometown football teammate
Tony Cecconi watched from his ship, LSM 238, as three B-29s roared down
the runway. America's newest and the world's largest bombers captured
Cecconi's full attention. The two leading Superfortresses, burdened with their
large bomb load, strained and lifted off. Near the end of the runway the
third bomber bounced, skipped, and suddenly disappeared in one giant,
orange fireball and a huge puff of black smoke. With his mouth ajar, Cecconi
stood there in a state of shock. For a moment he could not believe his eyes.
Then the meaning of the tragedy sank in, and he felt severe grief for the
dead crew members who had been physically blown out of existence in a
blink of the eye. In a little while he was sick at his stomach.

Later, the ships of these former Springfield football teammates and Dr.
Hamilton pulled anchor and headed for the high seas. They were on the last
leg of their journey to Iwo Jima, about 700 miles away. Tokyo Rose, a radio
broadcaster who had the job of demoralizing the Americans, had already
aired a message warning the marines that the Japanese defenders knew the
Americans were coming.

On February 19, 1945, in the wee hours of the morning, Paul Simms
enjoyed a grand meal of steak and eggs in the ship's galley. Marines joked
and laughed. Simms stashed away an apple and orange to have when he got
ashore. From the deck, he saw Iwo Jima looming on the horizon. As his ship
moved closer to the porkchop-shaped island, the sounds of battle focused
his mind on what lay ahead. The jokes ended. The troop-carrying ships took
their assigned positions. Except for Cecconi, who had been at the Normandy,
invasion, the Springfield sailors and marines had never seen anything quite

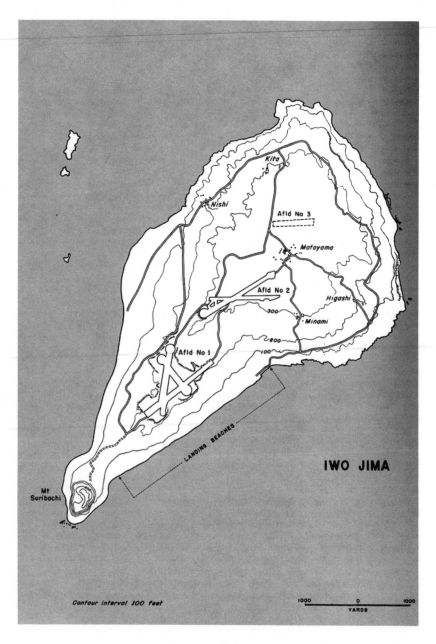

Courtesy of the U.S. Army Center of Military History.

like this display of combat power. It was the largest armada of ships ever assembled in the Pacific up to that time.

Then the big warships opened up on the island. The battleships' huge guns thundered, flashed, and hurled shells weighing over a ton; exploding in orange flashes, they sent up geysers of volcanic sand and dust. The island shuddered under the pounding from battleships, cruisers, and destroyers. Some 9,500 5-inch rockets roared off the new rocket ships, leaving white trails along their arching paths. Next, from the aircraft carriers anchored over the horizon and out of sight of the marines, came the airplanes. Watching from his ship, Dr. Hamilton thought the American bombers were going to sink the island; he did not see how anyone could survive the battering he was witnessing. But a combat-wise officer of the Fourth Marine Division thought otherwise. He told Hamilton, "Don't let that fool you. They are still there."

Meanwhile, as the island trembled and nearly disappeared under smoke and dust, numerous activities occurred in preparation for the assault. C.A. Milburn and Joe Simms, each with his own squad on a separate LST (landing ship tank), climbed aboard their amtracs (amphibious tractors). The armored tracked vehicles, which could move both in water and on land, lumbered up to the big opened doors at the front of the ships and onto the cleated ramps. As Joe Simms's amtrac, made of steel and carrying twenty-five marines, clambered down the ramp into the water, he thought, "This heavy thing is going to sink to the bottom of the ocean." But of course, it did not.

In the water, the amtracs circled Simms's ship while waiting for the exact moment to head for the shore. Slated for the first troop-carrying wave, the amtracs carrying Milburn's Company E, Second Battalion, Twenty-seventh Regiment, broke out of their circle and lined up on the line of departure in concert with the other units assigned to that wave. At 8:30 A.M. his company headed for Red Beach 2, about 4,000 yards away.

Scheduled to land at 9:10 A.M., the amtracs from Joe Simms's Company D, Second Battalion, Twenty-seventh Regiment, lined up with the third wave while the big guns fired over their heads. On shore the Japanese in their bunkers, pillboxes, caves, and tunnels did not fire back; they just waited.

On his ship to the north and opposite the Fourth Marine Division's four beaches, Hamilton watched the grand display of combat power and the coordinated teamwork with pride. But as the island shuddered under the onslaught, the marines climbing over the side of the ship onto the wide rope ladder wore somber looks. All kidding and laughter had stopped. Some had fear in their eyes; others trembled. It was serious business now. With heavy loads on their backs, they struggled down the rope ladder to the waiting

Before the landings on Iwo Jima, the navy shelled the island with big guns like these on the battleship USS *New York*. Courtesy of the Kentucky Historical Society.

Higgins boats—each capable of carrying thirty-six troops and their combat gear—bobbing in the water.

Later, Hamilton watched from the ship as the marines went ashore. At first he saw no signs of resistance and thought, "This is going to be easy." With the magnifying power of his binoculars he could even follow his shore-navy medical team as they moved ashore in the distance and began setting up their aid station. Thirteen other physicians and around forty trained medics (pharmacist's mates) aboard Hamilton's ship waited for their first patient. So far, neither the medics ashore nor the medics on ship had anything to do.

Meanwhile with the first wave of troops landing farther south, near Mount Suribachi, C.A. Milburn had trouble making a foxhole in the soft sand. The sides kept falling in. Suddenly, a bullet smashed into the front of his helmet, ripped a slight furrow across the crown of his head, and exited out the back. Jolted and stunned, he burrowed deeper into the black sand, hoping to get a little more protection.

As the third wave of troops approached the shoreline, Joe Simms's squad

Marines digging foxholes in the volcanic sand on the beach of Iwo Jima. More than 6,800 marines lost their lives on the tiny island. Courtesy of the National Archives.

leader, Sergeant Harkness, shouted above the roaring engine, "Everybody down." The big tracked vehicle lumbered up onto the beach and stopped. The navy coxswain tried to lower the rear ramp, but it would not budge. Marines with their heavy loads had to roll over the top and jump down eight feet to the beach.

Just as Joe started to jump, he heard a Japanese machine gun open up. With his heart pounding, he flipped over and hurtled to the ground. Quickly, the marines picked themselves up and made a mad dash across the narrow beach to the first of three steep terraces. Simms's feet thrashed and slipped in the ankle-deep black sand as he strained to get to the top. Breathing hard, the platoon flopped to the ground. Joe Simms heard sporadic enemy rifle fire. A voice shouted, "Everybody here? Anybody wounded?" About forty yards to his front Simms saw Milburn's company up near the crown of the second terrace. He knew his company was supposed to follow Milburn's company until it made a half-right turn to the north, and then Joe's company was to continue west across the neck of the island to the beach on the other side, less than a thousand yards away.

They had hardly hit the ground before Joe's platoon jumped up and sprinted across the second terrace and then to the top of the third terrace. In the more stable black sand, Joe Simms hastily dug a shallow foxhole. He rested there with his shoulders and head up in plain view of enemy eyes on Mount Suribachi until someone behind him yelled, "Hey Joe! There's bullets kicking up dirt behind you!" Desperately, he dug deeper and crouched down in his hole.

In about thirty minutes, they bounded out of their foxholes and took off running. Joe Simms darted from one shell hole or depression to another. Along the way he did not see a live enemy soldier, but he did see a few dead Japanese who had been badly burned by napalm bombs. Feeling no compassion, he hardly took notice of them. Once, on a sprint between holes, he heard a Japanese machine gun chattering away. He thought, "That can kill me." Still he kept going, always trying to stay in contact with his squad as he was trained to do.

About halfway to the other side of the island he discovered a huge hole and jumped into it—soon followed by the rest of his squad, platoon, and more. Voices would call out to a marine on the move under small-arms fire, the only kind they were receiving: "There's cover over here," and another marine would slide in.

Glancing back at the beach, Simms saw that waves of marines were still approaching, offloading, and then moving off the beach. Then, at 10:45 A.M., enemy artillery and mortar shells started raining down onto the beach and exploding. Chaos and destruction engulfed the men on the crowded beaches.

Meanwhile, just as Joe Simms had looked back, Doctor Hamilton raised his binoculars to his eyes. In concert, from pillboxes bristling with machine guns, tracers and bullets began ripping through the marines' ranks on the beaches; mortar rounds fired from concrete pits and artillery shells coming from the north exploded in their midst. While the island shook and volcanic dust filled the air around them, wounded marines called for help. So intense was the enemy fire that Hamilton, watching in a state of shock on his ship, thought the marines would be either killed or pushed back into the sea.

But the Japanese had aimed their instruments of death at the beaches, leaving Milburn, Simms, and the others already inland relatively safe, and the Americans would eventually prevail. The Japanese commander, Lt. Gen. Tadamichi Kuribayashi, had sprung his ambush a bit too late.

After the sixth wave, Higgins boats started taking marines ashore. Around noon, Paul Simms's boat roared toward the beach with the twelfth wave. He saw his own fear reflected in the eyes of his silent friends. Shells from American ships arced high over his head and struck well beyond the beaches. Soon he saw Japanese mortar and artillery shells kicking up black dust and sand. The beach looked as if a hurricane had unleashed its fury. Damaged Higgins boats, half-filled with water, rocked at water's edge. Wreckage and junk covered the beaches on the narrow neck of the island, running from the southern tip at Mount Suribachi for two and a half miles to the northernmost landing area. Some distance up the beach, Paul Simms observed smoke rising from a burning American ammunition dump. Marine bodies dotted the landscape. The wounded awaiting evacuation lay in the loose black sand. Boats coming and going created a huge traffic jam. A pall of smoke and dust covering Iwo painted a dismal picture. As Paul's boat nosed up to the waterline on the beach, he felt extremely tense and apprehensive.

Chaos reigned among the mass of human beings clogging the beaches. At the water's edge someone yelled, "Mines!" Nevertheless, the navy coxswain lowered the front ramp and ordered the marines out. Having no alternative, Simms stepped onto the cluttered beach. Someone shouted, "Move on up. Get off the beach." Fortunately, ribbons marked a safe path through a fifteen-foot-wide minefield. Struggling to climb the first steep terrace in loose sand nearly up to his knees, Simms took note of the casualties being loaded on boats. Enemy artillery rounds from guns hidden in the northern hills whistled in and exploded near his position. No one was hurt in his platoon, but no matter where an enemy round hit on the crowded beach, someone was likely to get it.

Just beyond the landing area, Paul Simms heard a voice shouting above the raging battle noise, "Get down. Get down and crawl!." Just under and slightly in front of the muzzles of an American artillery battery firing directly into Mount Suribachi to his left, Simms crawled along as fast as he could, considering the weight of his heavy load. The thundering howitzers belched out acrid-smelling smoke as the shells whisked by just above his head and exploded on the mountainside just 400 yards away, while incoming enemy shells burst in the midst of his company. Their combined thunder hurt Paul's ringing ears and made it difficult for him to focus on what he was supposed to be doing: staying with his squad while they fought their way to the southeast corner of Airfield 1.

Meanwhile, to Paul Simms's front and slightly to his left, his brother Joe in the big hole heard someone shout, "Gotta get the hell out of here!" He and his platoon crawled out of their relatively safe place and continued their drive toward the western shoreline. By this time, Dr. Hamilton and the medical team aboard ship were overwhelmed with casualties. Nothing in his training in Hawaii had prepared him for what he was seeing: missing limbs, shattered faces, and worse.

About the same time, Cecconi's LSM nosed up to one of the Fourth Marine Division's beaches and came to rest just beyond the waterline. When the big landing craft swung out its two large front doors and dropped its ramp, the tracked vehicles quickly rolled out and up the steep bank, but the trucks got stuck in the loose sand and clogged the offloading process. In training at Hawaii the marines and sailors on Cecconi's ship had taken great

Marines inch steadily up the slope in the soft, dark sand of Iwo Jima, with soon-to-be-famous Mount Suribachi to their left. Courtesy of the Kentucky Historical Society.

pride in their ability to offload the marines and their equipment quickly. Now, when it counted most, they were in trouble. As they worked diligently to push the trucks up the steep embankment, Japanese bullets pinged against the ship and at times even ricocheted around inside it. Cecconi saw a crewman take a bullet wound in his buttock. Thinking the wounded sailor would get to go home, he was almost envious.

The navy crew and marines struggled hard to get the stuck vehicles moving, and at last, about thirty minutes after landing, Cecconi's ship groaned, thrashed, and backed off the beach. The rest of the day his LSM carried casualties from the island to the medical evacuation ships. More than likely he delivered some casualties to Dr. Hamilton's team, but neither of them knew either about the planned reunion they had missed or about the other's presence off this tiny island in the Pacific.

Back on shore Joe Simms's squad was approaching the south end of Airfield 1, located midway between the east and west coasts. C.A. Milburn's unit had passed the southern end of the airfield ahead of Joe's and made the turn to head north. Simms had not yet seen a live Japanese soldier—they were underground; the Americans were not—but he ran full speed from one crater hole to another, or whatever cover he could find, always keeping an eye on his squad leader, the reference point for staying together. Moving as a team, usually spread out about thirty to forty yards wide and ten to twenty yards deep, the thirteen-man squad remained fully alert to the danger facing them. Some were down while others were up and running; Joe rarely saw all the other twelve men at the same time. Nor could he see the enemy's concrete bunkers, covered with black volcanic dirt and sparse shrubs, until he got within a stone's throw of them. Some, hit earlier by the big guns or bombs, were damaged, but most had not been hit. Either way, the squad leader told his men to throw a hand grenade into each bunker, even if it appeared to be empty.

Near one bunker, Joe Simms flipped out the folded bipod on his twenty-one-pound Browning automatic rifle (BAR), aimed, and fired a few rapid bursts into the opening. As he did so, a companion darted up to the bunker with a hand grenade. Knowing he could easily kill his friend, Simms aimed his weapon with care. Soon the grenade exploded in the bunker, and the squad moved on. At another bunker, Simms took his turn, dashing up to the bunker at full speed as the river of bullets streamed past him into the bunker's opening. Off to the side, with his back to the concrete wall, he pulled the pin and let the spring-loaded handle fly into the air, thus arming the grenade by starting the timer. He was trained to delay his throw for a moment so that the enemy would not have time to pick the grenade up and throw it back, but he was so charged with anxiety that he dared not wait. He flipped the grenade into the bunker and dived to the ground. He heard it explode inside and breathed a sigh of relief.

Farther along, looking to his right at Airfield 1, Joe saw demolished Japanese airplanes scattered about. He still had not seen a live Japanese soldier. Finally he and the others came to a point where they could look down and see the ocean on the island's west side. On the beach they saw Japanese mines that had washed ashore. The mines caused them to stop short of the beach and turn to the right. This put them on the left flank of the American forces moving northward. At the same time the Fifth Division's Twenty-eighth Regiment was attacking southward toward Mount Suribachi.

Just about the time Joe's platoon made the turn, a Japanese soldier sprang up like a flushed quail and sprinted northward. Supporting his BAR on the ground with the bipod mount, Simms rapidly aimed, sent a burst of automatic fire into the fleeing figure, and watched it tumble to the ground. Three of his friends had fired at the same time. Standing over the body riddled with bullet holes, Simms observed the effectiveness of their weapons. He felt good, felt he had done his job and done it well. He had no compassion for the dead man, for after Pearl Harbor he had learned to hate the Japanese enemy with a passion.

All day, Cecconi's ship carried marines, supplies, and equipment ashore from troopships anchored off the island and on return trips, delivered wounded marines to the medical ships. Late in the afternoon Cecconi looked down at wounded prisoners of war lying on the deck, strapped into form-fitting metal stretchers. Seeing Japanese soldiers for the first time aroused his curiosity. He thought they looked like "caged animals," and he felt sorry for them. He noticed one POW watching him eat a cracker. Thinking the man might be hungry, Cecconi offered him a bite. The POW locked his lips and refused the offer. Cecconi reached into a C ration can for a whole cracker and again offered the POW a bite. The man turned his head away to the side. Cecconi was baffled; at the time he did not know that it was against the law for a Japanese soldier to surrender and that to do so brought great shame upon the soldier and his family. On board his medical ship, Hamilton was equally baffled by a wounded POW he had treated; he watched in disbelief as the Japanese soldier pulled and tugged at the bandage, trying to rip it off. The medics had to restrain him.

Back on the island, Joe Simms's platoon, for the first time, came under heavy enemy small-arms fire. Until then he had rarely known where the light, sporadic enemy fire had been coming from—maybe from the caves, tunnels, or bunkers on Mount Suribachi. The openings in those fortifications were usually disguised with burlap sacks or something that matched the almost lunar landscape. Now and then an enemy soldier in a spider hole lifted the cover, popped up and fired off a round or two, then ducked back in. This time, however, Simms knew the enemy was engaging his company from an area sparsely covered with scrub. Soon the pinned-down American platoon started returning the fire. Bullets whizzed over Simms's head; the closest ones seemed to whisper as they zipped by and kicked up dirt around him. A clearer meaning of war unfolded in his mind. He did not like what he felt, but he fought on.

About fifteen minutes later the enemy's fire died down, and the company maneuvered toward a little piece of high ground where the men would dig in for the night. About twenty-five yards away from Joe, Sergeant White, noted for his friendly smile and good nature, stood and directed the adjacent platoon to the spot where he wanted them to dig in. Joe heard someone call, "Sergeant White" and turned toward him just as an enemy rifle cracked and the bullet zinged toward the sergeant. Joe saw White jerk and then tumble to the ground, blood pouring out of the bullet hole in his forehead. Simms thought, "Good gosh, that poor guy." He had known that the nature of battle involved death and dying and that a certain mental toughness was needed, but this was the first time he had stared up close at this particular ugly face of war. To help himself cope, he refused to see it in his mind's eye. Instead, he erased the terrible incident from his mind and went about digging his foxhole to defend himself against the expected and dreaded enemy night attack.

While Joe dug in for the first night on Iwo Jima near the northwest side of Airfield 1, Paul Simms's company organized a perimeter defense at the southeast edge of the airfield. Neither knew the other's location or how his brother had fared during the first day's fight. Both had had a relatively good day. Both had followed other marines most of the day, until Joe's unit became the lead company after passing the airfield. Except for the pounding Paul's unit took at the beach (while Hamilton and Joe had watched), he had had easy going and had not fired a shot. Paul dug his foxhole and set up his machine gun with confidence as darkness settled in. He had orders to shoot anything that moved, but he saw nothing in his immediate area and heard only the battle noises raging over the island: he heard American planes making their strafing runs to the north, American artillery and ships firing on Mount Suribachi to the south of his position. Japanese shells exploded on the beaches, but since his enemies were still aiming their fury at the busy activities there, it seemed to Paul that he was in a safe haven.

Later that night, a Japanese round slammed into a marine ammunition dump on the beach. The tremendous explosion rocked the island and hurled ammunition fragments in all directions. Hot fragments rained down around Paul. Suddenly, he felt a severe burning sensation on his left leg. He worked desperately to get rid of the red hot metal that had burned its way through his trousers and blistered his skin. Despite the pain, he continued to man his machine gun in the cool night.

On the other side of the island about 1:30 A.M. that same night, Joe Simms, also with orders to shoot anything that moved, was on watch while his foxhole companion, Rex Burch, slept through his hour off. In the pitch darkness Joe could not see even the outlines of the marines in the two foxholes only ten yards or so on either side of him. While the symphony of battle noises played on some distance from his position, Joe leaned forward in his foxhole with his finger on the trigger and listened for the expected night attack. Moving his head slowly left and right, he strained to hear a broken twig, a footstep, anything that might give him a warning. No one dared to whisper a word. In this lonely setting an hour's watch seemed an eternity. Suddenly, in rapid succession, Joe thought he heard footsteps, blinked as a bright parachute flare flashed and illuminated the area, and heard a rifle crack from the neighboring foxhole. He swung his BAR around as a second shot rang out. Two Japanese soldiers lay only ten yards away— dead, he thought, but he fired at them on the ground just to make sure.

Around noon the next day, while Joe Simms and Burch lingered in the foxhole, a marine unit that had been in reserve passed through their lines. Shortly thereafter, artillery shells roared in from the north and exploded around Simms's position. The violent thunderlike claps made his ears ring like a tuning fork. Dirt and debris rained down on the two figures crouched in their foxholes, and acrid smoke penetrated their nostrils. More enemy shells slammed down in rapid succession. Side by side, Simms and Burch clung tightly together and squeezed their bodies and faces against the north wall of their three-foot-deep foxhole. Amid the shock waves, smoke, dust, and ear-splitting noise, Simms fully expected to die. He thought, "God, I don't want to get killed."

A slight lull brought some relief, and then Simms heard guns thundering in the distance and said, "Jesus Christ, here it comes again." If he could have just found some logs—anything to cover his open foxhole—but there was nothing he could do. He couldn't even see the enemy guns, let alone fight back. He could only crouch lower and hope that no enemy shell would land in his foxhole and blow him to pieces. Multiple explosions rattled his foxhole and deafened his ears. He thought, "God, this is real war." A hot shell fragment dropped in on him; it burned a hole in his trousers before he could flick it off. The pounding went on for over an hour that seemed like an eternity. By the time the horror ended, his protracted high level of fear had drained his adrenalin, leaving his mouth dry as a desert and his body totally exhausted. He had seen the meaning of war, and he hated it.

By February 23, 1945, things were relatively quiet in Paul Simms's new position just behind the front lines on the west side of Airfield 1. Some incoming mortar and artillery rounds fell near but not in his immediate area. Soon his unit would move up into the front lines from their reserve status and relieve the marine company of another regiment to their front.

Glancing back over his shoulder to the south, Paul was pleasantly surprised to see the American flag fluttering in the breeze on top of Mount Suribachi. Enemy eyes would no longer observe his every action on the northern front. He felt a mild jubilation. The good news soon spread through the ranks of the marines on the island and around the fleet offshore. Later that day Joe Rosenthal made the most famous photograph of World War II, when the marines replaced the first flag with a larger one. His camera immortalized the Iwo Jima battle for the nation.

While Paul moved to take over the foxhole he was to occupy, a decapitated marine lying on the ground with the head off to the side caught his attention. The bloody cavity where the neck should have been sent chills up his spine. Observing the wedding ring on the left hand, he thought about the marine's family waiting for him back in the States. Paul recalled that the dead man had won several hundred dollars playing poker on the ship coming to Iwo Jima. It would do him little good now, he thought. Then he wondered why he would even think about such an unimportant thing at a moment like this. He had seen casualties before, but staring into the cavity, with the head nearby, left a memory he could not erase.

In his new foxhole Paul saw machine gun tracers whizzing through the company area and soon heard voices calling for medics: "Corpsman! Corpsman!" Off to the side, he saw a marine dashing up a steep incline, hell-bent on throwing a grenade into a bunker. Horrified, Paul saw a machine gun barrel in the bunker aperture point at the charging marine, and abruptly, a burst of bullets spewed out. Before the marine could throw the grenade, his body slammed into the ground. The bleeding corpse started sliding and rolling down the steep hill—picking up speed as it rolled, arms thrashing in the breeze—and came to a violent halt at the bottom of the hill, where it lay motionless. Something about the tumbling body disturbed Paul more than anything he had seen. Maybe it was one of the reasons he could not eat. Since coming ashore five days before, he had had only the porkchop sandwich he brought with him from the ship and a cracker or two now and then. His stomach just would not take food in this situation. Certainly, he did not want any at this moment, even though it was around noon. He did want a drink of water, but the marines were running low, and he decided to conserve his meager supply.

The next afternoon, Paul, now squad leader received his orders to support his company's planned attack with overhead machine gun fire. The company objective was a slice of the high ground near the west side of Airfield 2. Laced with bunkers and caves, the hill, about as high as a two-story house, loomed as a formidable threat to the marines making preparations in their dug-in positions about 300 yards away.

Feeling the pangs of thirst, Paul had his two gunners set up their machine guns and stock up on ammunition, while he studied the objective and selected targets for them. Around 5:00 P.M the American destroyers plowing back and forth off the west side of the island opened fire with their guns. The shells streaked over Paul's head and slammed into the hill above him. Minutes later the navy gunfire lifted, and American fighter bombers roared in, strafed the hillside, and dropped their high explosive and napalm bombs. Marines could feel the heat from the napalm inferno. The Japanese, crouching in their caves and bunkers, just waited.

As the planes droned out toward their waiting aircraft carriers, Paul's machine guns opened up. Marines rose out of their holes and dashed toward the hill under their own machine gun fire. Instantly, Japanese soldiers in their bunkers and caves filled the air with machine gun and rifle bullets. Marines darting from cover to cover, in and out of craters or whatever shelter they could find, heard Japanese bullets ricochet off the ground. Some heard close misses whisper as the bullets passed; others dived or fell back, bleeding, into their foxholes; some crumpled to the ground never to rise on their own power again.

Soon, enemy mortar and artillery rounds were dropping out of the sky in the midst of the marines. Still, Paul's machine guns blazed away; bullets spewed out so fast and long that the barrels of the guns got hot. More and more voices cried out, "Corpsman! Corpsman!" As the sun approached the horizon, Paul received orders to catch up with the company. His gunners snatched up their machine guns and ran forward. Paul jumped into a big crater hole on line with the others. Exploding enemy artillery and mortar rounds rained down on their position, and Japanese bullets flew everywhere, bringing the marine attack to a halt. Thirsty marines huddled in their holes, trying to stay alive, while casualties continued to mount.

As the sun touched the horizon, a lull came over the battlefield except for sporadic fire, and Paul heard an American amtrac roaring toward his position from the rear. Without sticking their heads up, crew members in the amtrac hurriedly slung five-gallon cans of water over the side as the amtrac approached, swung around, and scurried back to the rear. Driven by his thirst, Paul jumped up and made a mad dash for a can of water. An enemy gunner took aim, and two machine gun bullets smashed into Paul's hip, sending him crashing into a crater hole with two bloody gaping holes in his body. John Meyers, a section leader in Paul's squad, ran in leaps and bounds to the hole to administer first aid. He gave Paul a shot of morphine, then pulled out a pint of whiskey and offered him a drink. Paul took a big swig, and then another. He noticed an apprehensive look on Meyers's face as he handed back the bottle.

Still in his hole as twilight faded, Paul felt no physical pain, but anxiety filled him as he heard the bad news: the company was going to withdraw, and since there were so many casualties, the marines would have to leave their wounded and dead.

About the time Paul Simms was wounded, his brother Joe's unit was preparing to withdraw from front lines in the same general area. On the signal Joe and his comrades bounded out of their holes and ran toward the rear. Volleys of enemy artillery crashed down, exploded, and filled the air with dust and debris. In a lull, Joe jumped up and took off again. Jolted by what he saw, he stopped running at a big hole and looked down on the bloody and mangled bodies of five dead marines who had worked for the quartermaster battalion. One shell must have landed right in the middle of them. He recognized a handsome young man who had enjoyed a reputation as a great singer. His eyes swept by the corpse whose legs were missing from its bloody torso to the one whose head hung on by a shred. Joe could only think, "God!" This sight, which his brother Paul had seen a short time earlier when he too encountered a headless marine, froze Joe in place, although he thought he had become hardened. Someone said, "There's not a thing you can do, Joe." Quickly, he snapped himself back into his real world.

Moving back at a fast pace, Joe heard Japanese howitzers thundering up north, and in seconds the roar of the shells told him they were coming his way again. Diving for the nearest cover, he and Bob Wayner crashed into a shallow trench together. Volleys of shells whistled down and exploded in the general area while Joe lay face down in the trench. Then, under the light of parachute flares, Joe looked toward Wayner and saw between his head and Wayner's feet a huge dud from a sixteen-inch gun on an American battleship, needing only the shock waves of an incoming artillery shell to be detonated. In a trembling voice Joe told Wayner. Barely able to talk, he said, "If a shell gets close to us, we're gone." Wayner murmured, "Jesus." As more enemy shells rained down, the two men flattened themselves as close to the bottom of the trench as possible, petrified by the thought of being vaporized and blown out of existence by the big dud.

Meanwhile, his brother Paul, desperate not to be left behind when the marines withdrew from his sector, said to his neighbor. "If you'll help me, I think I can hobble back." His friend said, "Come on, let's go." At the first aid station many wounded marines lay outside the tent on stretchers on the ground, waiting their turn for treatment. In the darkness of the night, Paul Simms waited patiently with the others. He felt no pain and his wounds weren't bleeding much, but his apprehension about their seriousness mounted, and there was no one to talk to about it. The wounded lay silent, their thoughts turned inward. The medical people, working furiously, had no time to talk, and there was no chaplain there. Filled with loneliness and fear, he waited and waited. Finally his turn came, but the doctor and medics rushed about so much that he chose not to ask them about the extent of his injury, and they did not tell him.

About an hour later, strapped on top of an amtrac plowing through the water at full throttle, Paul noticed the water lapping at the top of the vehicle and thought, "My goodness." Soon litter-bearers transferred him to a barge tied alongside a ship staffed with navy doctors and corpsmen. Under heavy sedation he waited his turn to be hoisted aboard. Now and then the barge banged against the ship and jarred him out of his slumber. Repeatedly, he asked a corpsman, "What day is this?" Finally, the corpsman, in a gruff tone, said, "I just told you a little while ago that it's still February 24."

Even in his sedated condition, Paul discerned the chaotic conditions on the ship. He saw exhausted doctors and other medical personnel working frantically to save young men's lives. They had been working around the clock for five days, with only periodic catnaps, trying to deal with the unexpectedly large volume of casualties. When Paul's turn came at last, the doctor moved the leg around and announced, "Well, I don't think there's any bones broken." Paul's spirits soared. For the first time since going ashore at Iwo Jima, he was happy—but now he worried about his brother.

Back on the island the shelling eventually ended, and Joe Simms moved away from the big dud in the trench. Totally drained, he could not believe what he heard: his company had received orders to return to the front lines to occupy a position where another company had been overrun. An officer pleaded their case on the grounds of exhaustion to no avail, and the weary men moved toward the front, casting shadows as parachute flares drifted out of the sky.

Near the front lines a guide met the platoon and led them through a minefield. Joe anxiously kept his eyes fastened to the white ribbons marking the safe path. Ever changing shadows cast by the shifting illumination fashioned an eerie image over the battlefield. In the distant background Joe heard the individual instruments of death playing their battle sounds, and far away he heard Japanese artillery thundering. The exploding artillery shells clapped like lightning; incoming mortars went crump, crump, crump; chattering machine guns added their voices. None of this threatened him at the moment, but he knew it would come his way later if not sooner. Defining the nature of war kept nagging him. He thought, "This is war. Real war. It's killing or being killed." The hardening process had been advanced another notch.

At the front lines enemy fire again came Joe's way. Sgt. Joe Key yelled to his squad over the noise, "Jump into any foxhole you can!" Joe Simms didn't wait to be told twice. Off to his left, toward the ocean, he saw tracers spewing from a Japanese machine gun. Since the determined gunner aiming to the south was too busy at that moment to see him, Joe whipped his BAR around and pulled the trigger. He saw the Japanese gunner jerk and tumble over. The enemy gun fell silent. Joe knew he had killed his enemy now lying motionless only a few feet away, but did not yet realize that his company had advanced right into the middle of the Japanese line.

Under the glare of the flares and even before he could feel good about killing the enemy gunner, Joe saw a string of Japanese machine gun tracers going past his head while he was still crouched down in his foxhole. Suddenly a big glob of red danced before his eyes; that's all he saw. Sprawled at the bottom of his foxhole in a sitting position, he heard his foxhole companion yell, "Simms, are you okay?" He tried, but he could not answer. Again above the battlefield noises he heard, "Simms, are you okay?" As in a nightmare, he could not speak out. Not until the third or fourth query did his senses return, and after rubbing his hand over his head and feeling no blood, he said, "I think so." But there was no let up. All night the Japanese hammered away at the Americans with machine gun and rifle fire.

Finally, the sun cracked the horizon and the long, terrible night came to an end. Joe's buddy looked over and said, "My God! Look at your helmet."

Joe pulled it off his head. A big crease ran across the back, and the helmet liner had spiderweb cracks. Joe thought, "My God, I almost got killed," but so drained was his physical and emotional energy that he could not even generate any jubilation over escaping his close encounter with death. If he got out of the war alive, though, he was going to take that helmet home with him for everyone to see.

The other servicemen who had been slated for the grand Springfield reunion were having their own exhausting and horrific days. Elsewhere in the Twenty-seventh Regiment's area a mortar round had splashed down between C.A. Milburn's legs; between the time it hit the ground and the time it took him to realize it was a dud, he had gone stiff with shock and fear.

Aboard his LSM off the Fourth Division's area east of the island, Tony Cecconi had worked day and night hauling men and supplies to shore and wounded men back to the medical ships. At the northernmost beach near the rock quarry he had watched a marine carrying a flamethrower aim the nozzle toward a cave opening from an angle and send a long stream of fire roaring into the cave. While the marine was pivoting the long flame around to get in front of the opening so he could move forward, Cecconi saw someone bolt out of the cave. Horrified, he watched the flaming human form running full speed straight for the ocean; it slowed and tumbled to the ground not far from Cecconi's ship. The scene bothered the young sailor who had been raised in a peaceful little country town in central Kentucky. He reasoned that it had to be done, but he did not like it, and he was glad he did not have to use a weapon of fire to kill a fellow human being.

Just inland from the marines' landing beaches, Forrest Grider had come ashore with his army antiaircraft battalion and set up his radio in an empty Japanese bunker at Airfield 1, where he watched a crippled B-29 Superfortress make an emergency landing. Unknown to Grider, his high school football teammates had helped clear the enemy from the area, if not the bunker itself. Five of the Springfield men—Grider, Milburn, the Simms brothers, and later Cecconi—had been at the airfield without knowing the others were there. A global war had plucked them out of their little community, trained them for war, gathered them at Pearl Harbor, broken up their reunion in Honolulu, and exposed them all to bodily harm and death on Iwo Jima—a speck in the Pacific Ocean, thousands of miles from home.

On the medical ship, Dr. Hamilton continued working desperately to keep up with the patient overload, trying to keep the wounded and the maimed alive until they could be evacuated to better facilities. But racing against time to save young men's lives was taking its toll on the physician and his colleagues. What bothered him most were the combat fatigue cases. The stress of battle with its noises, sights, and constant threat to life and limb was too much for some men. Some were, he said, "scared to death!" A few were trembling uncontrollably, unable to relax; he discovered that no medicine would relax them, but four ounces of brandy would often help. He agonized over who was capable of returning to the front lines. With great regret he sent some back to battle. Others, especially those silent young men with the faraway stares, he had to evacuate to the rear.

Paul Simms was on a ship on his way to Guam in the Marianas, where the navy's huge Fleet Hospital 111 provided a wide range of medical services for wounded Americans. Paul was hopeful about his own situation, but fearing the worst for his little brother, he avoided talking to wounded marines from Joe's outfit. The folks at home worried about both of them. Paul Hubert and Rose Polin Simms knew that Paul and Joe's division was fighting on Iwo Jima and that the marines were taking heavy casualties. They waited anxiously to hear from their sons.

On the night of February 26, 1945, Joe Simms's company moved a little closer to Hill 362A, the marines' objective for the next morning's scheduled attack. The 362-foot cliff laced with caves and tunnel openings looking down on the marines made a formidable obstacle, and the 200- to 300-yard open space they had to cross lacked cover.

A little before 8:00 A.M. Joe opened a K ration and nervously gulped down a cheese and cracker sandwich. Peering over the edge of his foxhole at the naked approach route, he thought, "Damn, we have to cross that." He and his friends knew they were in for a slaughter. Just before jumping off in the attack, Joe looked over and saw the unit on the right pulling back. He thought, "Damn it, why aren't we attacking at the same time?"

Following Rex Burch, Joe bounded out of his foxhole at full speed. Running crouched over, he fired off a burst or two from his BAR into the side of the cliff. Twenty yards out he passed Burch, who had found a hole. As enemy fire swirled around him, he thought, "Jesus—there is no cover," and he knew he had made a mistake by not jumping into the hole with Burch. The Japanese machine guns rattled. Out in front of his comrades, crouched low, he continued running; he zigged, zagged, and fired his weapon some more. Japanese bullets kicked up dirt around him, and Joe decided to stop going forward. Glancing over to the right, he did not see anyone advancing; they were all pinned down. Off to his left he saw a man-high, narrow ridge. Running for his life, he practically flew over it and dived into the little dip on the other side. Bullets dug up dirt within a foot or two of his face. He thought, "Hell, I can't stay here." Up and out, he made a dash for a clump of scattered bushes to the left. He hit the ground running and rapidly rolled over four or five times as he was trained to do. He thought, "Good he's not shooting this way."

But Japanese eyes watched for him to make a move. Realizing he did not have any cover, Joe sprang up, and as he did so, a bullet smashed into his right ankle, tearing flesh and splintering bones on its way out. The force of the shot spun him around, whipped his BAR out of his hand, and sent him crashing to the ground. There he grimaced in pain. It felt like someone had hit him on the ankle with a baseball bat.

In a little while, numbness set in. Meanwhile, he discovered a wound in the left foot as well. A minute later, as he reached for his BAR, another bullet ripped into his right thigh, burning like a hot poker. He shouted, "Lame duck! lame duck!"—the code word for wounded marine. He yelled again, louder. No one responded. He thought, "Hell, no one's going to come out here and get me." Barely staving off panic, he shouted to the left, "Anybody over there?" He could not understand why no one would answer him. He debated whether to get up and run, but he realized he was in the enemy's field of fire—and he was not even sure that he could get up.

He knew Burch was about thirty yards to his right, and he thought Simon, another BAR man, ought to be off to the left. Joe yelled, "Simon!" At last he heard a reply: "Joe, I'm over here. Come over here." Though fearful that a Japanese soldier might be in a spider hole between them, Joe put his knife between his teeth and started crawling.

In a foxhole, Simon pulled Joe's shoes off and bandaged his wounds. Minutes later, the two marines eased out of the hole and crawled back about twenty yards, where they found other marines holed up. A corpsman gave Joe a shot of morphine. An hour or so passed before the little group of marines decided they could get Joe to an aid station.

On his way to the rear on a makeshift litter, Joe heard bullets whispering by, and he knew a whisper meant they were within an inch or so of his ear. Suddenly, his body crashed down and bounced off the ground. Behind him his friend Bob Pratt from Greeley, Nebraska, one of the litter-bearers, lay seriously wounded. As bullets continued to swirl around them, someone snatched Pratt into a foxhole, and Joe slid into another under his own power. They now occupied foxholes that the company had been in the day before the attack started.

To get the company out of the killing zone, Captain King ordered the marines to evacuate the area and leave the wounded. Joe thought, "Oh hell." Delirious in his foxhole a couple of yards away, Pratt kept pleading for water. Joe felt compassion for his wounded friend, but the corpsman had told him before the marines left, "Joe, you can't give him any water."

Under sedation, Joe found it difficult to stay alert, but he felt he had to keep an eye out to defend himself and Pratt. Time dragged by. To avoid drifting into a slumber, he pinched himself again and again. Pratt pleaded,

"Water, water." It was all he could say before he passed out again. Joe lifted himself up a little higher to look at the motionless form. He feared his friend might be dead, but before long the weak, pitiful voice pleaded for water again.

About fifty yards behind him his company kept a stream of machine gun bullets pouring into the cliff that towered over them. That comforted him and kept him from feeling so alone. Still, he agonized over what to do about Pratt, frustrated that he could do nothing to help a friend who had been wounded helping him. When a lull came over the battlefield, Joe examined his own wounds. He thought about his dream of being a football coach and said to himself, "Well, that's gone." It seemed funny to him that such a thing would come to his mind in his situation. Pratt's periodic weak plea for water grated on his nerves. Time dragged on, and so did his fear that Pratt would surely die without help. Joe's frustration became rage because the big guns—the artillery, the navy guns, the dive bombers—were not coming to their aid. It never occurred to him to leave his friend and crawl back for aid for himself. He felt he had to stay there and protect Pratt in case the Japanese attacked them. About the time he would think Pratt was dead, his friend would plead again in a suffering voice, "Water, water," and Joe would get madder and madder and say, "Where in the hell is the artillery?"

It was late in the afternoon before friendly mortars rained down on Hill 362-A. At last, as the sun fell below the horizon, marines dashed up and quickly carried Simms and Pratt out on litters rigged out of ponchos.

Back at the new front lines, Bob Wayner came to see Joe. Still upset over the long delay in getting them out and the effect it might have on Pratt's chance of survival, Joe asked angrily, "Where in the hell was the artillery?" A corpsman came and gave Joe a heavy dose of morphine. Stretcher-bearers picked up both men and started to the rear, but then mortar rounds dropped down and exploded nearby; the bearers dropped them on the ground and scurried into a foxhole; and Joe tumbled off the stretcher. Another mortar round went "crump" within twenty yards of him. Although heavily sedated, he knew the enemy was aiming at his little group, and he started crawling, trying to find a hole. In a little while, though, the shelling stopped and they went on.

About a mile behind the lines, in a tent complex, Joe saw wounded marines lying everywhere while medical personnel scurried about attending them. He thought, "A lot of people are getting hurt around here." Still doped up, he thought, "This is war," and wondered why the Japanese were not shelling the place, shining under the glare of electric lights.

Sometime in the wee hours of the morning, nearly a day after he was wounded, he lay on the deck of an LSM crowded with wounded. Alongside the medical support ship rolling with the waves, someone hooked Joe's stretcher to the ship's hoist. On his way up, the stretcher tilted his feet upward, and his helmet with the bullet crease in it tumbled off and splashed into the water. Joe had intended to take that helmet home with him, and the loss of his trophy angered him, but there was nothing he could do about it.

On board the ship, wounded marines crowded the deck and lay in nooks and crannies. A few had breathed their last and lay dead among the wounded. On a table in the operating room Joe heard Pratt on the table beside him moaning and whispering, "Water—water." A corpsman sponged Pratt's lips with a wet cloth, and Joe wished he had thought of that while his friend suffered beside him on the island. He reached over and squeezed Pratt's hand: "Hang on, Bob. Hang in there."

A doctor appeared and asked Joe, "How are you doing?" Joe said, "Oh okay. Get Bob first." The doctor wanted to know if Joe had seen many Japanese soldiers. Joe answered, "No. You can see the fire coming out of a hole. You don't see any Japanese out there attacking." The doctor said, "Well, that's what we keep hearing."

Holding on to Pratt's hand, Joe watched his friend's color change before his eyes. His skin faded to an ashen color, and the moans fell silent. The next thing Joe remembered was waking up in the recovery room. The next day the surgeon paid him a visit. Joe asked, "How about Bob Pratt?" "Joe, he died." Holding back tears, Joe asked, "What happened to his body?" The doctor answered, "He has already been buried." Joe let the tears fall.

At the fleet hospital, Paul Simms began to enjoy food again. The stark contrast between this peaceful setting on Guam and the horrific combat scenes on Iwo Jima made him keenly aware of and thankful for his own blessings. Yet the results of war and of battle stress surrounded him even here: he saw some wounded men who were maimed for life and, still more distressing, men in the psychiatric ward with the faraway look. These sights heightened his concern for his brother, and he continued to avoid the marines from Joe's unit. They might tell him Joe had been killed.

In Springfield, Kentucky, Julia Simms entered the post office hoping for some word from her brothers. The burden of family problems weighed heavily on her shoulders. She had brothers exposed to the dangers of war— two at Iwo Jima, and her mother was about to undergo an operation for a bleeding ulcer. At the Simms box, her face lit up when she spotted a letter from Paul, his first since the Iwo Jima landing. He talked mostly about the family, but at the bottom of the letter she read, "P.S. Don't worry about my wound." Julia sobbed, and a hush fell over the post office as she rushed out.

Relieved of his pressing duties back at Iwo Jima, Dr. Hamilton, tired to the bone, began recuperating back in the Marianas. Joe followed Paul, now on his way to the States, to the fleet hospital on Guam. On board a ship between Hawaii and San Diego, a marine friend from his paratrooper days spotted Paul and told him his brother was in the hospital: "He got shot through both legs." Alarmed and anxious, Paul said, "Well, is he all right otherwise?" "Yeah," answered his friend. Paul felt a surge of relief. With his brother's life spared and out of danger, he could now unwind and relax. Both had survived the ordeal; neither would ever be the same. A sense of pride followed them home and remained with them for the rest of their lives.

Back on the island as the final phase of the fight approached, a Springfield reunion of sorts did take place when Forest Grider joined his football teammate C.A. Milburn in a dugout just behind the front lines. Over K rations of cheese and crackers, the bearded, disheveled, grimy, and exhausted friends talked about hometown news. While battle noise echoed in the background, Milburn shared the news about the Simms brothers. He thought Paul would be all right, but Joe's wound was more serious, and he did not know what the outcome would be. Finally, Milburn said, "I was sorry to hear about your father." That was how Grider learned of his father's death. Milburn had received the bad news in a letter from Springfield.

Grider, Milburn, and Cecconi all remained on Iwo Jima until the battle for the island was won. After the war, Milburn's helmet with the bullet hole in it went on display in the window of McClure's Hardware Store in Springfield. Joe Simms regretted not having his creased helmet available to be exhibited with his friend's.

John Kelly's battleship, the USS *Maryland,* took another kamikaze hit at Okinawa, but Kelly and all the others whose grand reunion was canceled by the war returned home at different times, each to his own joyful homecoming. But each was a different man now, changed in many ways from those young servicemen who had arrived in Hawaii before the invasion of Iwo Jima.

Epilogue

Suffer or you end up accepting the world instead of relishing it.
—Author unknown

The combatants returned home with a stronger sense of pride in their country and a great pride in having served it. The suffering they had endured enhanced their ability to relish the world and to cherish their blessings. Even those whose suffering continued over the years said they would do it again, including Jack Reed, whose legs have ached every day from his bout with beri-beri and who falls if the lights go out. Every waking moment, in spite of medication, Bernell Heaton's back and leg pained him, but that did not rob him of his sense of humor. The Simms brothers had numerous operations because of their wounds; neither felt self-pity or regret, even though Joe, a natural athlete, never ran again.

Some of these men returned home to wives and children; the single ones soon married and started their own families; and all enjoyed long and successful marriages and cherished the blessings and burdens of raising and educating their children.

Many returnees took advantage of the GI Bill, a federally funded education program for veterans. Lee Ebner completed two years of schooling at the Louisville Art Center before attending the Chicago Academy of Fine Arts. John Barrows earned a Ph.D. The Simms brothers, Paul Mudd, and Forest Grider completed undergraduate degrees.

All the combatants put their war experiences behind them—a few with difficulty—and went to work building successful careers. Lee Ebner served as staff artist for the *Louisville Courier-Journal* and *Louisville Times.* John Barrows retired from the faculty of the University of Kentucky to a farm near Versailles, Kentucky. Bernell Heaton made a career in the U.S. Air Force. Willis McKee practiced medicine in Shelbyville, Kentucky, and rose to the rank of colonel in the reserves. Paul Mudd and Tony Cecconi worked for the Kentucky state government. Grider worked and raised his family in Springfield, Kentucky, while C.A. Milburn's career took him to Texas, where he raised his family. Richard Hamilton practiced medicine in his hometown into his eighties. Of the five who had been farmers, only Hanly Davis returned to the land and farmed for a living. Paul Simms, an accountant, worked for the Internal Revenue Service out of Danville, Kentucky. Joe Simms was an advanced production planner and methods engineer for General Electric at Bloomington, Illinois, until he retired.

Thomas Murphy and Skeets Kelly owned their own businesses in Springfield, Kentucky. Murphy deliberately worked longer hours than many, hoping the resulting fatigue would protect him from another nightmare of the wounded calling to him for help. When he recognized a voice in his dream and a forgotten name returned to his memory, he had to work harder for days to keep the painful scene from reappearing over and over in his mind.

On many mornings, Jack Reed did not feel like going to work and could have called in sick, yet he routinely reported to International Harvester for thirty years. His hard work earned him promotions to supervisor, general foreman, and assistant division head before he retired. He could have chosen to live off his disability pension, as did some of his fellow POWs who also suffered permanent physical damage and psychological stress due to brutal treatment by their Japanese captors. But watching some of them medicate themselves with alcohol convinced Reed that going to work, despite chronic pain, was the right thing to do.

Robert Haney cannot forget the horror of Dachau the day after it was liberated. The emaciated walking skeletons with sunken eyes and broken spirits, the stacks of the dead with their frozen stares, the silent crematorium smokestacks, and the stench emanating from the living and the dead together crushed his spirits, and the knowledge of what human beings could do to one another still persecutes his soul when he thinks about it. He tries to bury the painful scenes deep in the recesses of his memory and go on about his business as a gentle, friendly, and helpful realtor in Oldham County, Kentucky. Except for the agony of recalling that terrible day he enjoyed telling his World War II story. Both Haney and Reed said that their experiences with such evil had strengthened their compassion toward others.

After the war Ben Butler rose to the rank of major general in the U.S. Army Reserves. At his retirement, Gen. Mark Clark told the audience that Butler was one of the best combat leaders he had observed during the three wars of his military career. The 100th Division Reserve headquarters was renamed the Major General Benjamin J. Butler Army Center, and recently he was chosen as an inaugural member of the U.S. Army Reserve Hall of Fame. Butler also distinguished himself as a civilian: after serving as Fayette County agent, he was elected Kentucky's state commissioner of agriculture.

The artillery of time, as Abraham Lincoln once said it would, has begun to take its toll of the men whose stories are recounted here. Some fifty years after their combat experiences, Bernell Heaton, Jack Murphy, Paul Mudd, the Simms brothers, and Dr. Willis McKee have joined their young comrades who were killed in action in the bivouac of the dead. They have left a legacy of good citizenship to their children and to future generations.

Sources

The primary sources for this book were my interviews with the combatants whose World War II stories it tells and with others who were involved in the same actions. Sometimes, the protagonists provided me with information in articles by others whose publishers could not be identified and thus could not be included in this list.

The sources listed here are those that I found most useful for locating details needed to assist the reader's understanding and to verify the accuracy of the narrators' recollections.

Books

Ambrose, Stephen E. *Band of Brothers: E Company, 506th Regiment, 101st Airborne from Normandy to Hitler's Eagle's Nest*. New York: Simon & Schuster, 1992.

Ardery, Philip. *Bomber Pilot: A Memoir of World War II*. Lexington: Univ. Press of Kentucky, 1978.

Bradley, Omar N., and Clay Blair. *A General's Life*. New York: Simon & Schuster, 1983.

Breuer, William B. *The Great Raid on Cabanatuan: Rescuing the Doomed Ghosts of Bataan and Corregidor*. New York: Wiley, 1994.

Clausewitz, Carl V. *On War*. Ed. and intro. Anatol Rapoport. Baltimore: Penguin, 1968.

Cook, Haruko Taya, and Theodore F. Cook. *Japan at War: An Oral History*. New York: New Press, 1992.

Costello, John. *The Pacific War*. New York: Quill, 1982.

Featherston, Alwyn. *Saving the Break Out: The 30th Division's Heroic Stand at Mortain, August 7–12, 1944*. Novato: Presido, 1993.

Gailey, Harry A. *The War in the Pacific: From Pearl Harbor to Tokyo Bay*. Novato: Presido, 1995.

Graham, Dominick. *Cassino*. New York: Ballantine, 1970.

Hapgood, David, and David Richardson, *Monte Cassino*. New York: Congdon & Weed, 1984.

Hart, B. H. Liddell. *History of the Second World War*. New York: Putnam, 1970.

Hastings, Max. *Overlord: D-Day and the Battle for Normandy*. New York: Simon & Schuster, 1984.

Hoffman, Alice, and Howard Hoffman. *Archives of Memory: A Soldier Recalls World War II*. Lexington: Univ. Press of Kentucky, 1990.

Keegan, John. *The Face of Battle*. New York: Dorset, 1976.

Kelly, Brian C. *Best Little Stories from World War II*. Charlottesville, Va.: Montpelier, 1989.

Kerr, Bartlett E. *Surrender and Survival: The Experience of American POWs in the Pacific, 1941–1945*. New York: William Morrow, 1985.

Love, Robert W., Jr., *History of the U.S. Navy,* vol. 1, *1941–1945.* Harrisburg, Pa., 1992.

Ross, Bill D. *Iwo Jima: Legacy of Valor.* New York: Vanguard, 1985.

Ruhe, William J. *War in the Boats: My WWII Submarine Battles.* Washington, D.C.: Brassey's, 1994.

Selzer, Michael. *Deliverance Day: The Last Hours of Dachau.* Philadelphia: Lippincott, 1978.

Shirer, William L. *The Rise and Fall of the Third Reich.* New York: Simon & Schuster, 1960.

Toland, John. *Some Survived.* New York: Warner, 1984.

Von Senger and Etterlin, Frido. *Neither Fear nor Hope.* New York: Dutton, 1964.

Reference Works

Bombing Squadron Eighty-Four. *Bombing 84 at Sea.* N.p., n.d. [1945].

Dear, I. C. B., and M. R. D. Foot. *The Oxford Companion to World War II.* New York: Oxford Univ. Press, 1995.

Parrish, Thomas. *The Simon and Schuster Encyclopedia of World War II.* New York: Simon & Schuster, 1978.

Salmaggi, Cesare, and Alfredo Pallavisini, comps. *2194 Days of War: An Illustrated Chronology of the Second World War.* Trans. Hugh Young, ed. Malcolm Falkus. New York: Gallery Books, 1979.

The United States Army in World War II. 77 vols. Washington, D.C.: United States Army Center of Military History, 1950–.

Articles

Berens, Robert J., Col. "Pantano." *Army,* Nov. 1993, 41–44.

Frantz, Lisa K. "Witness at the Gates of Hell." *Retired Officer Magazine,* April 1995, 24–30.

Hammel, Eric. "Week of Relentless Bombing." *World War II,* March 1994, 26–32.

Harris, James Russell. "The Harrodsburg Tankers: Bataan, Prison, and the Bonds of Community." *Register of the Kentucky Historical Society* 86 (1988): 230–77.

Keegan, John. "History's Greatest Invasion." *U.S. News & World Report,* May 23, 1994, 57–70.

Parshall, Gerald. "Freeing the Survivors." *U.S. News & World Report,* April 3, 1995, 49–67.

Robbins Peggy. "Deciding the Fate of Monte Cassino." *World War II,* Feb. 1996, 35–40.

Wilson, William. "The 'Hellfires' of Bastogne." *Army,* Dec. 1994, 34–41.

Wukovits, John F. "War's Greatest Sea Fight." *World War II,* Sept. 1994, 30–37.

Index